Brown

everything
you ever needed to know about
training
3rd edition

kaye thorne   david mackey

**KOGAN
PAGE**

London and Sterling, VA

First published by Kogan Page Limited in 1996
Reprinted 1997, 2000
Second edition 2001
Third edition 2003
Reprinted 2005

120 Pentonville Road
London N1 9JN
UK
www.kogan-page.co.uk

22883 Quicksilver Drive
Sterling, VA 20166-2012
USA

© Kaye Thorne and David Mackey, 1996, 2001, 2003

The right of Kaye Thorne and David Mackey to be identified as the authors of this work has been asserted by them in accordance with the Copyright, Designs and Patents Act 1998.

ISBN 0 7494 4048 1

British Library Cataloguing in Publication Data

A CIP record for this book is available from the British Library.

Library of Congress Cataloging-in-Publication Data

Thorne, Kaye.
   Everything you ever needed to know about training / Kaye Thorne and David Mackey.--3rd ed.
      p. cm.
Includes bibliographical references and index.
   ISBN 0-7494-4048-1
   1. Employees--Training of. I. Mackey, David. II. Title.
   HF5549.5.T7T4625 2003
   658.3'124--dc21

                                   2003009009

Typeset by Jean Cussons Typesetting, Diss, Norfolk
Printed and bound in Great Britain by Antony Rowe Ltd, Chippenham and Eastbourne

To my parents who started my journey of learning, and my children Matthew and Louise who daily inspire me to continue it.
Kaye Thorne

To my mother who ensured that I understood the value of learning and to my wife Sally who has provided the inspiration and time to allow me to complete this book.
David Mackey

Contents

Preface to the third edition

Welcome to this third edition of *Everything You Ever Needed to Know about Training*.

Much has changed and developed since we wrote the first edition in 1996. Any form of sponsored learning and development or training programme, if it is to be successful, has to fit into the broader context of what else is happening in the business world, which currently has a level of uncertainty following the events of 11 September 2001. One of the realities is that businesses are having to embrace the new technology and increasingly operate in a 24/7 global environment: their customers and suppliers demand and expect it. Sitting in the corporate boardroom can be an unnerving experience in a world where certainties are being challenged and introducing any learning and development initiative may be seen as a low priority in the corporate agenda, so developing a persuasive business case will be vital.

As part of our research for this edition we talked to fellow practitioners for their views on what was important for organizations in today's climate. Here are some of their responses:

❑ 'Big issue is the "war for talent" and the part development can/ should play in recruitment and retention. Also whole issue of rapid capability building – how to build individual and organizational capabilities to meet the needs of the rapidly changing business environment.'

❑ 'Career planning and development is still a hot topic, particularly in flatter organizations, which challenges the traditional concept of hierarchical career progression.'

❑ 'Leading and managing change is a core capability for most organizations – challenge is how to build and embed in the organization, and how important it is to have a consistent change methodology and underpinning tools.'

- 'Leadership models based on releasing potential and coaching.'
- 'Performance measures – where do organizations need/want to be world-class/best in class? What are the implications for capabilities required and the organization model to deliver?'
- 'Specific to training and development functions still – how do they really step up to being a true business partner? How do they organize to deliver, and how do they measure their "value add" to the business?'
- 'Increasing focus on cost – also means organizations are having to think about different ways of delivering learning.'
- 'The use of technology seems to be on the radar a lot, particularly the "blended learning" debate, which most folk are trying to nail both from a client perspective as well as a cost issue.'
- 'Outsourcing bubbles along for the more fundamental stuff... Executive development though still seems to be hanging on in there from a strategic perspective and linking this with corporate strategy and competency frameworks.'

We have incorporated this feedback into our revisions, particularly in certain key areas. 'E-learning' has evolved to become 'blended learning' and, to reflect this, we have updated the new chapter introduced in the second edition, Getting the Best from E-learning, to include blended learning.

There has also been a continuation of the trend that we highlighted in the second edition: the reduction of traditional, menu-driven training courses, which have been replaced by a variety of learning solutions.

The role of the trainer has continued to evolve to include internal consultant, learning adviser, facilitator of learning, e-learning designer and workplace coach. Coaching in fact has grown considerably in significance, and to reflect this we have included a new section in The Trainer As... chapter specifically focusing on personal coaching. The scope, complexity and challenge of the trainer role are ever growing. Line managers have been encouraged to be more pro-active in the training and development of their teams and, with many new aspects to training and learning, there are more opportunities for trainers to work in partnership with line managers.

Importantly one of the key development areas for trainers and development specialists is the ability to cope with ambiguity and to be able to respond rapidly to the needs of their customers. As one of the responses in our research above indicated, there is a very real need for internal training functions and any professionals engaged in working with an organization to be able to identify exactly what value they are adding and what their contribution as business partner is.

As with the earlier editions, this book is designed to highlight the key stages of identifying, designing and delivering learning and development that is dynamic, positive and challenging. Above all it is about recognizing that the quest for learning should never stand still – it is about sustaining curiosity and always seeking better ways of helping others to learn. In supporting that, it is about learning to encourage learners to have a thirst for knowledge, striving to be inspiring and innovative, and wanting to lead in the field of training and development.

We wish you every success in your continuing journey to inspiration.

Acknowledgements

In a lifetime of learning we have met many people who have contributed to our own learning. Particular influences are David A Kolb, Tony Buzan and John Seymour, and the other authors mentioned in our bibliography. Specifically in the development of this third edition we should like to thank the following:

- ❑ Chris Dunn, TDA Transitions Ltd, for sharing his vision, imagination and entrepreneurship in the development of a leading example of an innovative training business.
- ❑ Andy Pellant and The Research Initiative for his inspiration, personal support and creative challenges in the development of personalized learning.
- ❑ We also acknowledge the work of those who created the models and concepts which underpin many T&D activities, eg SMART. David A Kolb for the inspiration behind *How People Learn* and for permission to reproduce his Experiential Learning Model. Tony Buzan for his innovative Mind Map Method®. Peter Honey and Alan Mumford for the Learning Styles questionnaire.
- ❑ Roger Greenwood, Esprit, Richard Graham, Huthwaite, and Dermot Bradley – three inspirational leaders in UK sales training.
- ❑ Paul Ewins, HSBC Bank plc; Chris George of Styles & George; John Murray; Trevor Tribe and Philip Mason of MacIntyre Hudson; Steve Eastham, Federation of Small Businesses – for their creativity, expertise and helpful input in our chapter on Training as a Business.
- ❑ All the staff at the CIPD and IOD Libraries for their very professional and responsive help in compiling the bibliography and the international training contacts.

All authors need support and we owe a particular debt of gratitude to the following for their encouragement and interest:

❑ Vivien Dunn, Barbara Bonner and the whole TDA team of staff and associates, for their professionalism, dedication and support. Alex Machray, Mark Woodhouse, John Kenney, Paul Allen, Cheri Lofland, Keith Bastin, Doug and Lisa Twining, Alan Smith, Lesley Shaw, Mark Sinclair, Kevin McGrath, Ian and Rosemary Anderson, Rob and Sue Ford, Bill Eldridge, Keith Harriss, Al Dunn, Margaret Burnside, Mike Brewer and the Garside family. The Kilby family and staff at the Garrack Hotel, St Ives, Cornwall, for providing an inspirational environment in which to write.

❑ Philip Mudd, Heather Langridge and Catherine Gibbons, our editors, and all those who have worked on previous editions, for their refreshing approach to publishing and for providing superb technical support and advice.

But above all, the very special clients and individual learners who ultimately have been our inspiration, and without whom this book would never have been written, our particular thanks to you.

Introduction

Our vision in writing this book was to create a compendium of concepts, ideas and resources to help those who help others learn.

You may be one of the following:

❑ a member of a training and development (T&D) function
❑ a line manager with responsibility for on-job training
❑ an external training consultant
❑ a lecturer in further, or higher education.

You may be called a trainer, performance coach, facilitator, developer, internal consultant or learning designer. Whatever your job title is, you will be helping others to learn.

This book is designed as a dip-in guide. It will provide at a glance sources of information and, hopefully, inspiration.

We wrote it because we could not find such a book when we needed it. In true trainer fashion, since no one else had done it, we did it ourselves. It is based on years of experience and is our attempt to give the answers to 'everything you ever needed to know about training'. There will be a sequel when you write and tell us all those things you know and that others may not.

You can contact us at www.theinspirationnetwork.co.uk (Kaye Thorne) and www.ccfocus.co.uk (David Mackey). We look forward to hearing from you!

HOW TO USE THIS BOOK

This book is about a journey, and the stages are clearly signposted so that you will reach your destination quickly. You may have travelled on some parts of the route before, and we anticipate you will wish only to look at the headings or checklists to ensure you are familiar with the content.

We hope you will find in the text everything you need to help you create exciting and interesting journeys for the learners with whom you work. The focus is on self-discovery and helping others enjoy the same delight and curiosity on their own development journey.

A book of this nature should provide connections to the larger world of learning. We hope that the information provided will help you find other more detailed books on specific topics highlighted in our text. We have used 'he' and 'she' variously throughout to avoid gender bias.

The book gives key points and triggers that enable the beginner, as well as the more experienced trainer, to assimilate the concepts quickly and to develop individual pathways to learning. You can start reading at the beginning, the middle or the end.

It was very difficult to stop working on this book. Just when it seemed finished, another thought would occur to us or we would hear of some new development. That is how lifetime learning is: just when you think you know everything about a subject, somebody discovers something new. Learning is never static, it is constantly changing and adding new dimensions to your understanding of yourself or others. In this the third edition we have updated the chapter on e-learning to reflect the broader perspective of blended learning. We have also included other additions to reflect the changing world of training and development.

WHAT IS TRAINING?

You can run a very interesting half-hour session with a group by asking them to define training. Some of their responses may be as follows:

'It happens off-job.'
'It happens on-job.'
'It is showing someone how to do something.'
'It gives a set of objectives that the learner has to achieve.'

Training is often seen as something that is work related – on-job training, off-job training or employment training schemes. In many cases it is perceived as being a formal process, ie with a trainer in a training room, often supported by materials such as a delegate guide. The underpinning principles of how people learn, learning styles, listening, questioning and giving feedback apply to training as well as teaching, lecturing, coaching and assessing. There is normally an expectation that the training will have an aim and objectives, structured contents and evaluation.

Within this process there is an enormous range of variations in delivery depending on the style and approach of the trainer and the context of the training. At one end of the spectrum there are highly facilitative trainers who use very few formal inputs, relying instead on their experience to generate ideas within the group – they are very much output driven. At the other end are the more traditional skills trainers, those who may be more comfortable in a 'tell' environment; their natural style is to input information. Both could be described as trainers delivering training, but the learning experience of the delegates will be very different in each case. Both approaches have advantages and disadvantages.

Facilitative trainers naturally work well with groups. Through their own personal creativity and energy they facilitate and encourage individuals and groups to excel.

The more traditional trainers may find this approach difficult to emulate. They have to learn new behaviours, their style may be more directive or they are used to adopting an 'expert' role.

In training today there should be a combination of active participation and information giving. Delegates like to feel that the trainer has 'given' them something. It might be a model, a process or information. They don't want to feel that all the trainer has done is to tell them what they already know. That gives substance to the old saying about consultants borrowing your watch to tell you the time and then charging you for the privilege.

As we discuss in the section on 'Changing role of training and development (T&D)' (p.8), training itself is changing. Many traditional centres of skills training have disappeared and been replaced by distance learning resource centres, line manager coaching and special motivational training events off-site. With the development of e-learning, some training has been completely removed from a classroom environment and made available online. In Chapter 6, Getting the Best from Blended and E-learning, this is discussed in much more detail. Today's organizations regard attendance at any training event as a serious investment and that it must provide value for money and relate to the objectives of the business.

Already, we are seeing an increasing reference to the use of the word 'learning', or 'learning and development', instead of 'training and development'.

CREATING A LEARNING ENVIRONMENT

Many organizations aspire to be learning ones, but it takes dedication to achieve this. It requires commitment from everyone to allow individuals to manage their own development and to support the process through coaching, feedback and ongoing performance management. Trainers have a key role to play in the creation of a learning environment; the role may be given different names, such as performance coach, team leader, or internal consultant.

The secret to success in creating a learning environment is an understanding of the learning process. Elsewhere in this book we shall discuss learning styles and how people learn, but it is important to recognize that we all learn differently and have preferred ways of assimilating information. The organization that recognizes this diversity is more likely to be successful in enabling individuals to unlock their potential.

Learning really is a lifetime process, and people working and learning together generate business success. Increasingly organizations are valuing innovation and creativity, but they are not clear about how to create the environment in which people are able to develop them.

Some organizations are paralysed by change rather than recognizing it as an opportunity to develop and move forward. At times of rapid change individuals need support to recognize the opportunities this presents, to think laterally, flexibly, and to identify their potential.

The learning organization

There is much talk about creating learning organizations, but less of what this actually means. In this section we attempt to identify what it is and how you can create it.

Our basic premise is that learning takes place everywhere, not just in the classroom. A learning organization has the following characteristics:

❑ There is a shift of emphasis from trainer to learner ownership.
❑ The whole range of learning opportunities within an organization is recognized: on-job, off-job, coaching, formal, informal, multimedia, open and blended learning.
❑ Managers are encouraged to develop coaching, mentoring and assessing skills.
❑ Additional learning opportunities are created, for example resource centres, learning centres, and continuous learning. Some companies sponsor such personal development, supporting their employees and encouraging them to gain qualifications or to retrain, or encourage creativity by sponsoring product innovation, for example.

Another idea worth considering is that of 'time-out' – one, two, three, six or twelve months' secondment into other industries or education, or to do something completely different to widen people's perspectives and to encourage the sharing of good practice between organizations.

HOW TO CREATE A LEARNING ORGANIZATION

Stage 1
Identify what currently exists: who has received training, what qualifications have been taken, what T&D structure is already in place within the company. Identify what resources, facilities, budgets are available. Also benchmark: how are other companies organized?

↓

Stage 2
Identify the opportunities within the working environment for coaching, mentoring and on-job training assessment. Match this back to Stage 1; are managers trained to coach, mentor and assess?

↓

Stage 3
Identify pilot potential and a starting point: who is learning what; what are the success criteria, implications on the budget, training requirements?

↓

Stage 4
Create an internal marketing plan, identify how to promote the concept, who to involve.

↓

Stage 5
The process starts, encourage people to take part, look at the big picture across the organization.

↓

Stage 6
Review the pilot: identify how it matches the success criteria. Promote success, for instance in a newsletter about people's experiences. Ensure there are measures of where it is working, an audit of where learning is taking place.

Importantly, review the process continually. Ask the questions, 'Is it working?', 'Is it working everywhere?', 'How can I as a trainer help the process?', 'What can the organization do to help me help others?

Knowledge management

Another word that has grown in importance is 'knowledge'. People talk about 'knowledge workers', and 'knowledge management'. What is interesting is that this is not something that is considered as a 'soft skill'. It is about the fundamental point that 'information equals power' and in today's organizations, when a relatively small number of people are developing specialist skills, if these people walk there is a very high risk of part of the business going with them. Today's younger employees are much more mobile than previous generations. In some cases organizations are offering financial incentives to join a company such is the need to attract new talent. Being enterprising is no longer a term just used for people who want to run their own businesses, people need to be enterprising within their own organizations.

Some of the definitions of knowledge management will describe how to develop systems to manage knowledge, in the same way as you might want to keep track of intellectual capital. However, the most important factor behind knowledge management is what people keep in their head.

Increasingly people are recognizing the importance of IPR (Intellectual Property Rights). In previous generations individuals who created new learning concepts were only too happy just to have their findings published, now those same findings can also have a value attached to them.

One of the key sources of information about knowledge management is @Brint.com and in an article about knowledge management they include the following:

> Bob Hiebeler, Arthur Andersen's managing director of KnowledgeSpace Intranet (profiled in the May 15, 1998 CIO magazine), observed at a recent panel discussion of knowledge management experts: 'to me, this is the essence of knowledge sharing. It's all about contribution, it's all about the respect for others' opinions and views, it's all about a good facilitation and synthesis process, it's all about the distribution of lessons learned from this knowledge process, and it's all about access to packaged knowledge and key insights that become the starting points for individual learning'.

A similar theme is taken up by Brook Manville and Nathaniel Foote in 'Strategy as if Knowledge Mattered' a Fast Company article, April 1996. In a thought-provoking article they identify the following as key steps:

1. Knowledge-based strategies begin with strategy, not knowledge.
2. Knowledge-based strategies aren't strategies unless you can link them to traditional measures of performance.

3. Executing a knowledge-based strategy is not about managing knowledge; it's about nurturing people with knowledge.
4. Organizations leverage knowledge through networks of people who collaborate – not through networks of technology that interconnect.
5. People networks leverage knowledge through organizational 'pull' rather than centralized information 'push'.

Linking this to a number of case study examples of how this is put into practice they explain that:

> These successes can be tracked to the superior use of knowledge. And they are much more compelling than the warm and fuzzy argument that companies should adopt knowledge as a philosophical goal since learning and education are 'good for the company' – or even 'good for society.' The point of a knowledge-based strategy is not to save the world; it's to make money. It's for hard heads.

When exploring the 'pull' rather than 'push' theory, they explain that the power should come from demand rather than supply and that companies run a real risk of overloading their employees with too much information. They also emphasize the importance of on-the-job 'just-in-time' learning, a term that is also used to describe some forms of e-learning – (see Chapter 6 – Getting the Best from Blended and E-learning).

They conclude by suggesting that: 'The essence of successful knowledge-based strategies is a company's capacity to raise the aspirations of each employee. These are the people whose contributions and ongoing development become the life-blood of performance gains.'

The implication of all this for organizations and trainers is a fundamental shift from training to learning, there is a distinct difference in ownership, the individual needs to own and take responsibility for their own learning and the importance of helping individuals realize their potential.

Emotional intelligence

Although it may seem that 'emotional intelligence' is a recent entrant into our vocabulary, it has in fact been acknowledged for a much longer period. Daniel Goleman, in *Working with Emotional Intelligence* (1999), suggests that a number of people have defined emotional intelligence including Howard Gardner who in 1983 proposed a model of 'multiple intelligence'. Peter Salovey and John Mayer in the 1990s, who defined emotional intelligence 'in terms of being able to monitor and regulate one's own and others' feelings and to use feelings to guide thought and action'. His own definition includes 'five basic emotional and social competencies':

❑ self-awareness
❑ self-regulation
❑ motivation
❑ empathy
❑ social skills.

Goleman's work moves emotional intelligence into the arena of emotional competence, by further defining 25 emotional competencies and explaining that individuals will have a profile of strengths and limits, but that 'the ingredients for outstanding performance require only that we have strengths in a given number of these competencies, typically at least six or so and that the strengths be spread across all five areas of emotional intelligence. In other words there are many paths to excellence'.

What Goleman and others have done is to introduce the concept of another type of intelligence, suggesting that our skills with people are as important to the organizations that might recruit us as our IQ, our qualifications and our expertise.

Many organizations are also recognizing the impact of this in their retention and development of key workers. This also has implications for the trainer working with learners in that there needs to be an acknowledgement that helping individuals develop in these core areas is as important as developing management or functional skills. It can also mean the need for a different approach and in this case personal coaching can be very effective (see The Trainer As... Personal Coach, Chapter 8, p.124).

THE CHANGING ROLE OF TRAINING AND DEVELOPMENT

Traditionally many organizations had large training and development (T&D) functions. They provided initial training support, designed and ran courses, and provided menus of training for other functions to select from. Some T&D functions were criticized for their lack of understanding of the business objectives. Also they were sometimes accused of being too slow when responding to the needs of the business.

In the last ten years T&D functions have changed enormously. In many cases they have been streamlined or removed altogether, and much more responsibility for training and development has been given to line managers. As highlighted in the preface of this edition, trainers as well as businesses are having to respond to rapidly changing environments, uncertainty and the need to recruit and retain key personnel often within limited budgets.

So, what should T&D functions do to survive in the current business environment? You may find the following checklist helpful.

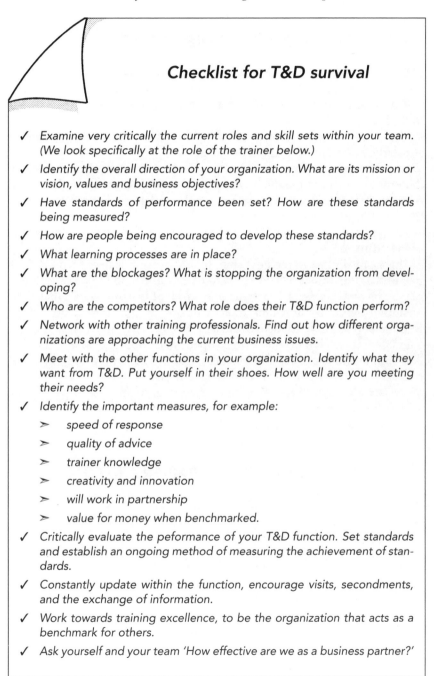

Checklist for T&D survival

✓ Examine very critically the current roles and skill sets within your team. (We look specifically at the role of the trainer below.)

✓ Identify the overall direction of your organization. What are its mission or vision, values and business objectives?

✓ Have standards of performance been set? How are these standards being measured?

✓ How are people being encouraged to develop these standards?

✓ What learning processes are in place?

✓ What are the blockages? What is stopping the organization from developing?

✓ Who are the competitors? What role does their T&D function perform?

✓ Network with other training professionals. Find out how different organizations are approaching the current business issues.

✓ Meet with the other functions in your organization. Identify what they want from T&D. Put yourself in their shoes. How well are you meeting their needs?

✓ Identify the important measures, for example:
  ➢ speed of response
  ➢ quality of advice
  ➢ trainer knowledge
  ➢ creativity and innovation
  ➢ will work in partnership
  ➢ value for money when benchmarked.

✓ Critically evaluate the peformance of your T&D function. Set standards and establish an ongoing method of measuring the achievement of standards.

✓ Constantly update within the function, encourage visits, secondments, and the exchange of information.

✓ Work towards training excellence, to be the organization that acts as a benchmark for others.

✓ Ask yourself and your team 'How effective are we as a business partner?'

Further information is available in Thorne and Machray (2000), *World Class Training: Providing training excellence* (see Appendix 3, p.237).

THE ROLE OF THE TRAINER

This book is about training, and, as we said earlier, training is about helping others learn. The techniques of effective training are also relevant to teachers, lecturers and consultants. What skills does a trainer need today?

First and perhaps foremost is curiosity to find out more, to want to support change and to want to develop.

Second is personal presence – that ability to rise above the mundane, that inner confidence which makes someone not afraid to lead, but equally able skillfully to facilitate and help people reach their own solutions and conclusions.

Third is a sense of urgency, to be able to respond promptly to the needs of the business.

This last is linked to the next skill, that of being business focused. This means that the trainer has the consultative skills needed to meet with line managers and heads of functions and to identify with them what their business objectives are, and then to work in partnership to design training and learning to meet those needs.

Finally, it is important to be open and approachable. Training is an important aspect of any business, but unfortunately some training functions and academic institutions have hung on to the belief that they alone set the objectives, the time frames and are the experts. The successful trainers of the future will be the change agents, the performance coaches, the facilitators and the business partners.

THE LINE MANAGER AS TRAINER AND COACH

If you are a line manager and have been asked to become a trainer or coach, you have a great opportunity to help others learn. Many managers have a natural ability to encourage people to learn, but this ability can be enhanced by a clearer understanding of how to coach (see Chapter 8, p.121) or how to train effectively (see Chapter 4, p.44).

Effective coaching has a lot to do with confidence. If you have never run a training session, you may be nervous, but by planning the session and thinking about the content you can minimize the nervousness and create a positive learning experience for those attending the session. (For details of how to design a training session see Chapter 3, p.29).

Many organizations encourage their line managers to take a more direct role in the development of their own team. The reasons for this are varied, but in many cases it is because of reduced training budgets. When businesses streamline, training functions may appear to be a costly overhead. They may also be viewed adversely because of their past performance (see the section on the changing role of training and development, p.8).

Apart from these reasons, many organizations have come to the conclusion that the person who can have most impact on the day-to-day development of the individual is the line manager. The reasons for this are that the line manager is accessible, that learning can be delivered in bite-sized chunks and that the theory can be supported by more immediate opportunities for practice.

The more progressive organizations are equipping their line managers with the skills of coaching, facilitation and performance management. If you are performing this role, the other underpinning skills as described in the role of the trainer are also important: understanding how people learn; how to design learning experiences; how to update your knowledge; and networking to share best practice. You may also be providing one-to-one support to those undertaking their learning online within an e- or blended learning environment. More information about this role is included in Chapter 6, but a key factor is to keep a dialogue going with the learner. It is very easy to assume that once people are behind a computer they do not need your support – but just as with any form of training, preparing people for the learning experience before and reviewing afterwards will enhance their understanding and demonstrate your own interest in their learning.

Whatever job title or role you have, the rest of this book is designed to help you in your personal development and to create learning experiences that are interesting, memorable and fun!

Being Professional

The training professional should continually want to develop. Your role is a key one in the development of other people. Whether you are working with a chief executive officer (CEO) and the board of senior executives, or inducting a new group of employees, the impression that you give to others is very important. You create the brand of training within an organization; whatever training role you have, you can make learning either a very positive, or a negative, experience.

Developing an understanding of yourself, your strengths, your style of training and your ability to facilitate and coach others, is an important part of this personal brand. Only from this understanding can you continue to build your skills and expertise.

We revisit this concept in several other sections of this book as we explore the different dimensions of the trainer's role. In this chapter we focus on the underpinning understanding of yourself.

BEING COMFORTABLE WITH YOURSELF

How well do you know yourself? When was the last time you undertook a psychometric test? Can you accurately describe your strengths and areas of development? When did you last undertake any personal coaching or training? As trainers it is very easy to neglect our own development – we have all the excuses: no time, too busy developing others, it's too expensive, etc. The real professional, however, recognizes the importance of having a personal development plan.

Where do you start?

In our experience, the better you understand yourself the better able you are to help others. We use the phrase 'being comfortable with yourself ' to describe the inner confidence that comes from knowing your strengths and areas of development. We can build a picture of ourselves through a variety of means, but the model of the training professional below illustrates the types of analysis that we can undertake to gain a clearer picture of ourselves and, even more important, how others perceive us.

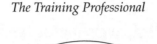

The Training Professional

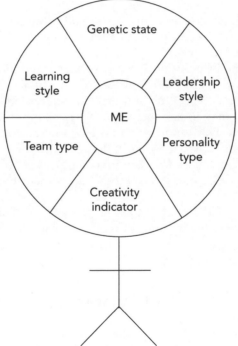

We can enlarge this picture by inviting feedback from others. Lifetime learning gives us the opportunity to explore ourselves and we build layers of knowledge as we work with others. There are a whole range of psychometric tests and other inventories and profiles, and new ones are being developed all the time. The important thing is not just to select one type, and not to just do it once.

As we mature, we change, finding new responses to situations. Some characteristics are inherent, but as you become more at ease with the ongoing process of self-development, you will discover other possibilities.

As a trainer or coach you can help others with the same process. It is important to mention here that people need to be trained and registered to give feedback and administer many of the tests. However, once the professional feedback has been given, the skilled trainer can help people explore how this knowledge affects their day-to-day working life and, importantly, how they interact with others in groups.

Why psychometric tests?

Psychometric testing is loved by many and questioned by others. The best approach is to be curious – by undertaking psychometric tests and receiving skilled feedback you are building up a picture of yourself similar to the model on page 13. Why we suggest undertaking a range of profiles is that, as in any piece of research, you will identify trends.

Some psychometric tests now incorporate features of others, so that by taking one you may in fact receive feedback about other dimensions of your personality. This is normally indicated in the information about the test. Our diagram illustrates some of the areas that are explored by search agencies and employers for recruitment purposes. However, we also suggest that you explore other areas, such as creativity and learning styles.

The purpose of the tests is to give you enhanced understanding of yourself, but, as with any form of feedback, you should review it carefully and test it against your experience of working with others and feedback you have received elsewhere.

Inviting feedback

Who gives you feedback? Do you invite it? Do you believe it? As professionals we should be able to ask for and absorb feedback into our ongoing development. Unfortunately too few people are really skilled at giving it. If you are training people to assess or coach, you will recognize the importance of doing it properly, but so many people give feedback in a way that is unhelpful during appraisals or performance management sessions.

If you do develop a clear understanding of your strengths, you are better able to help people to give you feedback. By asking the right questions, you will be able to elicit information about your effectiveness as a trainer. You will also, if you are an experienced communicator, be able to identify other people's responses to you. We mention several times in this book the importance of having a trusted colleague who can give you constructive feedback. This may be a line manager, a co-tutor or another team member, but the value of feedback from someone you respect cannot be underestimated.

THE PERFORMANCE

As a training professional it is important to recognize that people expect you to be able to present and facilitate with style. In running Train-the-Trainer programmes we encourage people to think about their performance (see Chapter 4, p.44). With an enhanced understanding of yourself you will find that you are better able to protect yourself from the stresses and strains of being a trainer.

Like actors, most trainers feel excited before some events. This can help you find the adrenaline and energy to run highly participative activities, but it is important to recognize the effect this may have on your body. We discuss this in more detail on p.17, but if you are regularly giving of yourself, you need to find ways of recharging your batteries and keeping yourself physically fit.

GUIDELINES FOR A WINNING PERFORMANCE

Step 1
Create a presence – who am I? Psychometric testing, reviewing the profiles. Talk to people, gain feedback from peers, your boss, family, mentors and friends.

Outcome: An accurate assessment of yourself, your strengths and areas of development.

↓

Step 2
What do I want to achieve? What does the company need me to do? Goals, aspirations, job role, outcomes from business expectations.

Outcome: Clear objectives – a route map.

↓

Step 3
Building the brand, being comfortable with yourself, the presentation, what to say, what to do, what to take, what to leave, what to wear.

Outcome: Creating presence.

Step 4
The performance – putting it into practice, first to role-play, then the real performance and then the feedback.

Outcome: The winning performance.

PREVENTING BURN-OUT

Trainers, like other creative, artistic and busy professional people, are potentially susceptible to 'burn-out'. Prevention is better than cure and all the measures mentioned in Recharging the Batteries are relevant (p.18). Equally with experience you are better able to balance the pressures in your life. There are specific actions that you can take to minimize the risk:

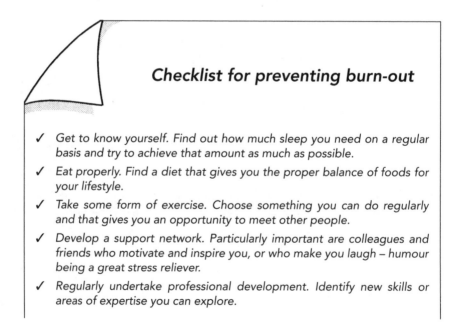

Checklist for preventing burn-out

✓ Get to know yourself. Find out how much sleep you need on a regular basis and try to achieve that amount as much as possible.

✓ Eat properly. Find a diet that gives you the proper balance of foods for your lifestyle.

✓ Take some form of exercise. Choose something you can do regularly and that gives you an opportunity to meet other people.

✓ Develop a support network. Particularly important are colleagues and friends who motivate and inspire you, or who make you laugh – humour being a great stress reliever.

✓ Regularly undertake professional development. Identify new skills or areas of expertise you can explore.

✓ Each day create space, however little, just for yourself. Whatever other work or domestic pressures exist, devote time to yourself. Use it to do something relaxing, such as reading a book, listening to music, telephoning someone, clearing something off your personal action list or just staring into space.

✓ Recognize your achievement. It's wonderful when other people give you positive feedback, but reviewing your own progress can be equally positive, particularly if you have logged your starting point.

✓ Be alert to the signs that the pressure is too much. Look for the signs beforehand and do something before you develop the symptoms of stress.

✓ Build variety into your working life. Try not to fall into a routine of doing the same things on the same days.

✓ Set yourself lifetime goals and regularly review progress against them.

HANDLING PRESSURE

Trainers, like anyone else, need to recognize the difference between stress and pressure. We can withstand a considerable amount of pressure, but the physiological changes that occur with stress can be debilitating, which is why the following section on recharging the batteries is so important.

Pressure for trainers takes many forms, depending on their role. For the self-employed independent trainer there is the ongoing pressure of diary management. In this business it is often either feast or famine: suddenly all your clients want you on 15 October, or alternatively no one wants you in July. All the time management and priority techniques in the world will not help you deal with these particular quirks of fate. You can, however, use your knowledge of the training business to protect yourself against these surges in demand. For instance, try to identify the likely requirements of your established clients during the more popular months of the year, and, where over-subscription appears likely, negotiate with each of them, trying to meet individual demands as closely as possible.

As in any business, trainers should aim to work in partnership with their clients, and alerting clients about the popularity of particular months in the year is part of that process. During the less popular months, identify design work, or other projects that require less direct training contact.

The need to win business can also create tension, as this need is a critically important aspect of business life (see Chapter 10, p.196). But being physically and mentally relaxed and feeling positive often help in successfully winning business.

Time management and prioritizing

Like any working professional, trainers need to plan and prioritize their work schedules. Making time for marketing or administration can often be difficult. It takes discipline to maintain a balanced schedule of direct delivery, design, marketing and administration. You also need to plan breaks to ensure peak performance. These breaks can take any form, but should provide you with the opportunity to focus on something completely different from your normal routine, such as sport, leisure or meeting friends.

Protecting thinking time is even harder, particularly when other people have access to your diaries. In offices with electronic networking it becomes even more important to protect your time. Very few people actually enter into their diaries 'thinking time', because there is a general fear of the comments that such an entry might generate. Many open plan offices preclude the opportunity to think creatively, and people often find it difficult to say assertively, 'I'm going to the leisure centre to think.' However, increasingly, more organizations are recognizing the importance of innovation and creativity and are encouraging a more positive approach to people's needs for space and thinking time.

The need to produce imaginative and creative development programmes can produce considerable pressure, because very few of us can be creative and innovative to order. If your role involves the design of development programmes or the creation of materials, it is important to find somewhere to work that is congenial.

Some of the more progressive training organizations create design rooms for their trainers equipped with flipcharts, lots of wall space, previous course material and other sources of inspiration.

For trainers working from home, the same principle applies. You need to be able to create a space which is comfortable as well as functional, and is surrounded by sights and sounds that help you to be creative. (For further guidance on generating ideas and being creative see p.26, and Chapter 5, p.67.)

Increasingly organizations are recognizing the importance of helping their employees achieve balance in their lives. If you are coaching individuals about their work, encourage them to adopt a more holistic approach, and apply this approach to your own work/life balance too.

RECHARGING THE BATTERIES

Trainers are expected to inspire others, but how can you inspire yourself? You need creative triggers (people, places) that you can use to recharge batteries and energize your thoughts, and it is important, because of the nature of your work, that you are able to recharge regularly and efficiently. And you need to identify the triggers and use them before you become depleted.

When we are running management development programmes, we talk about the need for everyone to visualize a place that is important to them, or a time when they were particularly successful. We want people to smile when they think of the image, and we encourage people to go to it regularly to reinforce positive messages about themselves and what they can achieve. The process can help you to relax, or it can energize you.

Music can have a similar effect; some trainers play it in the background during coffee/lunch breaks. Alternatively, it can be used during sessions to evoke memories and to encourage creativity, or as motivational entrance or exit music at large conferences. There are endless possibilities, but in every case the appropriateness of its use has to be assessed against the target audience.

On a personal level you can use music to energize you or help you relax. Many trainers have a selection for different occasions, such as rousing music to help them prepare for their performance, and more restful music to help them relax afterwards. You can create compilations to suit your mood and requirements. If you enjoy music, it can be a very effective method of re-energizing yourself.

HANDLING DIFFICULT PEOPLE

Most of us have to deal with difficult people at some time in our career. Knowing ourselves can help us handle others in potentially difficult situations. So much conflict is caused by lack of understanding on both sides. Tensions within companies often arise because people are too busy to talk to each other and to find out the truth behind rumours and hearsay.

Much can be achieved by identifying the other person's perspective. Customer-focused organizations are recognizing the importance of viewing issues 'through the eyes of the customer'. In any negotiating situation you need to use an enhanced skill set to identify the issue, explore the options and resolve the conflict. The following checklist may help in handling difficult people.

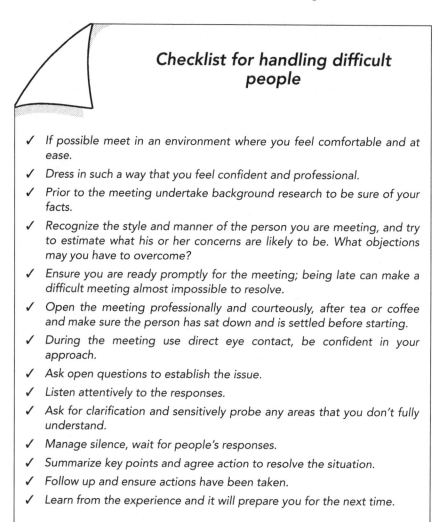

Checklist for handling difficult people

✓ If possible meet in an environment where you feel comfortable and at ease.

✓ Dress in such a way that you feel confident and professional.

✓ Prior to the meeting undertake background research to be sure of your facts.

✓ Recognize the style and manner of the person you are meeting, and try to estimate what his or her concerns are likely to be. What objections may you have to overcome?

✓ Ensure you are ready promptly for the meeting; being late can make a difficult meeting almost impossible to resolve.

✓ Open the meeting professionally and courteously, after tea or coffee and make sure the person has sat down and is settled before starting.

✓ During the meeting use direct eye contact, be confident in your approach.

✓ Ask open questions to establish the issue.

✓ Listen attentively to the responses.

✓ Ask for clarification and sensitively probe any areas that you don't fully understand.

✓ Manage silence, wait for people's responses.

✓ Summarize key points and agree action to resolve the situation.

✓ Follow up and ensure actions have been taken.

✓ Learn from the experience and it will prepare you for the next time.

In today's training environment the training professional has an important role to play, and the better you understand yourself, your strengths and areas of development, the better able you will be to help organizations and individuals fulfil their real potential.

How People Learn

LEARNING STYLES

One of the most important factors in the design and delivery of training is understanding how people learn. As a trainer you should recognize and take account of the differences between people's preferred styles of learning.

In the training professional model on page 13, we included 'learning style' as one of the components to measure for your own personal development. It is equally important to help the people you are developing to identify their preferred learning style. By doing this you can help them to recognize what they need to do in a learning situation to maximize their learning.

What are learning styles?

Initial research undertaken by David Kolb identified an Experiential Learning Model that had four phases (see the reading list in Appendix 3, p.237). He described the first phase as concrete experience, and the second as reflective observation, in which the learner rethinks through what has occurred. The third phase is abstract conceptualization, when the learner makes links with his broader knowledge base. Once this stage has been completed individuals must integrate this new learning into their active experimentation and then develop their own implementation plans.

This process is cyclical, so that a learner who has absorbed one set of learning experiences is ready to undertake the process again with another learning experience. Kolb's work underpins much of the current research into learning; one example of this is the Learning Styles Questionnaire developed by Peter Honey and Alan Mumford (see Appendix 2, p.234 for

The Experiential Learning Model

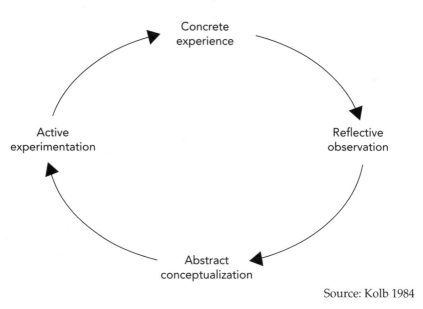

Source: Kolb 1984

further information). By undertaking this questionnaire learners identify whether they are:

❑ activists
❑ reflectors
❑ theorists
❑ pragmatists.

Each style is demonstrated through a series of behaviours and preferred way of learning. For example:

❑ *Activists* enjoy new experiences and opportunities from which they can learn. They enjoy being involved, are happy to be in the limelight and prefer to be active rather than sitting and listening.

❑ *Reflectors* prefer to observe, think and assimilate information before starting. They like to review what has happened, what they have learnt. They prefer to reach decisions in their own time and do not like to feel under pressure.

❑ *Theorists* like to explore methodically; they think problems through in a step-by-step logical way and ask questions. They tend to be detached and analytical. They like to be intellectually stretched and feel uncomfortable with lateral thinking, preferring models and systems.

❑ *Pragmatists* like practical solutions and want to get on and try things. They dislike too much theory. They like to experiment and search out new ideas that they want to try out. They act quickly and confidently, are very down to earth and respond to problems as a challenge.

By understanding Kolb's Experiential Learning Model you will be able to structure the learning experience to allow the learner to progress through the different stages of

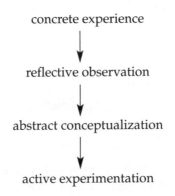

concrete experience

↓

reflective observation

↓

abstract conceptualization

↓

active experimentation

and to maximize his or her potential to learn.

You can also help the learner to recognize differences between the way they and others learn. In group activities you can illustrate the different styles within the group by asking the members each to work in a way that takes them away from their natural style.

Encouraging learners to find out about themselves is an important part of their personal development. As we discussed in Chapter 1, p.12, everyone should have a healthy curiosity about the way they learn and interact with others. Recognizing how they learn, or how they contribute to a team can be very helpful to the individual learner. A training programme that begins to explore these areas can be a very useful spring-board for further development.

Knowing and understanding the implications of learning styles is very helpful in structuring the learning. It has particular relevance if you are working on an individual basis with a learner. It can help you identify the most effective route, either through offering on-job training, coaching, practical experience or distance learning. It can also be used to help people overcome learning difficulties through helping them to recognize some of the factors that may have inhibited their previous learning.

It is equally important for the trainer to structure any training programme to include a range of activities that will reflect the different learning styles. For example, there should be opportunities for:

- ❏ theory input
- ❏ practical experience
- ❏ application of theory
- ❏ ideas generation.

Trainers also need to recognize that their delegates' learning styles may not be the same as theirs. This is where working with a co-tutor can be particularly helpful, as it is likely that your styles may be different.

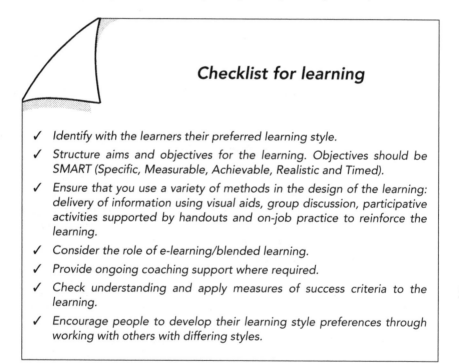

Checklist for learning

✓ Identify with the learners their preferred learning style.
✓ Structure aims and objectives for the learning. Objectives should be SMART (Specific, Measurable, Achievable, Realistic and Timed).
✓ Ensure that you use a variety of methods in the design of the learning: delivery of information using visual aids, group discussion, participative activities supported by handouts and on-job practice to reinforce the learning.
✓ Consider the role of e-learning/blended learning.
✓ Provide ongoing coaching support where required.
✓ Check understanding and apply measures of success criteria to the learning.
✓ Encourage people to develop their learning style preferences through working with others with differing styles.

DESIGNING TRAINING TO MEET PEOPLE'S NEEDS

Identification of client needs is discussed later in this book (see p.30), but as well as the sponsoring client you will also have the individual learner's needs to consider. The very skilled trainer is able to design the training experience to meet the needs of both the client and the learner.

Designing training to meet the combined needs is the application of much of the content in this book. In order to design the learning experience, the trainer should have the ability to identify together with the client the strategic overview and the business objectives and required outcomes from the training. However, once you are in direct contact with the learner(s) you should also be able to respond to their individual needs within the context of the overall desired outcomes.

Often trainers will present the overall aim and objectives and broad details of the content at the start of the training programme or coaching session and then ask the group to identify their specific training needs within the context of the planned learning. In this way you ensure 'buy-in' from the learner, providing you return to pick up the points during the course of the programme. Sometimes what is requested is beyond the scope of the programme, and this needs to be clarified at the time of the feedback, but it should be coupled with a suggested alternative route to meeting those needs.

It is an essential skill of a trainer that they put learners at ease and create an atmosphere where people can learn. We shall return to this point (see p.50). Many of us bear the scars of poor teaching or training, when we were told that we were 'no good' at a particular subject, or we have been humiliated in front of our peers, so the role of the trainer in creating a positive learning environment cannot be over-emphasized. The learner should feel accepted, supported and respected, and that the trainer has a genuine interest in their development.

Some people may have special needs, and these too need to be catered for in the design of training. Specialist support is available for people with learning difficulties (see Appendix 2, p.234) but trainers should always ensure that they provide equality of opportunity and are non-discriminatory in their approach to individuals and groups.

Once you understand how people learn you can then come closer to meeting the needs of individuals; this is particularly relevant when working with large groups, or in one-to-one coaching sessions. Use the content from Chapter 6, Getting the Best from Blended and E-learning, to explore different ways in which you can structure the learning. With the learners having potentially less time available for off-the-job learning, blended learning may be a more effective solution to meeting individual learning needs.

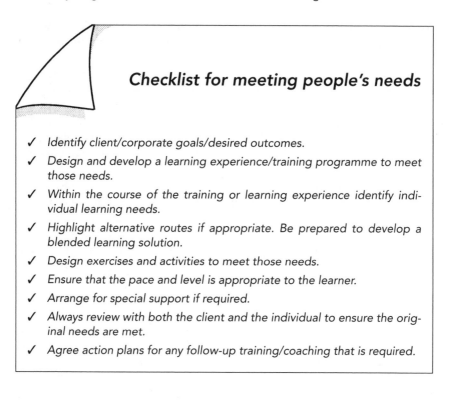

Checklist for meeting people's needs

✓ Identify client/corporate goals/desired outcomes.

✓ Design and develop a learning experience/training programme to meet those needs.

✓ Within the course of the training or learning experience identify individual learning needs.

✓ Highlight alternative routes if appropriate. Be prepared to develop a blended learning solution.

✓ Design exercises and activities to meet those needs.

✓ Ensure that the pace and level is appropriate to the learner.

✓ Arrange for special support if required.

✓ Always review with both the client and the individual to ensure the original needs are met.

✓ Agree action plans for any follow-up training/coaching that is required.

THINKING CREATIVELY

An essential skill of a trainer is the ability to think creatively and to provide learning opportunities that encourage the learner to explore all the potential of their learning style. Many of today's businesses want their employees to be creative and innovative without understanding how such skills are developed.

We discuss this further from a trainer's perspective in Chapter 5, but in the context of meeting the needs of the learner it is important to recognize the underlying principles of creative thought.

You may have heard the expression 'left brain/right brain'. This concept is attributed to Roger Sperry and Robert Ornstein from the University of California who showed that each hemisphere of the brain has a preferred way of operating, the left side being far better at performing logical, analytical tasks that require step by step logical progression, while the right brain, in contrast, is much better at free-flowing thought, seeing the overview, and likes colour, pictures and shapes and sees connections between things.

Sperry and Ornstein's work has inspired a number of present-day people developers to recognize both the differences and the potential for encouraging whole brain activity. Tony Buzan's Mind Maps® concept (see p.71) is an example of this.

The research showed that if you have always primarily used one side of your brain you may find it harder to use the other. Certainly many of us have been conditioned from an early age to believe that we have particular deficiencies, eg 'I'm no good at maths,' or, 'I've never been able to draw.'

What the work of Buzan and others is showing us is that we need not be totally left-brained, or right-brained; that we can, by using both sides of the brain in our activities, become more 'whole-brained.'

Equally right- and left-brained people have preferred, or predictable ways of working. Within a training situation the left-brained people will tend to be methodical, neat and tidy, and will complete tasks on time. Right- brained people will use acres of flipchart paper, and it will often be full of images and colour. They may either not have fully understood the task, because they rushed into it too quickly, or their lateral thoughts took them down another track, but they will present it enthusiastically.

These differences are important, because, once recognized, they will help the learner understand more about how they learn. For example, when you or your delegates complete a learning styles questionnaire (see p.21), some people may have difficulty in identifying one particular style because their scores may be more widely spread across a number of styles, reflecting both their left- and right-brain preferences. Others may have a high score on one particular style, indicating that they are predominantly left- or right-brained.

It is important that you help people to recognize the potential of whole-brain activity, but you also need to encourage people to respect the differences and to work together, drawing on each other's strengths in particular activities.

These learning preferences also have an impact on the style of the trainer. The left-brained trainer may methodically write down all the steps needed to lead a group through to reach a conclusion, and would be concerned if the group wanted to deviate from that route. The right-brained trainer may have less patience with a group of left-brained learners, who may be taking notes, asking questions or challenging the process.

Co-tutoring can help trainers to appreciate the benefits of the different learning styles, and it can be helpful for groups too because the trainers' combined style should match the preferred learning styles of the total group.

Within the learning experience there are a number of ways that you can encourage people to think creatively; brainstorming and mind mapping are just two such methods. Learning can also take place outside the training room: the concept of the learning organization (see Introduction, p.1) is based upon encouraging learning to take place within the work-place, individuals are being given the opportunity to pursue lifetime learning and to generate ideas for business improvement.

However, one of the constraints on real creative thought is the resistance to the implementation of new and novel ideas. We discuss this further (see the section on the trainer as change agent, p.151), but often really creative ideas founder when someone says, 'It won't work in our organization. Why change? We've always done it this way.'

Trainers need to help delegates not only to explore ideas but also to look at the practical application back in the workplace. In this way the energy and enthusiasm generated by thinking creatively can be channelled positively into action. Creative thinking, together with an understanding of how people learn, are important underpinning skills for any trainer. For much further support on this subject please see Chapter 5, Sources of Inspiration.

Designing a Training Programme

GETTING STARTED – THE INITIAL IDEA

Depending on your role, you may have full or part responsibility for this, but one of the key skills of a trainer is the ability to design a training or learning programme. At first it may seem daunting, but, like any other task, once you develop a process for doing it, it becomes much easier. The diagram below illustrates the key stages.

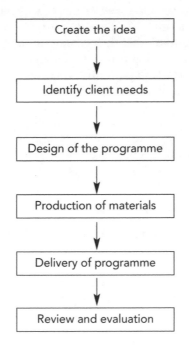

IDENTIFICATION OF CLIENT NEEDS

The starting point for a programme can come from a variety of sources:

- ❑ an idea that you have for an open programme
- ❑ a response to a client's request
- ❑ a follow-up to an existing programme
- ❑ a means of reinforcing business objectives.

In this initial stage you are only developing the idea, so you need to explore a number of options and questions:

- ❑ Should it be an open programme?
- ❑ Should it be an in-company training programme?
- ❑ Is it a training or a coaching need?
- ❑ Is there really a demand?
- ❑ Is training the right solution?

Whether you are working with an actual client or preparing an open programme, you need to identify outcomes that can be converted later into aims and objectives. One way of helping a client to focus on their needs is to ask the question, 'At the end of this training, what would you like people to be able to do that they cannot do now, or what would you like to be different?' By asking people to think about the future you begin to identify where to start. Importantly, you and your client should also consider if training really is the right solution. In today's organizations there are a number of ways including coaching and blended/e-learning that may be a more appropriate solution. Another important factor is the duration. One key feature in today's learning is the attention span of learners. Consider really carefully the overall solution and examine ways of pro-actively involving learners; make as much of the learning as possible personal to them.

LINKING TRAINING TO BUSINESS OBJECTIVES

You may also have to structure aims and objectives, or outcomes if you are submitting a proposal for funding (see Chapter 10, p.196). To help you identify the outcomes you need to spend time with the client and, ideally, a sample of participants, identifying their needs. This will help you refine the content and also ensure buy-in from the participants on the programme. This stage should not be too lengthy and should be based on meeting a representative sample of participants and structured around a sample of questions, such as those in the following checklist.

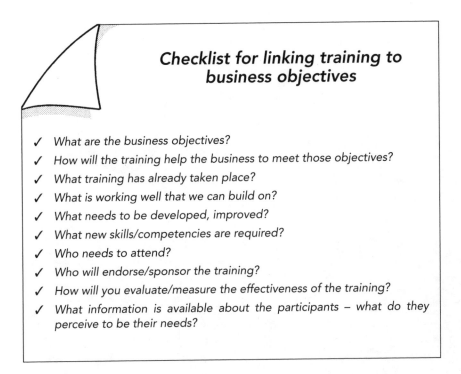

Checklist for linking training to business objectives

✓   What are the business objectives?

✓   How will the training help the business to meet those objectives?

✓   What training has already taken place?

✓   What is working well that we can build on?

✓   What needs to be developed, improved?

✓   What new skills/competencies are required?

✓   Who needs to attend?

✓   Who will endorse/sponsor the training?

✓   How will you evaluate/measure the effectiveness of the training?

✓   What information is available about the participants – what do they perceive to be their needs?

DESIGN OF THE LEARNING SOLUTION

This is the most creative part of the process, the stage when it is important to 'blue-sky' ideas, thoughts and approaches. Tony Buzan has developed a mind mapping technique that is an excellent way of developing training programmes (see Chapter 5, p.67, and Appendix 2, p.234).

The figure overleaf illustrates another model that allows your thoughts to roam as widely as possible, yet still to follow a structure.

Buzan's technique follows a particular process, but you can use the technique in an ordered linear style, or in a more creative way using colours and illustrations. In this way two people working together on a programme with different learning styles, one more imaginative and enthusiastic and the other more practical and logical, can both use this technique to build a programme. You will see from the model some other important factors to consider at this stage.

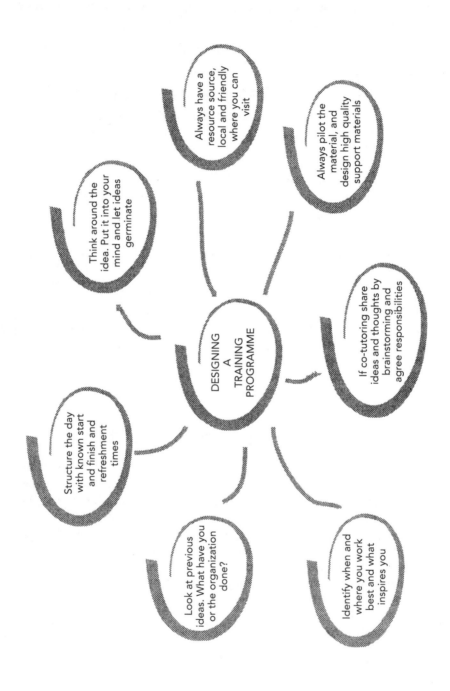

DESIGNING A TRAINING PROGRAMME

Always have a resource source, local and friendly where you can visit

Always pilot the material, and design high quality support materials

Think around the idea. Put it into your mind and let ideas germinate

If co-tutoring share ideas and thoughts by brainstorming and agree responsibilities

Structure the day with known start and finish and refreshment times

Look at previous ideas. What have you or the organization done?

Identify when and where you work best and what inspires you

Research

Very few trainers are able to create training programmes without some form of research, something to get them started. We have already mentioned talking to participants, but it is also useful to have other sources of inspiration. The more experienced trainers will have built up a resource bank of previous programmes, proposals, content or activities.

Trainers, like teachers and lecturers, are notorious magpies, gathering bright jewels of inspiration. Other people's material often gets recycled under new guises, hopefully acknowledged in the process!

However, aspiring trainers should also be capable of generating their own ideas because it can bring tremendous satisfaction. Often these ideas are generated as a result of the background research, or built on from other resources. You can also attend training programmes that give you the opportunity to learn techniques like mind mapping, or to help you develop your own creativity (see Chapter 5, p.67).

A good place to start in the actual design of a programme is to work with another more experienced trainer; as illustrated in the model (p.32) it is important to identify the best time and way for you to design training. One technique is to lock the outline concept away in your mind and let ideas about it germinate while you undertake other activities. If you keep a notebook handy, the ideas can be jotted down until you are ready to start the actual design process.

Another technique is to shut yourself away. Ideally this should be in a design room – somewhere with a flipchart and access to pens, paper and other resources so you can apply discipline to the project.

Setting the parameters

After the initial creative stage you need to begin to commit to a framework for delivery. If it is to be a training programme, one way to start is to divide a page of flipchart paper up, putting in the start and finish and refreshment breaks. As a first step this helps you to identify the size of the task. It also helps to make the process more manageable. Then divide the blocks of time into sessions that will later form the basis of your timetable for the day. You may also decide to create headings for the sessions to stimulate interest, eg 'The Art of the Possible' to describe a session on problem-solving.

By now you should have identified that it is going to be a training programme. For coaching and facilitation (see Chapter 8, p.121) you should also have decided the duration, although this may be revised during the pilot stage. Always aim to design a dynamic, packed programme rather than a stretched event. Sometimes training programmes can be too long and thus lose their impact.

Developing the content

Having identified the time parameters, set about filling the content, remembering pace, variety, attention span and learning styles. (For more information on learning styles see Chapter 2, How People Learn).

The key components are as follows.

Introduction

In the introduction you need to set the tone for the event. Ideally, if the programme is internal, arrange for a senior manager to introduce the programme. During a series of events you may need a number of senior people to share this responsibility through a rota system. Their brief should be to set the training into the context of the business objectives, and to illustrate the company's commitment to the training.

At this stage you should identify the potential senior people and work up a brief for them, of course allowing them the courtesy of creating their own, but as busy people they may appreciate some ideas from you.

Aims and objectives

Next you should be able to write aims and objectives. There are a variety of ways that they can be written, but normally an aim describes the overall outcome of the programme, eg:

Aim: To enable area managers to achieve real business success through the effective management of their people.

The objectives are something that participants are able to do at the end of the programme. Objectives should be SMART:

Specific
Measurable
Achievable
Realistic/**R**elevant
Timed

Always start with a verb, and try to avoid the use of the word 'understand' as it is perceived as too 'soft' and difficult to measure. Use such words as the following:

At the end of the programme participants will be able to...

... describe
... identify
... measure
... consider
... develop.

Beware of setting objectives that are unachievable. Sometimes trainers set over-ambitious objectives that come back to haunt them at the end of the programme. Some trainers prefer to use 'relevant' to 'realistic' in the definition of SMART.

Opening session

In planning the first activity it is important to recognize what you are trying to achieve. However well briefed the participants, trainers are often faced with a mixture of emotions when they first meet the group. Therefore, in the design stage, you need to think carefully about the first activity. What are you trying to achieve?

1. Impact:	You don't want observers, or passengers, you want to generate interest and involvement.
2. Buy-in:	You want the participants, whatever their initial reservation, to have bought into the training, ideally before the first coffee break.
3 Curiosity and intrigue:	You want them to find out more, to take part in the event.
4. Energy and rapport:	You want their active participation and willingness to work with you.

With this in mind the first activity needs to help you meet this criteria. It should be quite short and dynamic and may be followed by a short break to allow people to mix with each other. Either during this activity, or after it, you need to provide a vehicle for people to introduce themselves, often described as an 'ice-breaker'.

There are many products that contain ice-breakers; however, if you are not comfortable with the ice-breaker that you select, then do not use it. Almost any task can be used as an ice-breaker if you include an opportunity for people to introduce themselves within the feedback. Also recognize that, if the group already know one another, it may simply be that you need to introduce yourself. Always try to avoid any activity that seems contrived – be as natural as possible. Use a conversational approach rather than the 'expert' style.

Expand on the content

Following the first activity, the programme needs to be structured around meeting the objectives. The content should be built around a balance of input and participation. The sequence may be as follows:

❏ input
❏ practical activity
❏ feedback
❏ review of learning points.

Now let us look at each in detail.

Input

Within the initial input you can invite guest speakers, use 35 mm, video presentations, or you can present the information yourself. Always remember the attention span of your audience and encourage involvement through active participation in discussion or by asking questions of the group. Always provide copies of this information either by printing out copies of your slides with spaces for their notes, or just the copies themselves. Think carefully about when you distribute these. There are advantages in giving these out early as it allows participants a chance to make notes. The disadvantage is they may lose concentration in what you are saying by reading ahead.

Practical activity

The practical activity can be an exercise, case study, a game/simulation or a role-play. It should encourage the active involvement of all participants. Never provide a task or activity which does not link to an objective, or one in which you have no faith, it won't work! Participants are very shrewd and will reject anything that has no depth.

Designing an activity can take some time, and your sources of inspiration can be varied. It may be based on a tried and tested technique that you have used before, amended to meet the needs of the new group, or it may be something completely new.

You must always research your client group to discover their attitudes, style, energy levels, etc. In your design you should provide relevant examples, case-study, or role-play material to which the participants can relate. The material should be meaningful and practical, eg giving the participants the opportunity to work through case-studies and to develop solutions based on actual scenarios that they recognize provides a safe environment for them to test out their ideas and approaches.

A well-structured role-play carefully organized with supportive feedback can provide participants with a real learning opportunity. Equally, business games or simulations can encourage creativity, problem-solving and team working. Building up these examples takes time, and once you have established examples use them as models for future exercises.

Experiment with a number of formats until you find the one that works best for you and your delegates.

Feedback

This needs careful handling – it is worth spending time with the group prior to their undertaking the activity to explain what you expect in their feedback. It will also provide an opportunity for participants to present their findings. They need to be given clear guidelines on the time and quantity expected, ie one or two flipcharts, feedback to last for approximately ten minutes, and encourage them to identify someone to present the group's findings.

Review of learning points

Unfortunately this can sometimes get forgotten, or inadequate time is allowed for it. Participants often appreciate the trainer highlighting the key points after an activity. It should not be too long, or repetitious, but take just enough time to reinforce the learning.

Co-tutoring

If you are co-tutoring you need to identify the best way to work together on the actual design; brainstorming, sharing thoughts and ideas about the initial structure and then writing it up separately, each taking responsibility for particular sections. Whichever technique you use, you need to recognize each other's strengths and development areas and divide the work accordingly. (See also Chapter 4, p.44.)

The overall programme should be seamless in its structure while benefiting from different styles and approaches.

Action plans

Like the review of learning points, people often run out of steam by the time they reach the action planning stage. Your approach to this will vary depending on the organization. In some cases an organization will have performance management systems, and the outcomes from the course will be linked into their personal development plans.

Others may have a competency framework in place, and the outcomes may support their demonstration of competence. At the most fundamental level you should aim to encourage participants to commit to taking action as a result of being on the course. One way of doing this is to issue stick-it notes and ask each participant to write down one thing that they intend to do differently as a result of coming on the course.

The group then shares their action by sticking the pieces of paper on a flipchart. These commitments are collated by the trainer and sent back to the participants as part of the follow-up from the programme. This can be enhanced by putting the participants into pairs and encouraging them to exchange telephone numbers and to contact each other in three months to review their actions.

Evaluation

Each programme that you run should be evaluated to provide feedback to you on the effectiveness of the experience, and to provide feedback to your client (see Chapter 7, p.98).

Checklist for designing a learning solution

Here are some important points to remember:

✓ However exciting it may seem in the design stage, any new activity needs to be planned carefully and ideally dry-run through a pilot programme.

✓ Never ask participants to do something that you would not be prepared to do yourself. Although trainers are often working to change attitudes, real development does not take place if the participant is resenting the tutor for exposing them, or making them feel uncomfortable in front of their colleagues.

✓ Therefore do not create activities or situations which peel layers off people, as it is unlikely that you will have either the time, or possibly the skill set to put them back together again. If someone has a real difficulty, it is often more appropriate to raise awareness, but to follow up with one-to-one coaching or counselling support.

✓ Try to find a local resource centre where you can view videos, games and other activities. This may be a commercial centre or a university/business school library. Membership of professional bodies, such as the Chartered Institute of Personnel Development (CIPD) or the Institute of Directors (IOD) can also give you access to libraries and other sources of material (see Appendix 2 for useful contacts and addresses). Always try to avoid using outdated materials. Look at the date of publication before ordering and always try to view them before using with a group.

✓ Once you have designed a programme, review it at regular intervals to ensure it is still meeting the needs of the participants and the organization.

PRODUCTION OF MATERIALS

This is an important part of the training process, yet sometimes is an area that is neglected. Well-produced clear information provides a valuable reinforcement of the learning.

What approach should you use?

Your approach will very much depend on your group and the type of event and budget. There are, however, some common guidelines:

❑ Always produce information that is easy to understand and clear to the participants.

❑ Use a variety of mediums, eg OHP slides/PC presentations should have clear bullet point information or illustrations that make key points. Always check font size for projection.

❑ Use handouts for the more detailed text.

❑ Use video to provide variety in the delivery of information, but use short inputs, maximum 20 minutes, unless it is used in a trigger format (ie short video input followed by discussion).

❑ Flipcharts can be used for brainstorming, or outputs from syndicate activities; again prepare where appropriate, write neatly and clearly using dark colours that are easy to read, such as green, blue, purple and black. Avoid red, which is more difficult to read.

How to produce materials

Like many aspects of this book, the production of materials is an enormous area. The breadth and scope of the various methods merit a book in their own right. Our approach is to outline choices and options and to alert you to some of the pitfalls and other areas you should consider when producing materials. However, we also suggest that you seek specialist help in these areas.

Poor materials are actually worse than no materials, therefore it is very important to plan carefully any material production. The simplest form of material production is to desktop publish hard copy and then to reproduce it either using an in-house photocopier or an external copy shop. You can, if your systems are compatible, take the disk from your PC to a specialist printer for longer print runs or for a more sophisticated design process.

Some people generate their presentation on their PC and then use specialist equipment to provide a presentation to a group or individual.

For larger conferences, video, audio or 35 mm slide or PC presentations can be used.

Trainers often focus on delegate material but forget their own. Within training organizations, or in-house training functions, more discipline is usually applied because of the need for consistency in the delivery of several courses using a number of trainers.

Even the most intuitive trainer can benefit from having written some notes to define the content of their input. Writing a trainer guide for others to deliver from is an important skill. We include a sample layout in Appendix 1 (p.224), but writing short notes can help you trigger your thoughts and also ensure that you remember key points in your presentation. Again, the production of a trainer's guide will depend on your budget and specific requirements.

If you are working within an organization, or are producing a guide for someone else, the normal corporate presentation for both delegates and trainer is a binder of either A4/A5 format, either two- or four-hole with tabbed dividers that guide delegates through the various sections of the programme. In writing the content you may wish to adopt the following format:

background to the programme

↓

introduction

↓

session 1, 2, 3 etc

↓

exercises

↓

action plan

↓

course evaluation

↓

reading list

Include copies of OHP slides and handouts numbered for ease of reference within the session tabs.

Trainers have different preferences about giving out the material to delegates; some give it out at the start of the course while others give out session notes as the programme progresses. Some trainers are concerned that the delegates will read ahead, or not fully concentrate on the input if they are reading. Usually, if you draw the delegates' attention to the guide at the start of the programme and say you would prefer if they did not sit and read it but only refer to it as appropriate, most people will be content to wait. Some people will want to make notes on the guide as they run through the programme.

We have primarily discussed material to support programmes, but there are other types of learning material to consider, eg distance learning, management games, multimedia packages, video and audio. Each has special production requirements, and as a rule of thumb, however creative and ambitious you may feel, there is a distinct advantage in producing your first attempts with the help of experts in the different techniques.

The same principle applies to the design of materials. You should have an aim and objectives, the content should be structured in a sequence and it should engage the interest of the learner. It is possible, in the excitement of working in other mediums, to forget the basics of good practice, and end up with not very interesting content. Any form of learning support should have a structure and a purpose and should add to the learning experience rather than detracting from it.

Scheduling the production of materials

It is easy not to allow enough time for the production of materials. It is an important part of the planning process, and once the date for the event or the learning need has been identified, you should work back from that date to identify the production schedule. Whatever is being produced needs to go through several stages, all of which need a timescale attached to them, eg:

❑ overall aim/objectives set
❑ outline content set
❑ schedule for production agreed
❑ guidelines for format, typeface, font agreed
❑ outline first treatment produced
❑ client/author's amendments added
❑ proofing, final version produced
❑ client's approval given for production.

Depending on the involvement of other people, such as the client, the draft stage may involve the production of other draft versions, in which case you repeat the stages of amendments and proofing prior to the final sign-off. Although this may seem a tedious process, by adopting a methodical approach to the final stages, you will avoid the expense of re-doing materials because of errors, which can be particularly costly when the material is being produced for a large number of programmes.

Costings

As we highlighted earlier, the potential for escalating costs in the production of materials is a very real threat. For the inexperienced trainer, purchasing from outside providers is fraught with danger. Most corporate organizations have purchasing procedures that help to eliminate some of the problems. Whether you are part of an internal structure or a sole trader there are some important points to remember.

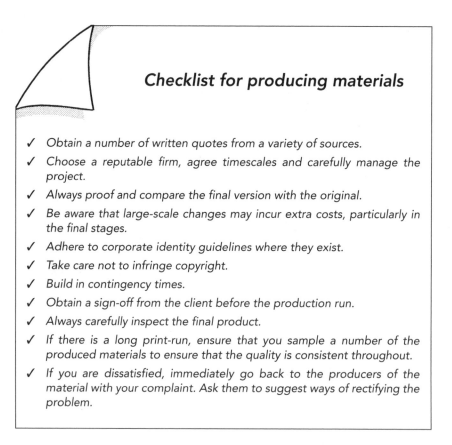

Checklist for producing materials

✓ *Obtain a number of written quotes from a variety of sources.*
✓ *Choose a reputable firm, agree timescales and carefully manage the project.*
✓ *Always proof and compare the final version with the original.*
✓ *Be aware that large-scale changes may incur extra costs, particularly in the final stages.*
✓ *Adhere to corporate identity guidelines where they exist.*
✓ *Take care not to infringe copyright.*
✓ *Build in contingency times.*
✓ *Obtain a sign-off from the client before the production run.*
✓ *Always carefully inspect the final product.*
✓ *If there is a long print-run, ensure that you sample a number of the produced materials to ensure that the quality is consistent throughout.*
✓ *If you are dissatisfied, immediately go back to the producers of the material with your complaint. Ask them to suggest ways of rectifying the problem.*

Designing training can be one of the most satisfying and stimulating tasks for a trainer as you begin to highlight and identify learning opportunities. Always dedicate quality time to the process, and ensure that the final stages of the production of materials are not rushed.

Delivering Training

METHODS OF DELIVERY

Having structured the training it is important to deliver it effectively. If you are regularly delivering training, you will be aware of many of the points that make for effective delivery; however, if you are new to training you should prepare very carefully for the delivery. No trainer or line manager should attempt to run a formal training session without being trained themselves. Most companies run train-the-trainer programmes for their internal trainers, or there are external providers (see Appendix 2, p.234).

Your style of delivery will very much depend on the type of event you are planning. As a trainer you will be performing a number of roles: direct training, one-to-one coaching, facilitating or presenting at a conference. (See Chapter 8 for specific input on different roles.) However, as we discussed in Chapter 1, there are important underpinning skills that every trainer needs in order to be successful.

In this section we look at delivering a training programme. If the programme has been carefully designed, your life as a trainer will be much easier. You should be supported with all the material necessary to run the event. There are a number of key stages within the delivery process.

Before the event

Ensure that all participant material is completed and ready for use. Your trainer's guide should be complete with your guidance notes, OHP transparencies, 35 mm slides, videos and other supporting material.

Take time to run through the content. Some trainers like to make additional notes to support their presentation. Always make sure that these are big enough to be seen at a distance. Start each key area with a new page, or a new card, and always number the pages. Sometimes, if people are delivering a formal presentation, they will use postcards with key points written on them. Again either join them together with a tag or number the cards.

Prepare a box containing all the support material that you may need. Sample contents could be:

- ❑ Pads, pens, tent cards/name badges for the delegates. If you are using a hotel check what they are supplying.
- ❑ Marker pens, blu-tack, masking tape.
- ❑ A3 paper for individual and group activities.
- ❑ Stapler and staples, paperclips, stick-it notes, scissors, glue, rubber, ruler, pencils.
- ❑ Calculator (sometimes required for group activities involving finance).
- ❑ Other items specific to group activities, eg rewards, prizes for games. Some corporate events include larger gifts for team games.
- ❑ Promotional material, pens, hats, T-shirts, polo shirts and other branded goods are sometimes requested at team events. These need to be ordered in good time with sizes checked and agreed prior to the event.

Ensure that the venue has been booked and that a letter with the details of the timetable, start and finish times, refreshment breaks, any special dietary needs and the equipment requirements is sent either to the external venue or to an internal facilities manager.

If you or the delegates need overnight accommodation ensure it is booked and confirmation is received.

Take time to run through the programme and have prepared any additional notes or comments to support your delivery.

Ensure that you and your delegates have a letter with full details of the day's timetable, the venue, maps and directions, any special clothing required (eg if there are leisure activities ensure that people know so that they can bring the correct clothing). Also people should be told if dress is to be casual during the day, or semi-formal in the evening.

Prior to the event you should also decide what you are going to wear so that if anything needs cleaning, or you want to buy something new, everything is organized in plenty of time.

Trainers often move from hotel to hotel, in and out of cars, sometimes aeroplanes, so investing in easy-care, coordinated outfits makes life much easier. Equally you often need clothes that are defined as 'smart casual'.

As a trainer you are often very active so wear things that look smart and professional but are also comfortable.

Some trainers also take a spare shirt/blouse to change into during the day, usually the same colour. Alternatively, they travel in very casual clothes and change once they have set up the room so they feel fresh at the start of the event.

Always allow plenty of time to travel to the event and have a back-up route planned. Consider staying at the venue the night before if there is a chance that you may not arrive in time, or you will have to get up so early to reach it that you will be tired during the day.

The night before the event work through the programme session by session. You will often find that fresh points occur to you. Make additional notes in your trainer's guide if you feel they are important. Resist massive rescripting at this stage.

If it is a particularly important event, arrange for a friend, relation or partner to call you to wish you good luck or simply to remind you that there is another world outside!

Finally relax, do something that you enjoy and go to bed at a reasonable time, having set up an early morning call or alarm and booked a taxi if required, or checked the car for petrol etc.

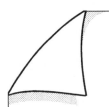

Checklist for delegate readiness

The greater the delegate's knowledge of the course, the more quickly the trainer can start the day and the more the delegates will gain from the event.

✓ *Distribute useful pre-reading at least two weeks before the event.*

✓ *Ensure delegates understand the importance of the course to the organization and to themselves.*

✓ *Provide an overview of the programme so that delegates understand what will be covered.*

✓ *Ask delegates to consider their needs from the course, to discuss these with their own managers and to bring a list to the course.*

✓ *Encourage delegates to 'read around' the topics of the course.*

✓ *Whenever possible, provide a list of questions for the delegates to research before the course to focus their preparation.*

On the morning of the event

Arrive with time to set up the room. Normally, the room will already be arranged in the formation you requested, but often some of the finer details may not have been understood. Sometimes, however, the instruction has not been given to the relevant people and there is a degree of furniture moving to be undertaken. Always elicit support if it is available.

Ensure that all the equipment works. Be particularly sure to check television and video connections, and make sure that the television is tuned to the video channel if you are planning to show a video. Put the video in the machine and make sure it is at your starting point. This can save you the embarrassment of trying to show a video to the delegates and it not working. Again, in-company technicians or hotel staff can help you.

Make sure the OHP projector focuses on the text by testing it with an OHP transparency, and make sure the projector glass is clean. Check the angle of projection and also ensure that the OHP projector is far enough away from the screen to project a clear image. Check from the back of the room, walk around and make sure that there are no blind spots for delegates. If you are using a PC-driven presentation ensure that the font size is large enough for your delegates to view. Also, check that the background colour is not too dark or too busy for viewing.

Very few rooms are ideal for training, many being hot and stuffy with poor air-conditioning. Do everything you can to achieve the right working conditions. This may mean resetting the temperature on the air-conditioning, or locating windows and opening them prior to the event. So many training programmes are marred by uncomfortable environments. This underlines the importance of checking the venue beforehand.

Lay out the material for delegates including the delegate guide, pads, pens, tent cards and/or name badges. Make it look welcoming and inviting.

It is often easier to prepare your first few flipcharts beforehand. Include an initial message, such as 'Welcome to... (insert title of your programme)'. Write your name on the corner of the page, or on a tent card at the front of the room, or put on a name badge.

Check on the arrangements for the coffee/tea on arrival and that water/fruit juices/squash are on the delegates' tables. Where possible arrange for all-day refreshments. This means that you can take shorter but more frequent breaks without having to wait for the arrival of refreshments. Giving delegates regular breaks often helps with the learning process.

Find the facilities manager or venue organizer and ensure that they have the latest copy of the programme, and impress on them the importance of the prompt arrival of refreshments.

Check the locations of the fire exits and washroom facilities, and if the event is residential, identify when delegates will be able to go to their rooms.

Locate syndicate rooms, dining rooms, photocopy/fax business centre support and agree arrangements for payment for these facilities. This saves escalating charges by over-enthusiastic delegates.

Locate in-house telephones and payphones.

Set out your slides, trainer's guide and other things that you need to run the sessions. You will find it easier if you have a table at the back or side of the room to keep additional handouts and exercise material. In this way you can keep the space at the front for your slides.

Make a final check that all the equipment works. If it is a formal presentation and you are working with an auto-cue, or someone else is running your slides for you, meet them beforehand and agree a set of signals between you to ensure it all runs smoothly. Remember, if you are given a battery microphone, to switch it off when you are not presenting!

Just before you start, allow yourself a few minutes for personal preparation. Walk outside for some fresh air, make a final visit to the cloakroom, check your appearance, relax, breathe deeply and walk back to the room ready to meet the delegates.

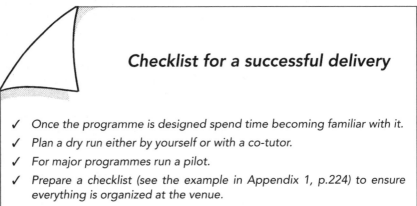

Checklist for a successful delivery

✓ Once the programme is designed spend time becoming familiar with it.

✓ Plan a dry run either by yourself or with a co-tutor.

✓ For major programmes run a pilot.

✓ Prepare a checklist (see the example in Appendix 1, p.224) to ensure everything is organized at the venue.

✓ Make sure your travel and accommodation arrangements have a contingency time built in. Always try to arrange overnight accommodation at the venue the night before your programme if it is far away.

✓ Be careful what you eat and drink the night before. Breathing garlic fumes over the delegates, or suffering from a hangover is not the best way to start a programme.

✓ Use relaxation techniques or favourite tracks of music to relax or energize yourself prior to the event. Have a tape in the car and play it on your journey.

✓ Just before you start go quietly outside the room and compose yourself.

The delivery

When you are ready and it is the correct starting time, encourage the delegates into the room and welcome them to the event. Always try to start promptly, or, if you know some delegates are delayed, tell the rest of the group and re-arrange a new start time. It is often better to start and allow latecomers to join the group than keep people hanging around. Ensure you spend time with those who arrive late helping them to catch up with the key information they have missed.

Sometimes you may have a senior person to open the event. Ideally, ask them to do their input first so that you can then run the rest of the programme without interruption. Hopefully they will be motivational and helpful in setting the tone for the day.

At the beginning of your input you need to introduce yourself, list the procedures in the event of an emergency and other domestic details like the location of washroom facilities. Agree the rules about smoking. Try to discourage smoking in the training room; encourage people either to go to a designated smoking area or outside. But do make the suggestion subtly so as not to destroy relationships with the smokers on your course! Many companies now have no smoking policies so the matter is less of an issue.

Follow this by encouraging people to write their names on tent cards. Do not assume that if they are from one organization they automatically know each other. Even if they do know each other it is quite in order to say, 'It would help me if you could all briefly introduce yourselves and say a little about your experience.' Normally this can be structured by asking for the following:

name
job title
years of experience
any previous training attended.

It is important to try to learn the delegates' names. If you have a problem remembering names try to find a way of overcoming this. The following points may help:

❑ As the delegates introduce themselves jot down brief details about them in the same formation as the seating. This can also help later in the day when you are dividing them into syndicate groups and you want each group to contain a range of expertise.

❑ Some people reinforce their recollection of people's names by repeating the names several times in the initial conversation, eg thanking them by name for their contribution.

❑ Talking to people on a one-to-one basis during the breaks helps to add other pieces of information to their name.

❑ One well-known ice-breaker is to ask people to give the usual information and then to tell the group something unusual about themselves that no one else knows, eg 'My name is George and I breed green canaries.' It's a test of everyone's memory to repeat this later and to identify what the group can remember about these initial introductions.

In running the first session, give delegates the opportunity to settle and to start participating. If the programme has been well designed there will be a good balance between input and activities. The development of the content was covered in detail in Chapter 3, p.29.

Your style

However well the programme has been designed it is the trainer(s) who bring it to life. As we discussed in Chapter 1, p.12, your role is critical to the success of the event.

You should encourage interaction, manage questions and help everyone to contribute and feel part of the event. While debate is an important part of the learning, you also have to oversee it to ensure that one or two delegates do not control all of the discussion, leaving the rest of the group as observers.

The experienced trainer develops the ability to answer the questions, widen the debate to include others as appropriate and then to move on. If your programme has been carefully timetabled, you will lose valuable time if you do not control the event, and then you lose respect from your group. Always acknowledge a good question and try to respond positively, even if it is a sensitive area. If you do not know the answer, or the questioner appears to want to monopolize the session, suggest that you discuss it with them later on a one-to-one basis.

Sometimes you may have to handle conflict, or facilitate the group to handle difficult situations. Always be sensitive. Recognize individual learning styles (see Chapter 2, p.21) and the differing needs and experience of individuals. During the event you should be ultra-observant, ensuring that the group stays with you and recognizing when someone is struggling or feeling uncomfortable.

Take time during the breaks to get to know them, and try to encourage them to articulate their concerns so that you can help them to overcome the issue, either during the programme or after the event, perhaps through coaching. It is not appropriate to discuss potentially sensitive areas in front of an individual's peers, and you need to respect their need for privacy.

As a trainer you are in powerful position. Never abuse it. Instead, use your skill to work with all the members of the group while recognizing the different individual starting points.

The more relaxed you are the better you will be able to work with the group. If you are co-tutoring you must establish a way of working that lets you both use your individual strengths to facilitate the progress of the event (see the section on co-tutoring, p.55).

The pace of the day should be carefully controlled to allow for maximum participation from the delegates. It is important not to have too much input from the trainer at one time; instead structure these slots throughout the day. Carefully watch your group for signs of boredom, discomfort or loss of involvement.

You also need to manage your own energy levels, as running training events can be exhausting. Eat and drink sensibly during the day to ensure a balanced sugar level. Sometimes trainers find themselves running out of energy or getting 'hyper' because they have eaten the wrong food or drunk too much coffee during the day. Five light snacks may be better for you, using fruit where possible.

This is also important for delegates too. Try to avoid the provision of heavy lunches and encourage them to get some fresh air, which will help them to maintain concentration. (This does not mean a visit to the nearest pub!)

If you have time, also take a break outside, it will help to clear your head from the morning's events. Use the time to review the progress of the group, either by yourself or with your co-tutor.

Always plan a practical activity for after lunch, traditionally known as the 'graveyard slot', because delegates often find it hard to concentrate at this time.

Keep checking the temperature in the room during the day. Sometimes there is a build-up of heat as the day progresses, which results in the delegates feeling lethargic.

You should also be assessing what progress is being made against the objectives. Are you achieving what was hoped for? Do you have any outstanding delegate requests that have to be met? Are you running to time? Do you need to amend any of the content? Have you encouraged the delegates to mix with each other through different pairings or syndicate work? Always be flexible, but stay in control of the overall process.

As the day reaches its conclusion you should either be summarizing and encouraging the group to identify their action plans, or setting up evening activities or plans for the next day if it is a longer programme.

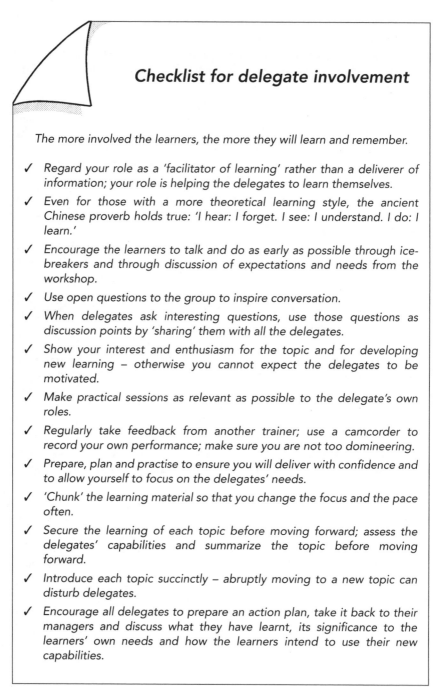

Checklist for delegate involvement

The more involved the learners, the more they will learn and remember.

✓ *Regard your role as a 'facilitator of learning' rather than a deliverer of information; your role is helping the delegates to learn themselves.*

✓ *Even for those with a more theoretical learning style, the ancient Chinese proverb holds true: 'I hear: I forget. I see: I understand. I do: I learn.'*

✓ *Encourage the learners to talk and do as early as possible through ice-breakers and through discussion of expectations and needs from the workshop.*

✓ *Use open questions to the group to inspire conversation.*

✓ *When delegates ask interesting questions, use those questions as discussion points by 'sharing' them with all the delegates.*

✓ *Show your interest and enthusiasm for the topic and for developing new learning – otherwise you cannot expect the delegates to be motivated.*

✓ *Make practical sessions as relevant as possible to the delegate's own roles.*

✓ *Regularly take feedback from another trainer; use a camcorder to record your own performance; make sure you are not too domineering.*

✓ *Prepare, plan and practise to ensure you will deliver with confidence and to allow yourself to focus on the delegates' needs.*

✓ *'Chunk' the learning material so that you change the focus and the pace often.*

✓ *Secure the learning of each topic before moving forward; assess the delegates' capabilities and summarize the topic before moving forward.*

✓ *Introduce each topic succinctly – abruptly moving to a new topic can disturb delegates.*

✓ *Encourage all delegates to prepare an action plan, take it back to their managers and discuss what they have learnt, its significance to the learners' own needs and how the learners intend to use their new capabilities.*

Residential events

Sometimes training events run for a number of days, but the same delivery principles apply to longer events. However, you do have to manage the learning process even more carefully. Residential events are more exhausting for everyone. The trainers often feel that they are never off duty, and the delegates often feel the peer pressure of not being the first to go to bed!

A balance must be set, with clear guidelines established at the start of the event. Residential programmes are an expensive investment and delegates need to recognize that the prime purpose is to help them develop new skills rather than an expenses-paid holiday. Heavy drinking into the early hours often has a negative effect on their ability to absorb any information the next day. Senior managers can often help the trainers in setting the scene and emphasizing the company's commitment to personal development. Equally, some companies do reward their teams by organizing residential events, and so activities should have sensible end-times to allow people to relax and socialize and switch off from the day's learning.

Ending the event

Whether it has been a one-day programme or a longer event, the key outcome should be that the delegates are able to go back and *do*. If the objectives have been achieved, then the delegates should be setting action plans ready to review them with their line managers.

Every training event should have a significant impact on the individual and the business. You want delegates to leave feeling positive and motivated and not just on an adrenalin 'high'.

We cover evaluation in much more depth (see Chapter 7) but you should always allow enough time at the end of the programme for both the action planning and the evaluation. Most trainers also finish with some opportunity for the delegates to comment on their own personal learning experiences during the event.

Always thank the delegates for their attendance, and ensure that you did meet the objectives and their needs. Highlight any follow-up training that has been organized, and offer a contact number for any individual follow-up needs.

After the delegates have left, gather together all the materials and put them into the right order ready for filing or to be used again at another event. Check the syndicate rooms for left resources. If you are writing a post-course report, remember to save any relevant flipcharts or other materials.

As you are leaving the venue, remember to thank the catering and facilities staff for their help. Also make a note of any difficulties that may have occurred to ensure that they do not occur again if you revisit the venue.

Finally, go home, relax and positively switch off!

Reviewing the training

It is important to set a time when you will review the event. This may be with your co-tutor, but should also involve the client. Normally this is agreed before the training, but always try to ensure that it happens.

Prior to this meeting, while the event is still fresh in your mind, make brief notes of the learning and action points. You may have identified further training needs with members of the group, or you may have identified follow-up business actions.

In Chapter 7, we refer to a checklist for reviewing other trainers' training delivery (see Appendix 1). Use this either to review your own input, or with your co-tutor. Ask yourself these questions:

- ❑ What did I do to involve the delegates?
- ❑ Which parts of the programme really worked?
- ❑ What parts need improving?
- ❑ How well did we work together as a training team?
- ❑ What would I/we do differently next time?

Checklist for good presentation

The following checklist is designed to highlight some key points in giving a presentation or delivering a training programme.

- ✓ *Reveal OHP transparencies by using a piece of paper under rather than on top of the transparency (this prevents the paper falling off).*
- ✓ *Do not read from the slides as this insults the intelligence of your group. Make key points instead.*
- ✓ *Use a pen to highlight points by laying it on the overhead projector itself rather than prodding the screen (choose one that does not roll).*

✓ Use laser beams or pointers only if you are comfortable with them. (Nothing is worse than an out-of-control laser or pointer.)

✓ If you are using 35 mm or PC-generated presentation ensure you are totally in control of the equipment. Check and double-check!

✓ The same principle applies to video equipment of any sort. Practise beforehand with the equipment to ensure that it all works.

✓ If in a strange venue, make arrangements for someone technical to be on hand to help you if there is a problem with equipment. Always check there are spare bulbs etc.

✓ Recognize that sometime in your career it may all fail and you will have to cope by using other means to illustrate your points.

✓ When using flipcharts try to have as much prepared as possible, and write clearly and in straight lines (some flipcharts come with feint lines or grids). Try to have perforated flipchart paper for its ease of tearing.

✓ Avoid the use of orange and red on flipcharts and OHP slides as they are difficult to read from a distance. Dark blue and green are an ideal alternative to black.

✓ Water-based board marker pens are kinder to the atmosphere than spirit-based pens, particularly in smaller training rooms.

As well as delivering training, trainers sometimes have other responsibilities, or need to work in different ways. The next sections deal with some of these aspects.

CO-TUTORING

If you are working as a team you need to agree how you are going to work together. There are real bonuses in working as a team, particularly if you have different styles, as it provides variety for the delegates and also helps you retain a freshness. The trainer not delivering can be observing the group and can give valuable feedback to their partner on the responses from the group.

It is important for people working together to agree styles and approaches and to give each other feedback on how the relationship is working. It is worth spending time on this because a good delivery team not only benefits the delegates but can be a tremendous source of feedback and personal growth as the trainers learn from each other.

Sometimes you co-tutor with a client or a line manager. This too may need careful handling and agreement of roles and responsibilities, particularly if the client is less experienced than you. A client will not thank you for making them look or feel small in front of their colleagues. Planning the inputs carefully and having a dry run can help the situation.

With experience and careful feedback you will identify people with whom you can work. You should set the ground rules so that you have a clear understanding on how you will work together. Healthy debate is positive, but delegates do not want to witness trainers competing with each other, or to be confused when they argue or give conflicting views.

Equally important is agreeing how to add supplementary information. Sometimes the other trainer wishes to contribute to the discussion, which should be done at an appropriate moment by giving an agreed signal to the trainer who is delivering, who can then bring the co-tutor into the conversation.

This technique can also be used very effectively to support a trainer who may be experiencing difficulties with a group. The co-tutor should never take over, only make their point and then hand back to the main tutor. It is worth continually giving each other feedback on the workings of the relationship, because when it works well a training partnership can really inspire a group.

TRAIN-THE-TRAINER

As you progress through your career, there will be times when you need to develop new levels of expertise. One way of doing this is to be trained. When trainers are being trained in a new area this is normally called train-the-trainer. In its purest sense the training may be designed for people who are already trained in the techniques of training but who wish to develop new areas of expertise.

In these cases you are normally given a trainer's guide and trained in the content of the specific new area. If it is part of a much bigger roll-out programme, you will normally not be allowed to run the programme until you have been trained and had practice runs at delivering the material.

Equally, you may attend a train-the-trainer programme to help you develop the basic skills of training; once you have attended this you should then have the opportunity to practice with extra top-up sessions as required.

Developing as a trainer is a lifetime process, and it is likely that you will attend many such events during your career.

USING EXTERNAL SPEAKERS

If you are using an external speaker there are a number of factors to consider:

❑ Why are you using a speaker? What are your objectives? What do you hope the speaker will add to the event?

❑ Identify the area of expertise required and set the objectives.

❑ Identify potential speakers; at this stage look internally as well as at external providers.

❑ Having identified potential speakers, narrow your choice by identifying their fee, their specific area of expertise and availability.

❑ Once satisfied with these details, confirm with the speaker the date, the timings, venue and outline content. Clarify their details for any publicity material that you plan to produce.

❑ Be aware that once booked the speaker may require a cancellation fee if you subsequently call off the event.

❑ Matching a speaker to an audience is very important. Speakers vary enormously in style, approach and content detail. Their fee will also vary depending on their status.

❑ It is important to find a speaker who has been recommended, depending on the size and scale of the event. An uninspiring speaker can be very demotivational and damage your reputation.

❑ Prior to the event send the speaker the same details as the delegates.

❑ In addition, out of courtesy, you may wish to send the speaker copies of your aim and objectives, the programme outline and your introductory content. If there is more than one speaker, you may wish to send each of them outline details of each other's presentation, or ask them to contact each other to ensure that they do not overlap each other's content.

❑ Prior to the event ask them for their equipment requirements and, like the delegates, any special dietary needs. Also ask for hard copies of their slides, ideally before the event, so that you can include this in the delegate's guide.

❑ Confirm that they have the details of the venue and establish their travel arrangements.

❑ Always write and thank them for their input after the event.

ORGANIZING VENUES

Like speakers, organizing venues takes time and patience to get right, and often forms part of the trainer's role. If you have administrative back-up, it is something that can be delegated once you have established the guidelines. You need very clear criteria to help you identify your ideal venue.

First, identify what you require in terms of the venue, which will vary depending on your event. If it is an in-company programme, you may have to use in-company facilities; however, increasingly organizations are prepared to use off-site facilities if they feel it is important to create different environments for the learning.

If you are going outside, shop around to find the best prices and range of facilities in your local area. Sometimes organizations want a venue that is further afield, and you are then reliant on brochure information or the recommendations of others. If you have an established network of other trainers or other company contracts, you can hopefully ask for advice from them.

There are some specialized venue finding organizations that will identify your needs with you and then give you a range of options. Normally there is no charge for this service as they receive commission from the venue. They can be a valuable resource because they can negotiate on your behalf, and if you use them on a regular basis they will begin to understand your needs. Alternatively, you or your administration can build up your own file of contacts.

Although time-consuming, finding the right venue is a very important consideration of any event, but is particularly important when running a residential one, or a conference, because of the additional requirements in terms of numbers attending or the facilities required. You need to research the venue under the following headings.

Main room

❑ Is it large enough, and well ventilated with natural light?
❑ Is the seating comfortable, with a facility for the delegates to write on?
❑ Are there syndicate rooms nearby?
❑ Are there toilets nearby?
❑ Is there a business centre, or somewhere where you can photocopy or send and receive faxes?
❑ Are there any likely planned disturbances, eg refurbishment, decorating or rebuilding?

❑ Are other large events being organized at the same time at the venue? (Sometimes small events can be overwhelmed by other large conferences.)

Refreshments

❑ How are the refreshments organized? Will coffee/tea be available in the room? Can it be available all day if required?

❑ Is there a separate facility for buffet lunch? Can you have part of the dining room kept separate for your group? This is particularly important for a residential event, where people prefer to eat together away from other guests. Some venues have private dining room facilities.

❑ What additional refreshments are available: mineral water, squash, mints, biscuits, cakes, fruit, etc? How are these items costed? What's included in the rate, what is additional? It is very important to establish the real costs when comparing one venue with another. Benchmark a variety of venues.

Accommodation

The standard of accommodation is another important feature at a training event. These too need to be checked and the following questions asked:

❑ What are the standard and quality of the rooms included in the day delegate rate?

❑ Where are the rooms located? You ideally want accommodation that is free of airport and traffic noise.

❑ Most hotels have a standard of accommodation that is now expected by corporate delegates, ie double rooms with single occupancy, ensuite, television, tea-making facilities, sometimes mini-bar. While not every organization may wish to provide this level of hospitality, people normally expect reasonable sleeping accommodation with a minimum level of facilities.

❑ Increasingly people expect there to be some form of leisure facility, particularly if it is residential. This can vary from a swimming pool or fitness suite to golf, or tennis. Whatever facilities you require it is important to confirm everything in writing and to identify a contact person with whom you can liaise both prior to and during the event.

Further information is available in Thorne (1998) *Training Places: Choosing and using venues for training* (see Appendix 3, p.237).

DEALING WITH THE UNEXPECTED

However well prepared you may be you may find yourself having to deal with the unexpected. We list below some of those situations.

Handling delegates' resistance or reluctance

Despite your best preparation and working in your most facilitative style, you may find yourself in a situation when you have to handle delegate resistance. There may be a number of reasons for this:

❑   lack of notice about a training event or resentment at being 'sent'
❑   nervousness on delegates' part about attending
❑   not wanting to be 'shown up' in front of peers
❑   personal reasons unrelated to the event
❑   personal chemistry issues between delegates, or between delegates and the trainer
❑   issues with the organization or the management.

Any of the above can create tensions within the learning environment/ training room. This may manifest itself in many ways, sometimes by a delegate not getting involved in the course, or by a delegate arriving late, wanting to leave early or creating verbal challenges. A delegate may show a lack of interest or possibly challenge the trainer, demonstrating 'When you cannot reach me, you cannot teach me.'

The event itself, including the trainer, can be questioned through comments such as 'You don't understand our situation', 'Your examples wouldn't work in our set-up' or 'This has been tried before and the management didn't follow it through.' The flow of a training session can be disrupted when delegates want to vent their own issues.

Our suggested strategies for coping with these situations are split over four areas.

Before the training event

Part of the pre-event planning should involve identification of any potential organizational issues. Talk to delegates' managers, ensuring that the managers and the delegates are clear about the importance of the course and that delegates are being prepared appropriately. Discuss any potential issues with the managers, particularly if there are personal or organizational circumstances that may influence your event.

At the start of the event, in the training room

Establishing some ground rules at the start of the event can help in terms of mutual respect and support. Demonstrating that you understand organizational issues, being flexible and adaptable in the way that the course is structured, allowing regular breaks and organizing access to all-day refreshments will all help to create an environment that is conducive to learning and supportive to the delegates. Simple strategies such as asking the delegates what they hope to gain from the event should identify areas of common ground. Remember that this does imply a commitment to try to meet their needs. It is easy to fall into the trap of identifying their needs only to ignore their input and to carry on and deliver the content that you had in mind with no further reference to their ideas. This works best as an interactive session, writing up their suggestions on a flipchart and being very honest about what will be covered and what needs to be addressed outside of the event or potentially on a one-to one basis.

During the training event

Once the event has started, the intuitive trainer will be working to develop positive relationships with the group, recognizing when the group needs a break and recognizing all the issues about attention span. Hopefully in the design and planning of the event there will be variety in pace and content, but don't be afraid to change the plan if the delegates are not responding positively. If you are co-tutoring, recognize the support that the other trainer can offer; by mixing and matching styles and approaches, the delegates' interest can be maintained.

Once you understand the cause of resistance, you can plan to handle it. All trainers need to be aware of their own natural fears, including 'Am I good enough?', 'Have I the authority I need?' and 'They don't like me.' It is key not to take situations personally and to consider the reasons behind challenging situations. Experience helps with these situations, but first courses can be daunting – an excellent reason to run pilots and to build in feedback sessions within the event and, if possible, co-train with an experienced facilitator. Remember your sources of confidence, keep eye contact with your delegates, move closer to them and discuss their issues. All our coping strategies rely on our ability to keep our cool and our ability to choose the appropriate response to the situation. Fear can result in our making the wrong choice.

We need to be aware of the form the resistance is taking, being alert to what is happening at all times during the course. We will *sense* resistance, *see* resistance when someone is not participating, sitting back, arriving late, not paying attention or distracting others, and *hear* resistance with muttered comments, direct challenges and hostile comments in small groups as well as unnatural periods of silence. We need not be paranoid, judging that the first time something happens (or is said, asked or refused) we accept it at face value, the second time become diligent and the third time believe it to be resistance and take action.

If there is a general feeling of discontent or restlessness, be prepared to take time out to identify the cause. You may need to refer back to the objective and main agenda of the event including the delegates' expressed needs and, adult to adult, seek to identify the reasons for lack of concentration and establish a joint commitment to work together to overcome any issues.

With an individual attempting to disrupt the event, you need to exercise mature judgement on the best course of action. Ideally you need to take time with the particular person, one to one, to identify what the real issues are. Sometimes people are unaware that they are being overbearing or taking up too much airtime in a group discussion. If there is an opportunity to play to people's strengths, ask the more experienced members of the group to allow others to contribute; this can be another way of avoiding direct confrontation. The last thing that you want to occur is an open 'spectator sport' between a trainer and a delegate. If the situation becomes particularly difficult, suggest a coffee break and handle the situation one to one with the particular delegate. During the coffee break take the individual aside and try to identify the root of the issue. If it is appropriate, allow the individual to suggest he/she leaves the course – hopefully this will only occur as a last resort.

Following the event

As highlighted elsewhere in this book it is really important that you carefully review all training events, as well as the formal evaluations; it is equally important that you undertake your personal review or review the event with your co-trainer. You should always be running a sense check during any event, recognizing the signals and trying to be in tune with the needs of the delegates. Regularly discuss progress with the programme sponsors and be open to any feedback that they have received. Equally, even with careful preparation and with all possible care on your part, there may be events that are less successful than others. The important factor is to learn from the experience, seek to identify areas for improvement and work to make sure that at the next event the lessons learnt can be applied in the new context.

(Additional coping strategies can be found in Chapter 1, Being Professional – see the section, Handling Difficult People.)

Coping with nerves

Running a training programme is very much like a stage performance.

Trainers often experience nervousness before an event, and the same exhilaration or adrenalin 'high' during a programme is often accompanied by a 'low' as you come down to earth. With experience you learn to adjust, but these mood swings can be disruptive for those new to training.

Fear normally occurs when people feel unprepared, and the better prepared you are, the more confident you will feel. If training is new to you, or you are preparing for a particularly prestigious event, the following may be helpful:

- ❏ It is important to prepare physically for the event. However nervous you feel, try to sleep normally before the event, particularly earlier in the week. Try to avoid too many stimulants – caffeine, cigarettes etc.

- ❏ Make sure you know what you are going to say, and don't overcomplicate what you are presenting. If you are worried that you might stumble over words, take out anything that causes you a problem in your dry run.

- ❏ If you do stumble, don't apologize, pause, take a deep breath and continue. Everyone makes mistakes from time to time, and it will always seem worse to you than to your audience.

- ❏ Check the equipment beforehand, but also have back-up notes so you can cope if there is a problem with it.

- ❏ Do your research. Spend time understanding the company's objectives and the needs of the group. Try to meet some of the delegates before the event as part of your design stage. Make references to their business. People appreciate it when you appear to understand their business and it gives your input a more tailored approach.

- ❏ Learn a good breathing exercise and practise it regularly. Relax just before you are due to make your presentation, particularly your shoulders. If you have the opportunity, go somewhere quiet and just think about your opening sentences. If not just look down at your notes a few minutes before you are due to start.

- ❏ At a large event, if you prefer not to look directly at your audience, instead focus on something at the back of the hall just above their heads. This will give them the impression that you are looking at them, but it will not distract you.

- ❏ Try to be as natural as possible. Keep a level of humour that seems appropriate, remember the other times when you have been successful – and *just do it!*

Problems with the venue

Regular checking to clarify details and confirming everything in writing helps to avoid problems; however, the key is not to make assumptions but always to check and confirm any details. Try to visit the venue, or obtain recommendations from others. Be wary of room size, because sometimes these are very much affected by the proposed layout. Ideally, ask for rooms with natural light, check heating, air-conditioning and soundproofing, particularly if it is a room with thin partitions.

If, despite this, the room really is unsuitable, try to negotiate for another. This may be difficult if it is a busy venue, which is why it is much better to try and view the room beforehand. Over a period of time you will build up a list of preferred venues.

The same applies within companies. Work towards achieving dedicated space that is suited to training events. Whatever difficulties you experience, do not let this interfere with your presentation. Your delegates will forgive accommodation and catering difficulties, but not an uninspiring event, and then they really will have grounds to complain. Always be professional and put your complaint in writing, and try to negotiate a reduction in fee.

Problems with the equipment

Most of the problems with equipment or the venue are prevented by good preparation. However, even with preparation things can occasionally go wrong. If any of the equipment fails you, hopefully you can carry on, particularly if you have a delegate guide with the OHP slides copied. If the video fails, you may have to talk through the broad areas of content, or move it to a later part of the programme while the machine is repaired.

Always ask for help quickly rather than entertain the delegates with your attempts to make the machine work! You need to remain calm, and if the day is well structured the failure of one component can be overcome.

Non-arrival of materials

You should always check that the materials have arrived after despatch. However, sometimes they go missing within the venue after arrival. Finding them is a bit like solving a murder mystery. You will have to painstakingly establish step by step who delivered them and where, who received them and at what time, who signed for them and where they were put. If you have taken a hard copy with you, you can at least run the first session with photocopies while the search continues.

Emergencies

As a matter of course you should always check the emergency procedures at every venue and such things as fire exits, assembly points and first-aid facilities. An awareness of others' safety and survival should be your number one priority, and even if it seems like only a fire drill, you should ensure that all your delegates leave the building and take with you a list of the delegate names. Wait to be told before re-entering the building. In today's environment of uncertainty it is particularly important to ensure that everyone is aware of all evacuation procedures.

Security

Training programmes present a number of security problems. The delegates have often come to a strange building where other members of the public are allowed. During the course of the day it is likely that they will be taking off their jackets, and handbags and briefcases may be left unattended as people move from room to room undertaking activities. You need to encourage people at the start of the day to be vigilant. Arrange for the door of the training room to be locked at lunchtime, and encourage delegates to take their wallets and valuables with them.

Look after your own possessions and try to place them in a secure place, as you are more likely to be moving around from one syndicate room to another than anyone else. If anything is stolen inform the security officer within the building immediately and allow the delegates affected to contact their banks and credit card companies.

Cars stolen, damaged, broken down

Again, the person affected is not going to be concentrating on the event. Allow them time to contact the relevant emergency service, but encourage them to rejoin the programme while repairs or investigations take place.

Lack of delegates

Sometimes, for a variety of last-minute reasons, the numbers that turn up are severely reduced. One or two fewer people, or equally one or two more than are expected, should present no problem. However, a dramatic drop in numbers may mean that the programme is no longer viable in

terms of interaction or sharing of best practice. On these occasions you
have to make a series of judgements:

❑ If the programme is part of an internal roll-out programme, are there
    others nearby who could be released to attend? Always clear this with
    their line managers.
❑ Has everyone arrived, are any just late?
❑ When is a group too small? It is possible to run an event with small
    numbers, but it is likely to be less effective, because people have less
    opportunity to share other people's experiences. Success also depends
    on your experience, as a more experienced trainer can turn a small
    group into a coaching session.

Sometimes you have to take a decision to postpone or cancel an event.
Ideally this decision should be taken before the day of the event to avoid
anyone making an unnecessary journey. Once you find out that numbers
are low for an event, try ringing around for likely extra numbers. If it is an
internal programme talk to the sponsor and the line managers.

In today's climate, running a training event is an investment and as
such should be treated with respect and commitment. This takes time to
achieve, and some internal functions battle to have training taken seriously. Therefore the more professional and businesslike you are the more
likely people are to take the training seriously.

As a trainer you always have to be prepared for the unexpected,
although most events happen without any problems. Preparation and
identifying venues that are able to respond to your needs are the keys. It
is essential to keep a balanced and professional approach, but if you do
experience difficulties, ask to see the duty manager, who often will be
able to solve them for you.

Sources of Inspiration

BEING CREATIVE

How creative are you?

One of the key skills of a trainer is the ability to design training programmes and learning experiences that are innovative, exciting and fun. You also have to recognize individual learning styles and respond to the needs of the business. Often you will also be faced with delegates who have arrived at an event with business pressures still on their minds. This process is repeated over and over again in a trainer's working year.

For a trainer this means that you need tremendous energy and personal strength to respond to the myriad of demands that you deal with in your work with groups. You need to be able to think round problems and issues, to rise above what is ordinary to produce extraordinary results. This is particularly relevant in organizations where the trainer is being encouraged to become an internal consultant (see Chapter 8, p.121). People will be looking to you for inspiration, they will expect you to be outward looking, to be able to facilitate groups where new ideas are generated.

Creative and innovative people have energy, they practically run to places because they cannot wait to start things. They are animated, excited, they may think of many more ideas than they actually have the time to implement. They often work hard and play hard and in the playing often come up with even more innovation!

However, not everyone has this energy, some of us have to work at it, so where do you start?

IDEAS GENERATION

In Chapter 1, p.12, we discussed the importance of getting to know yourself and your preferred way of operating. The same applies to creativity and ideas generation: with experience you will begin to identify when you get your best ideas. Many people feel that often their best ideas occur when they are least expecting it, or doing something else. They rarely happen to order. Given the fact that most of us cannot afford the luxury of just waiting for ideas to happen, we often need to help the process a little.

From the minute you know you have to generate ideas, to be creative, or to design a programme, park the broad parameters in your mind. If you have the space, put the title or the development area on a large piece of flipchart paper, and, either using stick-it notes, or felt pens, add the ideas as they occur.

Make things as visible as possible and keep adding. As the ideas begin to flow, even the most insignificant points may ultimately become an important feature of the end result. Also have with you some means of recording thoughts when you are doing other things, such as a small notepad, a dictaphone or a laptop computer. But often your mind just races with ideas and you need to be able to capture them quickly before they disappear.

In these early stages it is important not to force the process, and if you find that the ideas are not flowing, leave it and do something else. Often people find that by doing something completely different their minds will suddenly start generating ideas. Creative thinking can also take place at night during sleep. If you focus on a problem before you go to sleep, something called the Theta process takes over and the mind produces its own solutions that are there when you wake.

Some people find it easy to generate ideas, but most find it a challenge. Everyone has a different approach, but we will share with you some methods that have been proven to work.

❑ Identify the times when you have your best ideas. Create the environment that works for you, perhaps a room with a special view and music playing in the background.

❑ Identify where you work best. Some people go away to write or have special rooms but prefer to have their family or partner nearby so that they can break off from time to time to talk to other people.

❑ Some people find that taking part in such leisure activities as swimming, running or climbing exhilarates them and helps the creative process.

❑ Equip yourself with the right resources, a bit like taking an exam, sharpened pencils, lots of paper, coloured pens, and so on.

❑ Spend time researching. Talk to clients and participants, visit resource centres and business schools.

❑ Review what has been done before, clients' material, your own material, videos, books and magazine articles.

❑ Build up your own sources of material, everything from photographs, press cuttings to more structured activities. If you have an idea write it up even if you are not going to use it on the immediate programme. It may be useful sometime in the future.

❑ Set up a filing system, either computer or paper-based, but it should be well catalogued and cross-referenced and updated each time you develop a programme.

❑ Build up a network of contacts, other trainers, managers, consultants, mentors, people you know who are a source of good ideas. Be generous with ideas and others will share with you.

❑ Regularly undertake self-development: go to training events and learn from the trainer, be an active participant.

❑ Really try to think from the point of view of your client, trying to identify their priorities.

❑ Some people find it hard to be creative on their own and need to bounce ideas around with other people. Again, using a dedicated space with good facilities can be useful. Some design teams go to leisure centres, where they can combine a sports activity with thinking and design time.

THE ART OF THE POSSIBLE

Really innovative organizations ensure that they are constantly improving. They encourage their employees continually to look for a better way of doing things. There is also a close link between senior managers and the workforce. In some organizations every senior manager spends time working at the sharp end of the business, while in others mixed groups of managers and employees regularly meet to discuss business improvement.

As a trainer or an internal consultant you may be asked to run sessions where people are asked to create ideas, often as 'away' days, where groups of people are encouraged to be innovative. As we discussed above, people often find it hard to be creative to order, and you can help by creating an environment that is conducive to ideas generation. Like any development event, the objectives need to be clear and people need to understand what outcome is expected.

The day, or event, needs to be structured to allow people to mix with others. You need to build in activities that help people to identify issues and to begin to find solutions. Even more important is to work with the organization before and after the event to ensure that ideas generated are seriously considered in the business environment. Too often people go away on an event and build tremendous enthusiasm and energy, only to lose it once they return to the workplace.

Many ideas founder because no one sponsors them. Sometimes organizations have product champions, which may be teams of people, but that should always include a senior manager or a member of the executive who can ensure that the business takes the idea seriously. Equally, product champions throughout the business can ensure that at every level there is a commitment to developing the idea further. We discuss this in more detail in Chapter 8, p.121.

Running an ideas generating event

As we discussed above, in running an ideas generating event you need to set very clear objectives as to what can be achieved. It is important to highlight that not all ideas generated will be suitable for immediate implementation. In order to maintain momentum and the motivation for the group, a process for planning the implementation should be agreed at the end of the event.

In some cases this may mean reconvening the group or setting up planning or design groups. Ideally, at the end of the event there should be agreement to meet again to review progress (this meeting may be quite brief), or if the event has been very successful it may become a regular part of the business calendar.

There are a number of techniques that you can use to foster ideas generation. Every trainer will develop their own preferred way of operating, but the ones listed below have been used successfully by many individuals and organizations.

BRAINSTORMING

This is one of the simplest yet most effective techniques for working with groups. It is either trainer facilitated or takes place in syndicate groups. Using a blank piece of paper and a single topic or heading you note as many thoughts as possible, randomly, without any attempt to rank or order. Write them up as single words or small phrases. Usually groups will generate two or three pages of ideas and comments before exhausting the process.

The technique is designed to help with the flow of ideas and there are important rules; eg no editing, no qualifying, no restricting. The concept works because one person's thoughts often stimulates others and, by not interrupting each other, the ideas flow very quickly. Analysis can take place later. The activity often also creates an energy and an element of fun within a group.

SWOT (Strengths, Weaknesses, Opportunities, Threats)

This is a way of adding structure to a brainstorm. By dividing a piece of flipchart paper into four and adding the headings Strengths, Weaknesses, Opportunities and Threats, a group may analyze their business, the workings of the group, future business potential, in fact any aspect that seems appropriate.

Strengths and weaknesses are often perceived as current and internal issues, and opportunities and threats as future and external issues. Once the areas have been identified, different groups can work on the outcomes, eg 'What can we do as a business to minimize the threats we have identified?'

MIND MAPPING

One of the most creative and enjoyable ways of generating ideas is mind mapping invented by Tony Buzan. Since the 1970s Buzan has been exploring the workings of the brain and helping people to understand how their minds work. He particularly has researched the works of Roger Sperry and Robert Ornstein and whole brain activity (see Chapter 2, p.21). The uses of mind maps are endless, and Buzan actively encourages people to send him their personal examples.

Some examples of their use are as follows:

❑ note-taking at seminars, conferences, meetings, school/college lectures
❑ summaries of visits, sales calls, monitoring/assessing records of observations
❑ problem-solving, decision-making
❑ planning and designing training
❑ life planning, career choices
❑ revision before exams
❑ writing articles/books.

Although mind maps may at first be perceived as a very creative and right-brained process, Buzan emphasizes the importance of seeing them as a whole-brain activity, and to ensure consistency in approach he has developed guidelines for the completion of mind maps which ensure that you maximize the potential of the process.

❑ Words should be printed in capitals. This helps with reading back the contents.

❑ The printed words should be on the lines and each line should be connected to other lines. This ensures the basic structure.

❑ Words should be in units of one word per line. This leaves each word more free hooks and gives note-taking more freedom and flexibility.

❑ The mind should be left as free as possible, and therefore you shouldn't worry too much about sequencing or order. The key is to capture thoughts as quickly as possible, but where possible use hierarchy and numerical order in your layout.

❑ Buzan recommends drawing a coloured image at the centre to focus the eye and the brain.

❑ Use of illustrations and colour can also add to the imagery.

One of the great advantages of mind maps is that large amounts of information can be summarized on one page, and from this initial map project plans can be developed. Certain aspects can be given to particular people for further development, but you always retain a very visual model of the total picture and also the start of the process.

Now widely recognized in business training and education circles further information about training and the uses of mind maps are available from Tony Buzan (see Appendices 2 and 3, pp.234 and 237).

CREATIVE PROBLEM-SOLVING

As we discuss later in Chapter 8, trainers in today's organizations are often called upon to act as internal consultants or facilitators. One area that often requires support is problem-solving. Problem-solving techniques are a common management tool, but applying creativity to problem-solving often involves using many of the techniques that we have discussed in this chapter to encourage people to think 'outside of the box'.

The skilled trainer will not offer solutions, but instead will use facilitative techniques to work with the group or with an individual in a coaching situation to enable them to reach their own conclusions on the best course of action.

The following checklist can help the process.

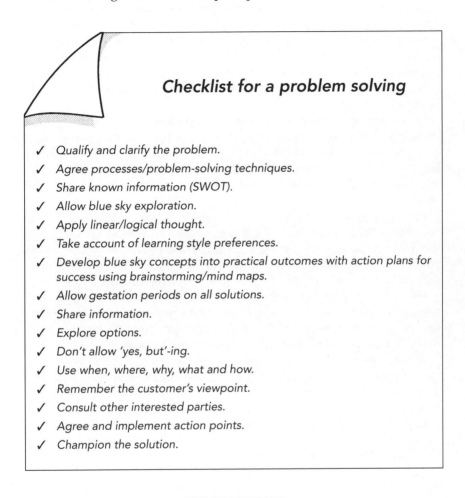

Checklist for a problem solving

✓ Qualify and clarify the problem.
✓ Agree processes/problem-solving techniques.
✓ Share known information (SWOT).
✓ Allow blue sky exploration.
✓ Apply linear/logical thought.
✓ Take account of learning style preferences.
✓ Develop blue sky concepts into practical outcomes with action plans for success using brainstorming/mind maps.
✓ Allow gestation periods on all solutions.
✓ Share information.
✓ Explore options.
✓ Don't allow 'yes, but'-ing.
✓ Use when, where, why, what and how.
✓ Remember the customer's viewpoint.
✓ Consult other interested parties.
✓ Agree and implement action points.
✓ Champion the solution.

NETWORKING

Recognizing the demands that are being placed on a trainer, there are some practical things you can do to help you maintain your performance level. Some are discussed in detail in Chapter 1, p.12, but another important source of inspiration is people. Being a trainer can sometimes be a lonely existence, particularly if you run your own business. You often have great responsibility for developing other people, and you are constantly giving of yourself, particularly if you are working in a high-performing organization.

In this section we look at networking as a source of inspiration, and we return to networking in more detail later (see Chapter 10, p.196). Every trainer recognizes the importance of generating ideas, concepts and activities that help people learn. Generating ideas on your own is possible but networking with others can be an invaluable source of inspiration.

Many informal networks exist around the country, where small groups of trainers either meet through professional associations or through informal networks to share best practice. Some of these networks are linked to industry sectors, some to voluntary groups, others are simply informal social events.

When people meet to share ideas or update each other on specific aspects of training, a high energy level is reached as people share concepts, visions and development plans. Sometimes these networks lead to mentoring situations. At their most creative level, people use the meetings to generate ideas, brainstorm or to identify future business opportunities.

Ideally, you want within your network people who match your learning style, people who will challenge your concepts in a constructive manner, and people who are just good friends, talking to whom makes you feel better. These people are invaluable in helping you to return to the real world after a particularly intensive training session.

Every trainer also needs at least one trusted fellow-trainer who will respond positively to those urgent late night requests for an ice-breaker or a team building exercise! The hope is that you too will respond positively in a reciprocal manner when they request the same of you!

As you become more experienced you may find yourself needing a special mentor, someone who really inspires you and will encourage you to push out the boundaries of your learning. It may be someone who has trained you in the past, it may be someone famous whose writing or whose video/audio tapes are a source of inner strength. Whatever the nature of the relationship they provide the ongoing creative inspiration to enable the trainer to develop others.

As we discussed earlier in this chapter and in Chapter 1, p.12, it is essential for trainers to recharge their batteries. This is particularly relevant if you are working in a highly facilitative or consultative manner. Both you and your delegates will benefit from exploring this area.

Finally, remember that you too can inspire people. Sometimes we get so absorbed in the day-to-day work of training that we forget how much experience we have actually gained, in sometimes a comparatively short space of time. Be willing to spend time talking to new trainers, share your experiences, the funny as well as the more developmental.

Offer to help others by giving them feedback, sharing in their brainstorms or helping them resolve issues. In this way you are giving as well as taking from a network.

USING RESOURCES

Despite advances in new technology, many of the materials that a trainer uses are paper-based, which often takes up a huge amount of space. There are often rooms occupied with previous course material, reference books and flipchart outputs, all of which was once useful, or could be in the future if only you could identify what exists!

The nature of training is such that few trainers are immediately able to file and store resources at the end of the programme. Often the trainer returns to his or her office or home and drops off one load of material before setting off with another load to another venue. Inevitably this leads to material stockpiling, which then means constant searching to find useful handouts or exercises.

However tedious it may seem, it can be invaluable to take time to organize this information into a manageable collection that can be easily accessed, which will take many forms, eg some of it may be stored on a disk, some in boxes, yet more in a library or in filing cabinets.

The format really depends on the space and facilities available. The key is organization and the discipline to set up client files, subject files and a retrieval system that is appropriate to the subject matter. You should also distinguish between materials needed for activities that go into an activities box, and specific OHP/handout material.

If your role involves presenting at conferences on particular subject areas, or you have a sales role, you will also have presentations that may be used on several occasions. Back-up promotional material may also be required. All this requires careful storing to allow ease of access.

Eventually it is likely that you will need a dedicated space labelled in the same way as a resources centre might be where training material can be stored and filed either under a client's name or under a subject area.

One useful approach to organizing your own resources is to visit a learning resource centre, a library or a business school. Here not only will you see examples of how to organize your own resources, but equally you will have the opportunity to browse through their resources, and if you join as a member of the library or as a professional associate, you will have found a valuable source of information. Library staff can be excellent in tracking down information on your behalf; many libraries now have access to very sophisticated international databases.

Source materials should be an important part of your background research. Your delegates will expect you to be up to date with new ideas and the latest business developments, and to have read the most topical and recent publications. Subscribing to professional organizations will give you access to other sources of information.

Many consultants associate themselves to universities or business schools in order to keep up to date with the latest research (see Chapter

9). Do not restrict yourself to information from your own country, look internationally too. Many organizations are thinking globally and trainers need to also adopt a global approach in both their research and development. There are opportunities for international research and to present papers at international conferences.

Checklist for finding inspiration

✓ Use all the techniques from Chapter 1 to keep your mind at its most receptive and to stay physically fit.
✓ Create working environments that help you to be creative.
✓ Always have a facility to note down your ideas.
✓ Identify sources of inspiration that work for you.
✓ Build up your own resources, identify libraries, business schools, sources of information.
✓ Think globally, research international sources of information.
✓ Share ideas with others, build your network of support.
✓ Use techniques like mind mapping and brainstorming to facilitate other people's innovation and creativity.

Whichever route you choose, managing resources effectively can be a powerful tool in ensuring your effectiveness as a trainer, and an ongoing source of inspiration.

If you cannot generate ideas, do something else. Relax, revisit your sources of inspiration, look for support from your network, and remember no one is creative all the time!

Creative resources: actors in training

There is a growing use of drama and acting techniques in the training room, often using actors to supplement the trainers' skills. The major uses include:

❑ actors being used as role players when training topics cause nervousness or inability of learners to reproduce the required behaviours;

❑ analogy playlets when a business problem is represented by a parallel situation played out by actors and then analysed with the help of a facilitator;

❑ forum theatre in which a business situation is depicted by actors with learners having the ability to stop and redirect the action; this allows learners to use the actors to explore the learners' difficulties in the particular situation.

For more information on this particular resource see the CIPD (Chartered Institute of Personnel and Development) Web site under 'Topics for Trainers – Theatre' (or Training comes of age) www.cipd.co.uk

Getting the best from blended and e-learning

The information in this chapter has been adapted from *Blended Learning: How to integrate online and traditional learning* by Kaye Thorne (see Appendix 3, p.237).

One of the most important factors in creating blended learning solutions is to recognize where it fits in the broader context of organizational learning and development. Much of the underpinning concepts of learning and development discussed elsewhere in this book have important relevance in the development of blended learning.

The potential of blended learning is almost limitless and represents a naturally evolving process from traditional forms of learning to a personalized and focused development path. Importantly, blended learning should not be seen in isolation: it represents one of the most naturally evolving processes of developing your human capital. Therefore any strategy to introduce blended learning needs to be considered carefully and positioned within the broader context of not just attracting, retaining and motivating talent, but also addressing the more compelling arguments of ROI and cost savings. An important part of this consideration is based on answers to the following key questions:

❑ What could blended learning mean to our organization?
❑ How does it fit with our overall business strategy?
❑ How could it help us to attract, retain and motivate talent?
❑ What other tangible benefits could it bring us?

SO WHAT DOES BLENDED LEARNING MEAN?

Blended learning is an example of how e- or online learning has evolved from its first inception. Before discussing blended learning it is perhaps helpful to identify some of the different components, firstly e-learning. E-learning can be found through a variety of different routes:

❑ online learning programmes incorporating activities and information, which are very similar to other forms of distance learning

❑ online learning portals, which take people through a variety of online and offline provisions

❑ Web sites that focus on specific product and service offerings, high-lighting features and benefits in the same way as a corporate brochure

❑ specific sites that allow you to download articles or tools, either free or in the case of particular tools on a free trial basis prior to purchase.

Some definitions

When one considers the e-learning component it is worth clarifying some of the language. Below is a short selection of some of the terms that you may hear. However, new descriptors are being created all the time. The only way to develop your knowledge is to talk to service providers and colleagues and always ask for clarification if you hear a term that you do not understand.

WBT (Web-based training)

This primarily describes training packages that are available using the Internet. Linked to this is the concept of virtual classrooms where again the Internet is used to link up different individuals in various locations with each other and/or their tutor.

In the virtual classroom, learners assemble at their own PC for a session. The material is presented to them via multimedia. In some programmes there are whiteboard facilities, which allow learners to contribute comments or even draw, type text or paste images and each learner can see the end result, and chat-rooms, which allow people to talk to each other. This can be augmented by video or audio conferencing. It is also possible to share applications when learners can view or work on documents jointly, or alternatively can voice an opinion or answer questions in a test.

Synchronous communication

Synchronous communication or learning is facilitated by bandwidth, which provides a medium similar to the way fibre optics support telephone communication. Everyone needs to be connected via an Intranet or the Internet. Initially the sound and video quality may not be very good but as the bandwidth improves it will get better all the time. Most communications online are asynchronous, using time-delay methods, eg e-mail or bulletin boards.

Learning portals

These are hosted by service providers who allow clients to access online materials held on a 'host' server. Individuals may leave a corporate Intranet and go into the Internet environment to use one particular provider's materials or in some cases a number of providers may be available through a portal catalogue. Individuals may also create online learning communities. Learning portals can also be built and branded to link from a company's Intranet, so that a user has seamless access from one to the other.

Learning object

One of the features of e-learning is the need to provide learning that is chunkable, often described as 'bite-sized' or 'just-in-time'. Part of the rationale for this is that the learning often needs to be contained within a few screens as e-learners often have neither the time nor the inclination to stay in front of their screens for long periods of time. 'Learning object' is a way of describing these bite-sized components. They are also important because they allow learners to get exactly what they need to learn, and not information that they may have already learnt in the past. This saves time in training and time to productivity for the learner.

Learning Management System (LMS)

An LMS provides the technology infrastructure for companies to manage human capital development by tracking employee training information and managing, tracking and launching all events and resources associated with corporate learning. A Web-based LMS provides online course and event management, content and resource management, comprehensive assessments, enhanced skills gap analysis, content authoring, e-mail notifications, and real-time integration with human resource, financial and ERP systems. An LMS manages all training delivery types – third-party and internal – including classroom-based, e-learning, virtual classroom and technology-based training, books and video. An LMS also provides access to authoring tools, 360-degree assessments, learning content management and/or virtual classroom functionality.

Application Service Provider (ASP)

This usually refers to a hosted service, which involves 'renting' the software, for example an LMS from an external company, rather than installing it and managing it on an internal system. In addition to providing technology on a subscription basis, an ASP also provides all the IT infrastructure and support services necessary to deliver it to customers. ASPs typically host applications at a remote data centre and deliver them to customers via the Internet or a private network.

SCORM (Shareable Content Object Reference Model)

The US Department of Defense (DoD) established the Advanced Distributed Learning (ADL) initiative to develop a DoD-wide strategy for using learning and information technologies to modernize education and training. In order to leverage existing practices, promote the use of technology-based learning and provide a sound economic basis for investment, the ADL initiative has defined high-level requirements for learning content such as content reusability, accessibility, durability and interoperability.

The Shareable Content Object Reference Model (SCORM) defines a Web-based learning 'Content Aggregation Model' and 'Run-time Environment' for learning objects. At its simplest, it is a reference model that references a set of interrelated technical specifications and guidelines designed to meet DoD's high-level requirements for Web-based learning content. These requirements include, but are not limited to, reusability, accessibility, durability and interoperability.

The work of the ADL initiative to develop the SCORM is also a process to knit together disparate groups and interests. This reference model aims to bridge emerging technologies and commercial and public implementations.

IMS

The IMS 'Learning resource meta-data best practice and implementation guide' provides general guidance about how an application may use LOM meta-data elements. In 1997 the IMS Project established an effort to develop open, market-based standards for online learning including specifications for learning content meta-data. For more information, see www.imsglobal.org.

Personal Digital Assistant (PDA)

This refers to a hand-held computer that, using WAP (Wireless Application Protocol) technology, has the potential to provide mobile access to e-learning content. This is still quite advanced for e-learning and not many companies are using this medium at the current time.

Definition of blended learning

Blended learning is the most logical and natural evolution of our learning agenda. It suggests an elegant solution to the challenges of tailoring learning and development to the needs of individuals. It represents an opportunity to integrate the innovative and technological advances offered by online learning together with the interaction and participation offered in the best of traditional learning. It can be supported and enhanced by using the wisdom and one-to-one contact of personal coaches.

Blended learning is a mix of:

❑ multimedia technology
❑ CD ROM, video streaming
❑ virtual classrooms
❑ voice-mail, e-mail, conference calls
❑ online text animation, video streaming

combined with traditional forms of classroom training and one-to-one coaching.

WHY IS BLENDED LEARNING IMPORTANT?

The real importance and significance in blended learning lies in its potential. If we forget the title and focus on the process, blending learning represents a real opportunity to create learning experiences that can provide the right learning at the right time and in the right place for each and every individual, not just at work, but in schools, universities and even at home. It can be truly universal, crossing global boundaries and bringing groups of learners together through different cultures and timezones. In this context blending learning could become one of the most significant developments of the 21st century.

SO WHO NEEDS TO BE INVOLVED AND WHEN?

This very much depends on the business and its internal structure. As a first step, it is really important to understand and think through the implications of embarking on a process of blended learning before figuring out the who and when. What are the immediate needs? What are the must-haves? Who will benefit in the organization and how will the organization as a whole benefit?

The following represent some key steps:

1. *Strategic-level discussion paper.* One of the major considerations in creating blended learning solutions is the ability to enable different

parts of the business to talk to each other, for example the IT department and the training/learning and development department. In its initial stages of development it will be really helpful for these departments to be in communication so that they are able to work together to create a discussion paper to outline the potential to the Executive. Initial discussions with suppliers can also help in positioning the internal business benefits or benchmarking in the context of either your business sector or the wider global community. It is also important to look at the costing of the proposal within the context of the other business priorities. Working with suppliers about the proposed phasing of the costs can also be helpful. One vital component that is often missing is the presentation of the ROI potential or cost savings within the business case.

2. *Sponsorship from the IT Director and L&D Director or equivalent commitment and buy-in from the Executive.* As highlighted above, if the potential has been carefully outlined with all the business advantages it will be easier for the Executive to commit to the development of blended solutions. Do not underestimate the need to build the case for the Executive who will be making the purchase decision on new software and/or hardware buys. E-learning is neither cheap nor easy, so the business case needs to be made on the return on investment as a result of initiating a blended programme or the cost savings from switching from one form of training medium to another.

3. *Internal champion/co-ordinator appointed.* As well as the higher-level support, blended learning does need an internal champion or co-ordinator who will be responsible for the day-to-day integration of online learning and traditional learning. This person, or team, needs to be not just familiar with the learning processes but also able to paint a persuasive picture of the possibilities and to be able to co-ordinate the different ways of learning into tailored learning solutions.

4. *Discussion paper formulated into an action plan with clear accountabilities.* As with any learning development initiative, it helps to be able to articulate the key stages and to outline them in an action plan and importantly to allocate key accountabilities. In this context the action plan will range across a number of areas from internal marketing to individual personal development. If this action plan is linked to the planned expenditure and the potential outcomes it will be even more helpful in managing the planned expenditure.

5. *Internal cross-functional team selected to work on creating blended solutions.* One of the very real issues in the early days of the development of online learning was a lack of understanding of the potential of the technology available. To achieve meaningful blended solutions it is really important to consider fully the range of media available and to

create the best possible solutions. It will also be important to help this team develop the broadest understanding of the range of learning opportunities that could be created using blended solutions. People in this group need open minds and must not take fixed positions based on their own preferences.

6. *Undertake an audit of the current learning provision, analyse who is doing what to whom and create a relationship database.* One of the real issues within large organizations is gaining a full picture of what is happening in learning and development throughout the business. This is further complicated if, as with many large organizations, some of the responsibility for purchasing learning and development has been passed down into the business. The larger the organization, the wider the span of control. Introducing blended learning can provide an opportunity to undertake an audit of all the learning solutions that are available within the organization.

7. *Undertake research to identify key providers of online learning.* Online learning is still a comparatively new offering, and identifying excellence can be difficult. Like any form of learning and development it will be important to undertake research to identify providers who can meet your criteria. It is essential that you talk to companies that have direct relevant experience in implementing blended solutions. Not all 'e-learning' providers have knowledge of blended learning. Also, it is vital that the provider chosen can demonstrate the ability to work in partnership with a number of other providers and will be happy to share methodology.

8. *Try to refine this list to invite three to five external providers to tender to provide a blended solution.* It is not necessarily essential that you should go outside of your organization to build blended solutions; however, for many organizations it is the case because there is not the necessary expertise internally to handle the total implementation. Part of the selection process will involve identifying what support is really needed. This will vary enormously from one organization to another and may consist of you identifying the exact level of support required. This may include commissioning a Learning Management System (LMS) or buying an off-the-shelf online learning solution, or commissioning your own tailored content.

Once you have selected your provider there then follows the next phase of development, which is to start the implementation of a process of generating blended learning solutions. The process for this is detailed below.

WHAT MAKES FOR SUCCESSFUL BLENDED LEARNING?

In reality the underpinning principles of blended learning are no different from any other form of learning. The key criteria are based on the following:

1. *Identify the core learning need.* Identifying the learning opportunity in blended learning is the same as identifying any learning opportunity. However, what is important is recognizing the need to provide the right solution for your learner. One of the real advantages of blended learning is the opportunity to be more focused and specific about the learning need. Increasingly organizations are recognizing the importance of tailoring learning to the individual rather than applying a 'one-size-fits-all' approach. We all have preferred ways of learning and, despite all the research and recommendations to take account of how people learn, many organizations from school to work still continue to provide blanket solutions. As training solutions evolve into learning solutions the hope is that organizations will begin to recognize the importance of making the learning more appropriate for each individual. Blended learning provides a great opportunity to tailor the learning to the learner.

    At this stage it is also important to identify how you are going to create the different parts of the solutions. There will be a number of ways in which the learning objectives can be met, and it will be essential that whoever is responsible for commissioning the solution has the necessary ability to look creatively at all the options. This particularly links to how the learning might be tailored. For example, if you have a very generic need it may be possible that an off-the-shelf provision could be purchased. This generic provision, however, could be supported by personal coaching by a line manager, who could prepare the learner before the learning experience and follow it up afterwards. In this way the overall learning experience will feel more personalized.

2. *Establish the level of demand/timescales.* In any decision about developing learning solutions there will always be a need to assess the reality of the demand. However, blended learning represents a real opportunity to respond more effectively to individual demand and as such has an application that is as relevant to an individual within a very small business as it is to a team of learners in a large global company. The very nature of the blend builds in flexibility. As with the development of any learning solution it will be important to gain a real understanding of the shape and scale of the demand, not just currently but also in the future. This highlights the importance of

making sure that those who are identifying the learning needs really understand blended learning so that they are able to ask the deeper-level questions to understand not just the immediate learning needs but the future needs too. It will also help if they can explore with the sponsor the potential of creatively offering different approaches to learning including the full range of blended options.

3. *Recognize the different types of learning styles.* We know through the work of David Kolb and Honey and Mumford that we all have preferred learning styles (see Chapter 2, How People Learn). As well as considering the different learning styles, there are other factors to take into consideration in the way that people prefer to learn. A blended learning solution needs to take account of these factors. In fact a positive by-product of using blended learning is that it does provide a range of learning solutions. In structuring the learning solution it will be important to take account of the learning styles of others. It also represents a great opportunity to review and revitalize the full learning and development offer. Use blended learning as a real opportunity to ask yourself or your team the question, 'How could we really do things differently?'

4. *Look creatively at the potential of using different forms of learning, eg matching the learning need to different delivery methods, and identify the best fit.* One of the biggest criticisms of many of the early examples of e-learning was that they were either text driven by technology or technology driving text. In the former the criticism was that people had simply taken words and put them on the screen with little thought about the real creative opportunities offered by the technology. In the latter the criticism was about the Web designers who got carried away with the wizardry behind text manipulation and particularly animation only to find that learners were unimpressed, or frustrated by the time it took to download learning objects.

Like most learning initiatives, integrating blended learning represents an opportunity to take what exists and evolve it into a different dimension using new technologies. One of the first steps is identifying what exists. Depending on your size of organization this can be a comparatively simple or a more complex exercise. In large or global organizations it can be difficult to keep up to date with local developments. Learning and development professionals are a creative breed and a programme that may have been developed centrally can often evolve into something quite different as it is rolled out into local regions and districts, or even into different functions.

'Tailoring' to meet the need of customers can also mean that the approach or content may be different from the original. Equally the wisdom gained through implementation may mean that what is offered is different from the original interpretation. All of this normally represents the healthy stages of implementation and development. However, if you are trying to develop a strategy to incorporate e-learning it is important to recognize what exists so that it can be integrated and formulated into new solutions.

This is where blended learning can really come into its own, by presenting the learner with a wide range of options. An important part of this process will be based on all the key stages above; in particular, the level of demand will be an important factor in designing the solution.

5. *Work with the current providers, internal and external, to identify the learning objectives and to ensure that the provision meets the current need.* In many large organizations this represents the toughest challenge particularly if the different provisions are located in different parts of the organization either geographically or psychologically. IT implementation and creating an e-environment may not necessarily sit next to learning and development. If you are a strong advocate of classroom training, a facilitator or a one-to-one coach you may not necessarily look for an online learning solution. The power of blended learning is that it can enable more elegant and bespoke solutions by combining one or more methods. The secret is to analyse what the key learning needs are and the most appropriate way of meeting them. In the early stages it may need some really basic examples of how it could work.

One of the challenges may be helping others adapt to the new forms of learning. If you feel that you excel in stand-up training, you may be less enthusiastic about adopting different ways of developing others. If you are fascinated by the use of design and technology in developing learning solutions, you may be less aware of the different ways that learners learn. However, in today's learning environment there have been a number of changes including using the line manager as coach, shorter training sessions and the use of online learning and multimedia packages. Going forward, it will be important to help everyone involved with learning and development make their maximum contribution.

6. *Undertake an education process and develop a user-friendly demonstration to illustrate the potential of blended learning.* As well as the need to outline the potential of blended learning, there is also the need to undertake an education process with the rest of the business; this will need to be far-reaching as it will include fellow learning and development professionals, line managers and the learners themselves. Some of the potential issues are likely to be linked to the need to do things differently and people usually need support with handling change, so

it will be important to help people recognize the potential as well as helping them to identify the solution that works for them. There are a number of ways that this can be achieved, which can involve online demonstrations, PowerPoint presentations, small lunchtime meetings or workshops.

7. *Be prepared to offer follow-up coaching support.* Before e-learning became so topical some organizations had created learning resource centres. These centres provided learners with the opportunity to use technology to support their learning and development; in some cases large sums of money were invested in purchasing or developing multimedia solutions. One of the issues that determined the success or otherwise of these centres was the level of support available. This issue has remained throughout the development of e-learning and blended learning.

   This support does not have to be through the same person. It could be a line manager who starts the process and continues to monitor progress throughout the individual's development. Individuals may also have a mentor; they can be encouraged to talk through their life goals with a partner or someone close to them. There may be an online support coach, peer support teams or different tutors linked to both the online and classroom development. The most important factor is that when learners feel the need for support they have access to the most appropriate person available for them.

8. *Set up a monitoring process to evaluate the effectiveness of the delivery.* One of the criticisms levelled at many learning and development initiatives is that they are not effectively monitored and evaluated. This can have significant impact when the organization is trying to measure the ROI. With something as far-reaching as introducing blended learning it is important to track the development, the lessons learnt and what improvements can be made. Having an internal Learning Management System can really help in this process.

   Having identified the process, one of the major considerations will be the creation of the content.

DESIGNING AND WRITING ONLINE LEARNING

The principles behind designing online learning are no different from those for any other learning intervention. As highlighted earlier in this book everyone has particular preferences when learning. In designing the learning experience it is important to take account of these preferences and build a learning experience that provides enough variety to cater for this. The very nature of how we learn means that online learning can only ever be one part of a broader learning experience. Thinking creatively about the design, however, can mean that it can be stimulating, interesting and intimate for the learner.

Who should be designing the materials?

One really important consideration must be how to develop the materials. Although it may be challenging and interesting to develop Web design skills in order to develop your own online materials, it may not be practical or possible within your time-frame of introducing blended learning. There are a number of roles that you can valuably perform in the process, but, unlike some of the other roles, writing for the Web is more specialized, and you must ask yourself if this is the best use of your time.

Guardians of intellectual property

One way of achieving a best fit is to recognize the roles and expertise involved in the total process. Internally it may be more appropriate for you to become a guardian of intellectual property, recognizing your breadth and depth of knowledge about content, the users/learners and the learning and development process. Externally there may be Web designers and authors. By taking the expertise from the right people with the right knowledge it will be far easier to create a blended solution that has a higher chance of success.

Recording and protecting what you know

In order to protect your intellectual property it is absolutely vital to keep meticulous records of all the stages in development. One of the major issues is disclosure. You can issue confidentiality agreements and sign non-disclosure documents, but it is important to assess the level of risk you are taking when you start talking about your ideas and concepts. The best advice is to be careful, recognize the value of what you have created and take professional advice where appropriate.

Auditing content

Auditing and identifying where relevant content is located within an organization are also highly relevant. Benchmarking best practice externally and networking with fellow professionals is another important role. Assembling a team of sample users to pilot and test the material will be a major contribution to the final success of the product. Equally, introducing the concept of blended learning to colleagues and to the rest of the organization can help to ensure that the implementation is more successful.

DESIGN PRINCIPLES

What the online component of blended learning shouldn't be is a training programme simply put up on to the Web. Used properly there are excellent opportunities to make learning interactive, dynamic and fun, but it does require the use of specialist design software and IT skills to create an effective learning environment.

There are some important criteria to remember when developing online learning. You can also use this as a checklist for evaluating material developed by others. It is important to recognize the following:

- ❑ Content should be high-quality and interesting.
- ❑ Less equals more; remember your learner will potentially be reading off a screen.
- ❑ Think about print options; some information can be printed off to read rather than scrolling through a screen.
- ❑ Use a journalistic, conversational style rather than an academic approach.
- ❑ You can refer people on to other sites for articles and resources.
- ❑ Ideally use a designer to enhance your words on-screen.
- ❑ Recognize that many people may be viewing your material on laptops or smaller screens.
- ❑ Make careful use of illustration and animation.
- ❑ Remember that, unlike with some other forms of learning where the sequence may be more controlled, online learners may be entering a screen in a more random sequence. They may also drill down, so having clear forms of navigation will be important to help them find their way around.

As in the early days of video when people were coming to terms with the ability to photograph people moving, you now need to recognize the reason why you are using online learning. It should be giving the learner a richer experience than simply reading flat text. If all you put up on the Web is flat text, however well created, there is the question: is this the best way of presenting your information? Equally if you create space which is over-full with animation or illustration, your learner may simply find it a distraction.

Contract with the learner

One of the benefits of an online environment is that it can create an intimacy with the learner, which needs to be respected. One of the issues with e-commerce has been a very natural reluctance on the part of the user to giving personal information when undertaking a transaction, and learning is no different. Once users have started a process of interaction they will be revealing information about themselves that should be protected and treated with integrity. The very nature of the learning that they may be undertaking may include them recording their personal responses to different situations; they may be undertaking assessments; they may be sharing their views with others. The following checklist highlights some key areas.

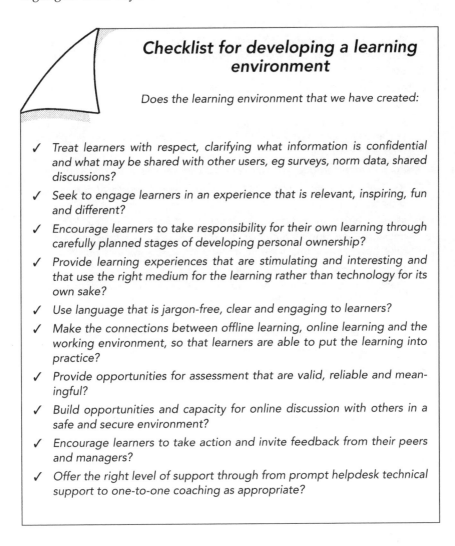

Checklist for developing a learning environment

Does the learning environment that we have created:

✓ Treat learners with respect, clarifying what information is confidential and what may be shared with other users, eg surveys, norm data, shared discussions?

✓ Seek to engage learners in an experience that is relevant, inspiring, fun and different?

✓ Encourage learners to take responsibility for their own learning through carefully planned stages of developing personal ownership?

✓ Provide learning experiences that are stimulating and interesting and that use the right medium for the learning rather than technology for its own sake?

✓ Use language that is jargon-free, clear and engaging to learners?

✓ Make the connections between offline learning, online learning and the working environment, so that learners are able to put the learning into practice?

✓ Provide opportunities for assessment that are valid, reliable and meaningful?

✓ Build opportunities and capacity for online discussion with others in a safe and secure environment?

✓ Encourage learners to take action and invite feedback from their peers and managers?

✓ Offer the right level of support through from prompt helpdesk technical support to one-to-one coaching as appropriate?

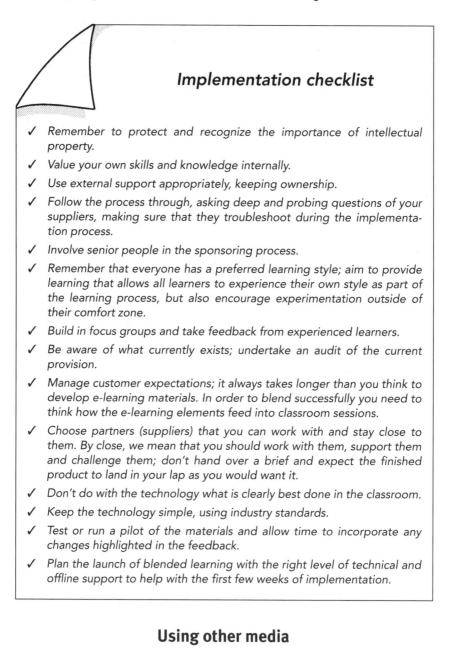

Implementation checklist

✓ Remember to protect and recognize the importance of intellectual property.

✓ Value your own skills and knowledge internally.

✓ Use external support appropriately, keeping ownership.

✓ Follow the process through, asking deep and probing questions of your suppliers, making sure that they troubleshoot during the implementation process.

✓ Involve senior people in the sponsoring process.

✓ Remember that everyone has a preferred learning style; aim to provide learning that allows all learners to experience their own style as part of the learning process, but also encourage experimentation outside of their comfort zone.

✓ Build in focus groups and take feedback from experienced learners.

✓ Be aware of what currently exists; undertake an audit of the current provision.

✓ Manage customer expectations; it always takes longer than you think to develop e-learning materials. In order to blend successfully you need to think how the e-learning elements feed into classroom sessions.

✓ Choose partners (suppliers) that you can work with and stay close to them. By close, we mean that you should work with them, support them and challenge them; don't hand over a brief and expect the finished product to land in your lap as you would want it.

✓ Don't do with the technology what is clearly best done in the classroom.

✓ Keep the technology simple, using industry standards.

✓ Test or run a pilot of the materials and allow time to incorporate any changes highlighted in the feedback.

✓ Plan the launch of blended learning with the right level of technical and offline support to help with the first few weeks of implementation.

Using other media

As well as online learning, there may also be other elements of learning that need designing, and the same principles apply; whether it is a CD ROM, video streaming, or distance or open learning, the focus must always be on the end user. Another question to ask yourself and the designers when commissioning any form of learning is whether this is the most effective way of transmitting the learning to the end user. Is it interesting? Does it take the right amount of time? Is the learning reinforced in different ways? Increasingly standards are being set, eg SCORM or IMS; therefore there is another layer of questions to ensure compliance with global standards.

Other key points to remember

One of the disadvantages with the growth of more technology-based learning is the lack of human contact; individual learners are losing the opportunity to talk through their embryonic ideas with other people. The whole philosophy of self-managed learning provides individuals with choices about how and where they learn, which has distinct advantages for both the individual and the organization. However, one of the potential losses from the reduction in training programmes is not so much what happens in the classroom or lecture theatre, but the learning that takes place on training events in those quieter, more intimate moments when two people start talking to each other at the end of a day, or in seminar groups before someone interrupts them and tells them to get on with the task. Therefore when introducing blended learning it is important to remember the need to include opportunities for this level of personal contact as part of the learning experience.

Working virtually

One of the distinct advantages of technology is the ability to transmit messages rapidly around the world. Globally, technological advances mean that organizations rarely sleep, working virtually. While Europe is asleep the business runs through the Pacific Rim, paying less for services provided by workers who are inducted into the culture of the country they are representing.

Below is a series of questions designed to prompt reflection and hopefully highlight some key areas of development that could make working virtually more effective:

1. How often do we take time to think through projects properly?
2. Do we use planning techniques?
3. Do we have analytical thinking skills?
4. We will need to plan this process. Have we undertaken a SWOT yet?
5. How creative are we? Are we hungry for information? Are we curious?
6. Do we share ideas with others? Do we take advantage of global time-zones to work virtually in teams?

7. Do we use idea-generating techniques? Do we take time to identify what really inspires us?

8. How open are our minds? How often do we say 'Why don't we try this?' as opposed to 'We've tried it before; it won't work'?

9. What do our customers need that we don't currently give them?

10. What do we have that works really well that could be adapted? What could we do more quickly or more efficiently?

11. Do we build teams of people with different styles of thinking? Do we take time to explore how we can work together? Do we play to people's strengths?

12. Do we tend to keep to the same pattern of working or do we regularly explore new options?

13. When we are presented with a challenging situation, do we take time to explore the 'what if' and develop a plan for contingencies?

14. Do we develop a 'worst case' scenario and plan how we would deal with any issues that might arise?

15. Do we ask 'Who?', 'What?', 'Why?', 'When?', 'Where?' and 'How?' when testing possible links, and consider all possible consequences of new product development and project management?

16. Do we always consider the bigger picture?

17. Do we consider the following: the strategic implication, the people implication and the customer?

18. How often do we review the decisions that we have made?

19. Do we allow time to review our assumptions before passing our conclusions or decisions on to others?

20. Are we driven by a deadline or do we build in a contingency time that allows for reflection and consultation?

You may want to reflect on these questions or discuss the key issues with another team member or colleague.

One way working virtually can help is in the design of learning, particularly when designers do not need to be in the same location. As well as the application of this globally it can also apply more locally. Disney uses a technique called 'displayed thinking' where projects that are being worked on are literally displayed on the wall. What this achieves is a number of things: people working in different areas can potentially add their own suggestions, but also it serves as a valuable communication tool. This same process can be used to share information with others using e-mail or company Intranets. Again, as mentioned above, you can use techniques such as mind mapping, sticky notes or other methods to transmit a lot of information simply. There are a number of advantages to this approach:

1. It allows for the natural and creative development of ideas.
2. A number of people can contribute at the same time.
3. Using simple techniques, ideas can be commented upon, amended or added to, while retaining the original document.
4. It is possible to work through different time-zones and shorten the development time.
5. Working in this way can help to forge global links and overcome cultural differences.
6. Everyone can work at a time, place and pace to suit their preferred learning styles.
7. To be successful, designers need to follow the same principles as mentioned above.
8. The same disciplines of meeting deadlines and responsiveness also need to apply in this virtual environment.

E-technologies have particular relevance in supporting virtual teams. This can involve you in being part of a global team, or working with teams that are working virtually. Importantly, with virtual teams there is an even more pressing need to establish the ground rules for working together. This can include the following:

❏ identifying what technology support is available and how to make best use of it
❏ agreeing the frequency of meetings
❏ commitment to attendance, on time and uninterrupted
❏ agreement of team rules, eg responding to e-mails, within a certain time-frame
❏ ways of using time efficiently, eg defining the purpose of virtual meetings
❏ using other methods to share information, eg circulating material prior to a meeting allows everyone to come prepared to contribute
❏ ideally from time to time physically getting together to form more substantial relationships
❏ understanding each team member's expectations and needs when working virtually
❏ constantly reassessing the opportunities for extending the technology support as systems improve, but using it appropriately, eg not using valuable conference airtime on something that should have been e-mailed.

By remembering the ground rules above you have the opportunity to exploit the advantages and minimize the disadvantages of working virtually.

USEFUL CONTACTS

There are many providers of e-learning information, but one organization that provides an international source of useful information about e-learning is the MASIE Center, which hosts the TechLearn and the World e-Learning Congress. Its Web site is at www.masie.com.

Another organization is WOLCE. The WOLCE event celebrated its 10th birthday on 2–3 October 2002 at the NEC, Birmingham by taking on a new name. The event is now called the World of Learning Conference and Exhibition; the 'Open Learning' aspect of the title has been replaced with 'of Learning'. Its research indicated that 89 per cent of all senior training professionals advocate using blended solutions to complete the rounded training package they offer to their companies. Thus the WOLCE event will now encompass all delivery methods of training, which will be reflected not only by the exhibiting companies but also in the conference programme. WOLCE's Web site is at www.wolce.com.

Also contact your regional professional association, many of which will have useful contacts on e- and blended learning.

WHAT ARE THE BENEFITS OF BLENDED LEARNING?

Using online learning within a blended solution helps to focus on individuals and their interaction with learning technologies using the Internet or an Intranet (in-company Web-enabled system).

There are a number of advantages to be gained by using blended learning in its various forms:

- ❑ Learning can be more targeted, focused, delivered bite-size, just-in-time.
- ❑ Learners can interact with the tutor.
- ❑ Learners can interact with their peers.
- ❑ Learning materials are readily accessible.
- ❑ Blended learning can make use of a variety of techniques by maximizing different technologies.
- ❑ Blended learning can build on other off-job provision.

There are very few disadvantages, but there are aspects to be aware of when introducing blended learning:

- ❑ Launch it on- and offline.
- ❑ Identify the support networks, both technically with help lines and with coaching support.

❑ Encourage learners to announce when they are engaged in online learning so that they are not interrupted.

❑ Encourage learners to recognize how they learn best, and that they should create a learning environment that works for them, which may be at work or at home.

❑ Encourage learners to share successes and support each other.

❑ Create learning that is stimulating and visually compelling, and recognizes different learning styles.

❑ Integrate online learning with other forms of learning.

WHAT IS THE FUTURE FOR BLENDED LEARNING?

The future for blended learning will very much depend on the pace of change in your organization and the level of commitment to doing things differently. Introducing the online components of blended learning does require investment, but the cost savings could be significant in the longer term. It does also represent a very positive way of targeting learning and development. However, it also requires sponsorship and commitment at the highest level to exploit its full potential.

On the technology front there are new developments all the time. Some will work and others may be more experimental. One of the opportunities for online learning in the future is the development of hand-held devices or PDAs. Using wireless technology the PDA has the potential to provide mobile access to e-learning content. The growth of the use of mobiles handling other facilities means that in time learning could be available through an individual's mobile phone. Learning could be adapted from the PC to a hand-held machine. If this is the case the learning would need to be tailored even further, but already text messages are becoming a very popular form of communication, and a similar technology could be developed to share learning content. If organizations are committed to providing online learning there will be the need to explore different ways of accessing the material, particularly in areas such as manufacturing and service environments such as retail and catering.

Whatever the technological advances, one key message about blended learning is to remember to stay focused on the learner. It is important that the learner's needs are fully captured and documented at the start of the project and that any success measures are based around these.

Evaluation of Training

BACKGROUND

The importance of evaluation

This has always been a key topic for trainers. T&D that is not delivering the expected results is likely to be potentially harmful to the organization, demotivating to learners and damaging to the reputation of trainers. Meaningful evaluation of T&D allows you to monitor results and to make any appropriate changes. Meaningful evaluation also provides you with information that you are 'doing a good job', and allows you to celebrate your successes!

In today's business world evaluation has taken on even greater significance than in the past. We are constantly reminded that the business world is rapidly changing. Almost every organization in both the private and public sectors is making important internal changes to develop a more customer-focused approach. T&D functions have rarely ever had such priority as in those organizations seeking to rapidly modify skills, knowledge, behaviours and styles of working of their staff. The rule for everything associated with T&D in these organizations is 'business focused, fast and flexible' and we hear expressions such as 'just-in-time' training. Everything needs to be done quickly but needs to be done correctly, and using the correct processes of evaluation is of the highest priority. The key to success is in the choice of evaluation processes that can be implemented with minimum difficulty and then followed up with urgency.

Why then, with this need for emphasis on evaluation, do we see that not every organization gives it sufficient focus? Some will direct vast energy into planning, developing and delivering T&D programmes, yet apparently direct minimum thought to evaluation. There have been examples of major training initiatives, costing large amounts of money and involving much precious resource, that have included almost no monitoring or evaluation. No mechanisms were included to monitor the potential benefits for the business or for the development of the staff. It will never be known how much of the money and resource were wisely used!

Evaluation is undertaken with the purpose of encouraging improvement. When evaluation is planned, it is done with the intention of analysing results and implementing suitable changes in a timely manner – followed by further evaluation. Such cyclical approaches – agreeing standards, evaluating, improving, checking standards, evaluating, and so on – are the bases of really useful evaluation processes for each aspect of the training and development process. The focus is on maximizing the use of resources, maximizing the likelihood of business success and maximizing the impact on staff motivation.

What to evaluate?

Organizations typically monitor their T&D operation to understand the extent to which:

❑ training and development objectives and strategies are aligned to the business;

❑ training and development initiatives are assisting in improvement of the 'bottom line' and in the organization's overall progress towards its business objectives;

❑ resources applied to T&D are being used in the most effective manner;

❑ specific components of the training processes, including the T&D function, individual trainers and individual training programmes are meeting agreed standards;

❑ specific training and development initiatives are appropriate for the staff for whom they are designed and are helping to produce the planned business results.

To ensure that the appropriate evaluation processes will be used, organizations need to consider the following questions:

❑ Which aspects of training and development should be evaluated?

❑ Against what standards should evaluations be undertaken?

❑ What mechanisms of monitoring and evaluation, both quantitative and qualitative, are available?

❑ What sort of changes to our T&D programmes can be implemented as a result of the evaluation?

❑ With whom will trainers discuss the required changes?

❑ When there are changes to be made, how and by whom will the changes be made and the results of change analysed?

❑ How quickly can changes be implemented?

Once the appropriate evaluation techniques have been implemented, full records of the results of evaluation need to be maintained. 'One-shot' evaluations of a particular training event are obviously important, but the real usefulness of evaluation will come from tracking progress against the agreed objectives of T&D.

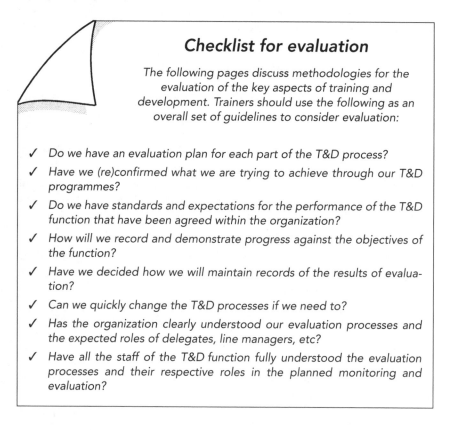

Checklist for evaluation

The following pages discuss methodologies for the evaluation of the key aspects of training and development. Trainers should use the following as an overall set of guidelines to consider evaluation:

✓ *Do we have an evaluation plan for each part of the T&D process?*

✓ *Have we (re)confirmed what we are trying to achieve through our T&D programmes?*

✓ *Do we have standards and expectations for the performance of the T&D function that have been agreed within the organization?*

✓ *How will we record and demonstrate progress against the objectives of the function?*

✓ *Have we decided how we will maintain records of the results of evaluation?*

✓ *Can we quickly change the T&D processes if we need to?*

✓ *Has the organization clearly understood our evaluation processes and the expected roles of delegates, line managers, etc?*

✓ *Have all the staff of the T&D function fully understood the evaluation processes and their respective roles in the planned monitoring and evaluation?*

EVALUATION OF T&D FUNCTIONS

It is worthwhile remembering that it is not just T&D that should be singled out for evaluation! The role, responsibility and business impact of every part of an organization should be reviewed regularly and rigorously. Each function needs to achieve its objectives within budgetary constraints in order for the overall organization to prosper.

Evaluation can, however, have a specific urgency for a T&D function. In common with other 'service' functions, there is a danger of T&D being trivialized and having its existence queried at times when there is 'bottom line' business difficulty. Unfortunately, this attitude has existed in too many traditional organizations, and the well-known adage about 'cutting training budgets first' can still be heard in some quarters. In resisting such dangers and in promoting itself as a vital part of an organization, the T&D function must be prepared for constant and strict evaluation. Indeed, as a potential 'leader of change and improvement', the function should be encouraging evaluation to prove its own worth and contribution within an organization.

Among the ways that T&D functions are evaluated are the measurements of:

❑ the perception across the organization of the function's worth;
❑ the overall view from summaries of the feedback provided by delegates following T&D events;
❑ the business effectiveness of delegates before and after they attended a T&D event;
❑ the commitment and competence of the function's own staff;
❑ the usefulness of the function's operational systems and processes.

Consistently implementing these and other measurements and reacting to the results is a constant responsibility of the function. This can be particularly challenging in organizations where the business environment is changing rapidly. The willingness and ability of the T&D function to be 'business focused, fast and flexible' can be severely stretched in an organization dedicated to continual change and refocus. The function needs to be able rapidly to evaluate its current effectiveness and be ready to make quick changes in its operation in support of the organization. Below we have discussed examples of evaluation processes that have been successful in assisting T&D functions to initiate proactive evaluation and significantly to improve their service.

Methods of evaluating the T&D function

Evaluation for the T&D function is based on the results from a number of measurement techniques.

The most frequently used of these techniques, which include a mixture of qualitative and quantitative processes, are outlined in the diagram and are discussed in the following paragraphs.

Establishing acceptable standards

If you are going to evaluate the impact of the T&D function, then you should be prepared to define appropriate standards. Obviously, the function will be evaluated against the objectives and plans that have been agreed with senior management. There needs to be an emphasis on sustaining improvement month on month, year on year. The standards will be both the commercial standards applied to every function in the organization and specific standards concerned with the implementation of T&D. Techniques to establish these specific standards are discussed in the final section of this chapter.

Surveying individuals across the organization

Ask a wide range of individuals from across the organization to complete a straightforward questionnaire (see Appendix 1, p.224). The chosen people should include:

❑ members of senior management
❑ managers of functions that frequently use training
❑ managers of functions that rarely seem to use training
❑ a selection of recent delegates and their line managers.

Look for trends as well as for the specific details that are indicated by the answers to the questionnaire. Identify particular situations that apparently need improvement. You should be starting to build a clear picture of those areas of the organization that would benefit from improved or extended services from T&D.

A selection of the people who have responded to the questionnaire should now be interviewed. Choose those who gave 'average' answers and those who gave answers that varied significantly from the average. As a rule, if people are interested enough to write additional comments on the questionnaire form, they are worth adding to your list of interviews; they are showing that they have a real interest in your work. The results from this wide range of interviews will allow you to add specific knowledge to that built from the completed questionnaires.

Summarizing learner feedback

Learners in all forms of training initiative, including distance learning, formal training courses, performance coaching and mentoring will normally be requested to provide evaluation of the initiative. There may be issues that require rapid attention, but the overall aim here is to further understand how T&D is generally perceived. All evaluations are collected and summarized and the results are carefully analysed.

The use and meaning of these learner evaluation forms is further discussed in the section on the evaluation of trainers (p.114).

Function reviews

This is an opportunity for T&D management to take the team 'off site' and critically to evaluate the function and its usefulness to the organization. The prime sources of information for these reviews are:

❏ the agreed T&D strategy for the function that should include the current roles and responsibilities within it (see the section on the trainer as a consultant, Chapter 8, p.143);

❏ the results of all the evaluation processes described above,

❏ benchmarked information about sources of training excellence (see the section on establishing appropriate standards, p.115);

❏ the knowledge of the training world held by the team members.

Sufficient time should be made available to discuss fully all the information and its impact on all the aspects of the function, and to make plans for progress. The meeting is likely to revolve around a number of brainstorming and problem-solving sessions (see pp.70–73) using guiding questions, including:

❏ What are our functional objectives and how well are we discharging them?

❏ Do the aims and objectives of the function match those of the organization?

❏ Do we understand the business priorities of the organization? Is T&D focusing on these priorities?

❏ Are we regularly checking that the organization's objectives have not changed?

❏ Are there business evaluation techniques in common use in the organization that could usefully be adopted by T&D?

❏ Are we regularly updating senior management and our clients about our strategies, our plans and our current training programmes?

❏ How are we regarded by our clients and the rest of the organization?

❏ Are we making a real contribution to the organization? Could we proactively extend our contribution by offering new services such as coaching?

❏ What are the important gaps between what we are doing and what we should be doing?

❏ What, in priority order, should we be doing differently?

❏ Are we advertising our successes?

❏ Are we regularly researching and benchmarking externally to the organization to keep abreast of current training trends?

❏ How can we present all the information we have gathered in a manner that will support our proposals?

❑ How are we going to gain agreement for these proposals from senior management and from the remainder of the organization who will be our clients?

At the end of the review the team should ask itself about the evaluation processes that are regularly being used by the function. Are they providing enough of the correct information to allow the function to evaluate and improve? Are there other, potentially more powerful evaluation processes that should be considered? Finally, the team will discuss the review process. What have they learned in this review about the review process itself? Could it be improved?

The results of these ongoing functional review meetings should be:

❑ opportunities to (re)confirm aims, objectives, strategies and plans with the whole organization;
❑ the agreement within the team and with senior management on the manner in which the function will continue to be evaluated.

Modifying the training and development function

Modify those aspects of the function and its work that do need to change, and ensure that the organization understands what has been changed and why. Communicate with those who undertook the questionnaire, thanking them for their help and indicating the positive result of their input. Senior management should be regularly advised of progress, using summaries of your information in an interesting and digestible form. There should be an emphasis on the way that the function is continually being integrated into the business objectives of the organization. This progress report should be set against the current T&D strategy and implementation plans.

Be prepared to identify where the problems really lie!

At the same time as you are surveying and reviewing all the T&D processes, be checking elsewhere. If there consistently appear to be issues between the function's work and other parts of the organization, trainers should satisfy themselves that it really is T&D that needs modifying. Fault and misunderstanding may lie within other areas of the organization. When an organization decides on new business directions or new internal processes, it can take several months for the new messages to be communicated. At any time there may be wide differences across the organization in the perceived meaning of the messages. Training should be reflecting the current needs of the organization, but occasionally trainers can be faced with learners who are not yet familiar with the new organizational messages. Be wary of deciding, and having others decide, that T&D initiatives are not supporting the business directions of the organization before all the facts are known.

The way ahead

This section has so far discussed well-accepted methods of evaluation for the T&D function. Surveys and benchmarking provide qualitative information, but the majority of the information made available by evaluation is quantitative. Trainers have always wanted to introduce 'softer' evidence to balance the weight of numeric information. We are beginning to see organizations where 'soft' measures of evaluation are being implemented. These typically involve:

❑ measuring the abilities of individual delegates and teams before and after training programmes, normally against changes in competency;

❑ the use of staff satisfaction surveys and the measurement of staff retention levels;

❑ measuring operational performance against reference groups, for instance with groups of salesmen, by comparing the performance of a trained group with a non-trained group.

These soft measures are beginning to win acceptance, although there is strong debate about their real meaning! There are so many other influences in addition to training. Relating change to training alone is difficult to fully justify.

Questions and answers on evaluating the function

 Is it really possible to evaluate a T&D function effectively?... Aren't there just too many external influences on the success of the function to make effective evaluation meaningful?

 It certainly has always been a challenge to establish meaningful evaluation for all the aspects of training. Often organizations have not gone beyond qualitative evaluation at the broadest levels, and results have tended to be at too global a level really to assist. Basically, the T&D function must be constantly evaluating its approach and its impact in order to implement changes to approach, in specific programmes, in specific training events. Unfortunately, the function too often needs to be seen to be self-evaluating for political reasons! And it is currently still true that the methods will be mostly quantitative or qualitative at a very broad level; the skill of the trainer will be the interpretation and the use of the results.

Q *Where do we start?*

A As the T&D function you are firmly in the world of client service. Most significant evaluations of a T&D function will start by building an accurate picture of the organization's perception of the function. This starts by undertaking the questionnaire approach outlined above.

Q *What about continuous evaluation? Haven't we got enough to do in the T&D function in reacting to the changing needs of the organization in a 'business focused, fast and flexible' manner?*

A All the techniques in this chapter should be used as an ongoing process. The really interesting point for trainers is that as an 'agent of change' there is a responsibility beyond the evaluation of the function. There is a real opportunity, because the trainer works across many areas of the organization, to be part of an evaluation of progress towards overall business objectives.

EVALUATION OF T&D PROGRAMMES

When an organization introduces an operational business programme one of its components will normally be a T&D programme. This is true for 'soft' organizational programmes, such as management development, and for 'harder' initiatives, such as bringing a new product on line. The T&D programmes will be a mixture of training initiatives, including training courses, performance coaching and mentoring. Each of these will include evaluation procedures for the initiative to test success, including contribution to the associated business programme. The design, development and implementation of these evaluation procedures will normally involve the trainer working in a team that includes the sponsor(s) of the operational programme and line managers of the most likely learners.

The team will agree the use of evaluation procedures that will monitor all the vital aspects of the T&D programme:

❑ ensuring the training programme supports the organization's overall objectives and is an integral part of the particular operational programme;

❑ checking that the most appropriate methods of training and development are being used to achieve the agreed objectives;

❑ ensuring that the correct learners are selected and that the priority order is agreed for their attendance on the appropriate training and development initiatives;

❑ ensuring that each stage of the training and development programme is individually evaluated to test that it is fully contributing to the overall programme's success.

Checklists for programme evaluation

The following pages contain a series of checklist approaches to implementing evaluation for T&D programmes. Our suggestion is that trainers use these examples to build checklists they can apply in their own situation. Disciplined use of these approaches, working with the sponsors of operational programmes and line management, will:

❑ maximize the possibilities of implementing successful evaluation procedures for all T&D programmes;

❑ maximize the possibilities of quickly detecting and solving problems;

❑ maximize the chances of delivering T&D programmes that are acknowledged as making major contributions to operational programmes.

This approach will demonstrate the professionalism of the T&D function and of individual trainers.

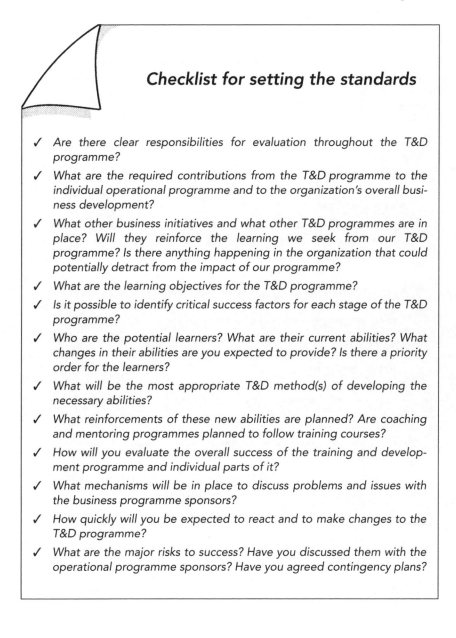

Checklist for setting the standards

✓ Are there clear responsibilities for evaluation throughout the T&D programme?

✓ What are the required contributions from the T&D programme to the individual operational programme and to the organization's overall business development?

✓ What other business initiatives and what other T&D programmes are in place? Will they reinforce the learning we seek from our T&D programme? Is there anything happening in the organization that could potentially detract from the impact of our programme?

✓ What are the learning objectives for the T&D programme?

✓ Is it possible to identify critical success factors for each stage of the T&D programme?

✓ Who are the potential learners? What are their current abilities? What changes in their abilities are you expected to provide? Is there a priority order for the learners?

✓ What will be the most appropriate T&D method(s) of developing the necessary abilities?

✓ What reinforcements of these new abilities are planned? Are coaching and mentoring programmes planned to follow training courses?

✓ How will you evaluate the overall success of the training and development programme and individual parts of it?

✓ What mechanisms will be in place to discuss problems and issues with the business programme sponsors?

✓ How quickly will you be expected to react and to make changes to the T&D programme?

✓ What are the major risks to success? Have you discussed them with the operational programme sponsors? Have you agreed contingency plans?

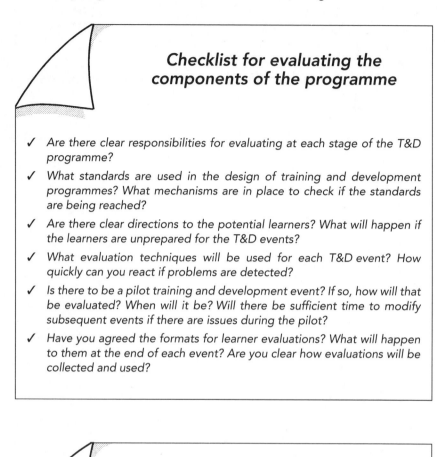

Checklist for evaluating the components of the programme

✓ Are there clear responsibilities for evaluating at each stage of the T&D programme?

✓ What standards are used in the design of training and development programmes? What mechanisms are in place to check if the standards are being reached?

✓ Are there clear directions to the potential learners? What will happen if the learners are unprepared for the T&D events?

✓ What evaluation techniques will be used for each T&D event? How quickly can you react if problems are detected?

✓ Is there to be a pilot training and development event? If so, how will that be evaluated? When will it be? Will there be sufficient time to modify subsequent events if there are issues during the pilot?

✓ Have you agreed the formats for learner evaluations? What will happen to them at the end of each event? Are you clear how evaluations will be collected and used?

Checklist for evaluating the overall impact

✓ Who will take the responsibility to analyse the impact of the T&D events on the abilities of the learners? Directly after the event and then after a further three months? Who will ensure the T&D function receives timely feedback?

✓ How will the business impact of the T&D programme on the organization and on the operational programme be measured?

✓ Who will summarize the result of the whole T&D programme against the original plan? How will this be used to improve future T&D programmes? How can it be used to improve T&D's contribution to the organization?

EVALUATION OF TRAINING EVENTS

You need critically to evaluate each T&D event in which you are involved. This is as true for a week-long course as it is for an individual coaching event. The more you evaluate, the more you learn, the more quickly the business will benefit and the more quickly your skills will develop. Each type of T&D event will have its own type of evaluation, but each has the common aim of change and improvement.

Training courses

Each will have an overall aim and a series of specific objectives (see Chapter 3, p.29). These frame the expectations of the course's impact for both the delegates and for the sponsor of the course, who is normally the business manager with whom it has been planned. As the course is evaluated, there will always be an all-encompassing question: 'Did it achieve its stated aim and objectives, and if not where and how did it fail?' In reality, the meaningful evaluation of a training course will involve all aspects of the course, from the impact on the business, through the delegates' perception of the trainer's performance, to questions about the venue and the food!

End of course evaluation forms

These are a topic that will generate discussion with most trainers! They are traditionally labelled 'happiness sheets' and are regarded with lively cynicism in parts of the T&D community. The cynical view says that the forms are no more than an evaluation of how much the delegates have enjoyed their time away from work and how much they were entertained by the trainer. This view gives little credence to the significant improvement that can result from the correct use of the forms. However, the trainer needs to be wary of delegates' reactions and may need to emphasize that evaluations will be taken seriously.

Although there are arguments that question their value, for most trainers and most T&D functions the forms provide instant feedback on a course's outcome and on the perception of a trainer's performance. The trainer needs to stress to the delegates that completion of the form is part of the course, that their input is meaningful in improving courses and is their contribution to business goals. If there are any examples where delegate feedback has led to significant changes in training events or in training programmes, then discuss these with the delegates.

Design your evaluation forms in a way that is appropriate to the event, to the delegates and to the manner in which you will use the results of the evaluation. Often, most of the questions have numerical responses or are multiple choice. Ask the delegates to spend time in thoughtfully answering all the questions, particularly those that need a full written answer.

The example forms we have shown in Appendix 1, (p.224) are designed to concentrate the delegates' minds on the real impact and usefulness of the course they have attended.

If more than one trainer is delivering the same training course, use the 'happiness sheets' to monitor the difference between the ratings given to each of them. Why are the ratings different? Is it because:

❑ One trainer is delivering a course that delegates are genuinely finding of greater value?

❑ One or more trainers are having difficulty in the delivery of this course?

❑ One or more trainers are having difficulty in building relationships with the typical delegates on this course?

❑ Different trainers are using different training methods, or supporting the event in novel ways?

❑ Some trainers are managing to entertain delegates and make friends with them in such a manner that poor evaluations are unlikely? This could be shown when the trainer is rated highly, but there is little indication of any commitment by the delegates to do anything after the course or to change their working patterns.

The trainers delivering the course should regularly meet and discuss their ways of delivering the course against the background of the evaluation sheets. They should be able to help one another to improve their individual performances and the course's contribution to the organization.

Using the results of evaluation forms

The summarized results of the training courses should be discussed with the sponsor of the training programme. Together you should decide on any modifications to the course and how they would affect:

❑ the likely level of benefit to the business from the delegates using their new skills, knowledge and behaviours;

❑ the commitment of the delegates after the course to put the learning into practice;

❑ any mechanisms that are in place to reinforce the learning of the course.

Other methods of evaluating training courses

The end-of-course 'happiness sheets' are by far the most usual way in which training courses are evaluated. There are other methods, some of which were mentioned in the previous section when we considered the evaluation of T&D functions. These methods tend to focus on evaluation of the impact of the course on the delegates. This involves measuring delegate abilities before and after a training course, normally by using standards set by the competence bank adopted by the organization. These evaluations can involve multiple choice checklists, written examinations or interviews conducted by line managers.

As experience of competencies is gained, these newer techniques of evaluating training courses are taking on more significance for trainers. You should continue to be aware of the concern that surrounds the 'soft', quantitative evaluations that were also mentioned in the previous section. There are many different things that can impact a person's performance and attitudes, in addition to that of being a delegate on a training course. It can be difficult, therefore, really to isolate the impact of that particular course. When appropriate, a follow-up with the delegates after a period of time could be really helpful both for the delegate and to provide feedback for the trainer. The nature of the conversation could be built around their agreed action plan.

Pilot courses

It is normal to pilot a new training course, particularly when the course is likely to have a high business impact, and when a number of new training/learning initiatives are to be introduced. The audience for a pilot course should include delegates with the same background and potential learning needs as the delegates who will eventually attend the regular courses. In addition, pilot course delegates may include other interested parties, typically members of the business function who have sponsored the course and other trainers who will subsequently deliver the course. Time should be made available for the pilot course to run one day longer than the planned regular course for which you are preparing. This will provide sufficient opportunity for detailed discussion of all aspects of the course, and even, should it be necessary, for sections of the course to be tested more than once. Delegates should be selected based on their ability to give useful and valuable feedback.

Evaluation during the pilot will be even more detailed than for the regular course:

❑ The trainer and the sponsor should agree SMART aims and objectives for each session, as well as for the whole event. (See Chapter 3, p.29.)

❏ Evaluation forms will be completed by the delegates at the end of each learning session or each module of the course, as well as at the end of the whole event.

❏ The progress of the course should be reviewed regularly, either at the end of each day or first thing each morning.

Coaching and mentoring events

These sorts of events are generally one-on-one events as opposed to the one-with-many of a training course. Evaluating the progress of a mentoring or coaching programme, or of one specific session, should therefore be a straightforward process. The relationship that is being built is open and forthright, and giving feedback in either direction should be part of this relationship. As the format of each meeting is planned, 10 minutes is scheduled at the end to allow the coach and the learner to discuss progress and the coaching/mentoring techniques that are being used. These 10-minute evaluation sessions will employ the same skill sets that have been used throughout the coaching and mentoring session (see Chapter 8, p.121). The coach/mentor questions the learner's view of the success of the session and the learner's views of potential improvements in the coaching/mentoring process. The coach/mentor and the learner agree any changes and how they will be introduced.

An occasional session should be devoted to a review of the overall objectives of the coaching and/or mentoring. The trainer and the learner should agree that the objectives are still appropriate, that the sessions are working towards those objectives and that the techniques of coaching/mentoring in use are appropriate.

The trainer/coach/mentor should ensure that these evaluation discussions and their outcomes are recorded. This will obviously promote the success of the coaching/mentoring sessions and the perceived professionalism of the trainer. Also, the results of such evaluation sessions should be fed into overall evaluations of the trainer personally, the T&D function and the techniques currently in use for coaching and mentoring.

EVALUATION OF TRAINERS

Those working for the majority of organizations will have corporate annual performance management and appraisal systems available. Such systems provide trainers with overall performance evaluations and with agreed personal development plans. The organization for which you work may already have developed a competency model for your job and be using this for your ongoing evaluation and development. Here we are discussing ways in which trainers can evaluate themselves in the area of training competence beyond these general annual appraisals. The ideas are also applicable to other people, such as line managers who are asked to take on a training responsibility. The results of all of these evaluations should be added to the considerations of a personal development plan and a skill development plan (see Chapter 9, p.170).

The essence of the approach is for the trainer regularly to build evidence from a number of sources for use with a personal checklist (see Appendix 1, p.224), against which he can evaluate himself and monitor his own progress. The sources include:

❑ the results of 'happiness sheets' from delegates at the end of courses;
❑ direct feedback from people to whom you are providing mentoring and coaching;
❑ direct feedback from your manager;
❑ direct feedback from delegates from conversations during courses;
❑ personal benchmarks against acknowledged excellent trainers.

This personal development checklist should be honestly scored, giving a mark out of 10 for each point. Over a number of months, check the improvement in the overall total and individual scores. Those scores that continue to be consistently low highlight those areas of performance that need improvement.

This approach will constantly remind the trainer of the importance of self-evaluation, and also of the importance of personal learning. Trainers should be ready to benchmark themselves against colleagues and against external trainers, and should seek to find time in their busy schedules to attend courses within the organization as well as external ones.

A checklist called 'So you want to be the best' is available in Chapter 4 of Thorne and Machray (2000), *World Class Training: Providing training excellence* (see Appendix 3, p.000).

ESTABLISHING APPROPRIATE STANDARDS

This chapter has been devoted to key aspects of evaluation in T&D. Such evaluation only has meaning when it is done against meaningful, agreed standards. Some of the measurement standards are straightforward. For example, a standard could be set that a trainer should undertake at least 100 days of delivering training programmes in a year.

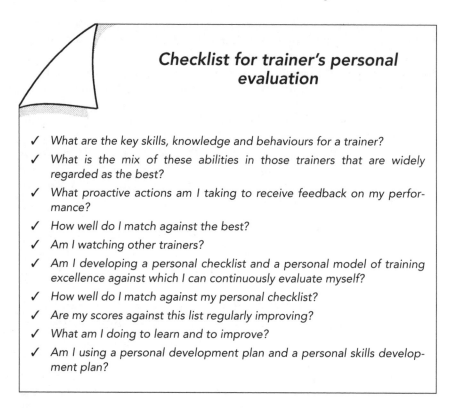

Checklist for trainer's personal evaluation

✓ What are the key skills, knowledge and behaviours for a trainer?

✓ What is the mix of these abilities in those trainers that are widely regarded as the best?

✓ What proactive actions am I taking to receive feedback on my performance?

✓ How well do I match against the best?

✓ Am I watching other trainers?

✓ Am I developing a personal checklist and a personal model of training excellence against which I can continuously evaluate myself?

✓ How well do I match against my personal checklist?

✓ Are my scores against this list regularly improving?

✓ What am I doing to learn and to improve?

✓ Am I using a personal development plan and a personal skills development plan?

However, at the other extreme you may wish to evaluate situations where standards are very difficult to express. What would be a standard that could be implemented to evaluate the contribution of an individual course to the business success of the organization? In between these two extremes there are standards in regular use about which there is significant debate. If a standard is set that a trainer should regularly be achieving a mark of at least 90 per cent delegate satisfaction on a 'happiness sheet', what does that mean? Is such a standard realistic given the environment in which the course is being given? Was it realistic last week? Will it be realistic next week? Standards in T&D are vital and necessary, but not always easy to implement. They will always be a mixture of 'hard' and 'soft'. The vital concerns are that the standards are set and they are agreed as being realistic for the overall good of the trainer, the T&D function, the delegates and the organization.

Appendix 1, p.224, lists areas of T&D to which evaluation procedures could be applied.

Setting standards through best practice

Standards employed in T&D have typically been implemented as the result of experience and best practice. This has generally been as the result of cyclical trial and error approaches. Based on trainers' experiences a performance standard is set for a T&D programme or for a specific training event. As experience grows of implementing the training initiative and evaluating results, the standards for performance can be discussed and modified appropriately. In most organizations this approach to the development of standards has occurred with little conscious planning. However, these best practice methods are widely used and regarded as successful. Training staff should recognize the current standards and adopt the cyclical approach to continue to improve them. The team should be asking the following questions:

❑ How and when were the standards set for the evaluation of T&D?

❑ Are the standards still appropriate? Are they regularly being updated?

Setting standards through benchmarking

Most trainers are familiar with standards set by some form of best practice approach. For many organizations this is in fact sufficient; the agreed internal standards for T&D are accepted as being appropriate for all evaluation needs. However, other organizations are attempting to set standards for key functions, including T&D, through benchmarking against acknowledged excellence.

Benchmarking with other organizations

Benchmarking all aspects of training and development, including evaluation, is in reality quite challenging. There is much published material about the results of benchmarking and about the implementation of training excellence; the evidence tends to be qualitative. For standards to be established through benchmarking you also need sets of quantitative data, and these are difficult to assemble. To handle this, trainers need to be proactive in their benchmarking initiatives, and the following provides a useful approach:

❑ Use your personal experience, recently published articles and your personal network, to develop a picture of the trends and important issues in training and development, particularly in the arena of evaluation. This will build your own knowledge of evaluation in training and development and build your credibility to undertake the next steps.

❑ Inquire within your own organization if external benchmarking is already employed on other topics; find out which external organizations may welcome benchmarking initiatives.

❑ Approach the management of T&D functions in organizations geographically close to you. Ask if they would be prepared to share knowledge and views, and, if so, to what level of detail. Our experience has been that companies will willingly trade such information if it is not commercially sensitive. There is normally sufficient benefit to each side to make meetings worthwhile.

❑ Be prepared to exchange information about the way in which you plan and prepare training initiatives and their evaluation, rather than the actual content. This will be less likely to cause commercial embarrassment to either side.

❑ In some commercial fields there are networks of T&D functions from several organizations. These groups meet regularly and exchange a lot of highly useful information. They tend to be reasonably informal and are discovered by inquiring through your contacts in the industry. If such a network does not exist, you might consider starting one. It can be of immense value to your training initiatives as well as to your own development.

❑ Once mutual agreement about the areas of discussion is reached then T&D functions can meet. The normal format of the meeting is for each team to make a presentation to an agreed agenda and for the meeting to discuss the issues raised. For most purposes a six-monthly meeting, perhaps lasting half a day, will be sufficient for each team to absorb a lot of useful information.

❑ Ensure that the debate on how evaluation is carried out has an important place on the agenda. Discuss, if possible, the important topic of how other organizations quantify the value of training to their business.

❑ It is not unusual for these meetings to promote less formal sessions between individuals from different organizations. There have even been examples in which a number of organizations have worked together with an external training consultant on a programme that each team needed.

❑ Trainers should be naturally inquisitive and be wishing to compare their personal contributions with those of other trainers both within their own organization and with those elsewhere. This comparison with others becomes very important if a trainer decides on self-employment in a training career. Trainers may well be able, through personal networks, to establish a personal connection with a trainer in another organization, and through this connection undertake significant benchmarking.

❑ If necessary, use external consultants to benchmark for you when the cost is appropriate. They should have a wide bank of experience and data as well as the contacts to undertake further searches on your behalf.

As you work to establish connections you will have to accept that some organizations will not take part in benchmarking exercises. You may try to sell the mutual benefit, but you may find the idea of benchmarking across organizations is totally unacceptable to them.

Internal benchmarking

Even if your organization does not have other T&D functions with which you can benchmark, there may be functions that are acknowledged for their excellence, particularly for client service. Discuss with them:

❑ how they set up objectives and plans;

❑ how they monitor those objectives and plans through to success;

❑ what exactly is evaluated and the methods of evaluation that are used;

❑ how they develop their evaluation processes with their clients, internal and external;

❑ how, and how quickly, they can change programmes in response to what is learned from evaluation;

❑ how responsibilities for evaluation and using the results are implemented;

❑ how they use benchmarking.

Final thoughts

Benchmarking is a powerful business approach. It does take a lot of time to undertake and the results can take time to turn into really useful information to improve your organization. When benchmarking evaluation, as in all benchmarking initiatives, it is really important to consider what benchmarked information would be useful and could be used. Do not be tempted into 'nice to haves' that will be of no real use. The section on aspects of training for evaluation and benchmarking, Appendix 1, p.224, lists those features of T&D, including aspects of evaluation, that are worthwhile for consideration in benchmarking initiatives.

Checklist for standards through benchmarking

✓ When I attend conferences and trainer meetings, do I consider if there are people present who would be appropriate for formal or informal benchmarking on evaluation and other topics?

✓ Have I thought through an approach to other people and organizations that includes the mutual benefits of benchmarking?

✓ Have I discussed benchmarking of evaluation techniques and processes with any other areas of my own organization?

✓ Have I decided which aspects of evaluation I should benchmark? What would be really useful?

Maintaining the standards

Building, interpreting and modifying standards for training and development are major tasks for trainers. It is, however, the foundation of successful evaluation. The standards that are to be implemented should be retained in a standards manual for the T&D function, and an individual trainer should be made responsible for them.

The Trainer As...

As we discussed in the Introduction, there are significant changes occurring in the role of both the trainer and the T&D function. In particular, the role of the trainer is evolving to encompass new responsibilities, including acting as an internal consultant, performance coach or mentor. Each of these new roles requires the development of an enhanced skill set. Each of them also provides a positive opportunity for career progression.

COACH

Creating a coaching environment

As highlighted in the preface to this edition, the corporate world is changing quite dramatically, businesses are facing challenges on an unprecedented scale and the retention of key employees is a major ongoing challenge. Employees equally are looking for organizations that value their contribution.

One major way of helping all individuals fulfil their potential is to develop a coaching environment. This is not something that will be achieved overnight, but if you can engender a sense of sharing wisdom you are more likely to create a real sense of personal development. This is very different from the process of 'managing'.

A coach guides rather than manages; throughout history there have been instances of guidance being given by 'elders'. What if instead of creating 'managers' we created guides? What if we gave respect to the wisdom of our experienced workers? The very best supervisors and managers are those who share their wisdom and give guidance to new employees. The very worst managers are those who play it by the rules with no flexibility or explanation.

Introducing a coaching environment may have a very far-reaching impact; individuals need to think about their very best learning experiences, remember what inspired them and think about how they can recreate special learning. Managers need to forget about being in control, and instead help their team members to explore by asking open questions and being provocative; although individuals should never be taken unsupported outside their comfort zone, they can be encouraged to push their boundaries beyond their normal learning experiences. Equally trainers could also perform the role of coach and may need to recognize that in the future classroom training may become much more focused on the individual, and as a result small discussion groups or one-to-one coaching may occur more frequently than classroom sessions.

Traditionally coaching was something that might only have been offered to senior executives or fast-track employees. However, as more and more people become aware of the benefits of one-to-one support, coaches may be found operating at a number of levels within an organization. Another major advantage is that if people really begin to adopt coaching behaviours the organization becomes much more of a learning environment. People really do start to learn from each other, but it needs attention to survive, and this is one of the major challenges; in any large organization it takes constant attention to maintain any initiative. Too many employees are introduced to an idea, process and way of working, only to find that it is not sustained. Creating a real coaching environment needs focus and nurturing rather than just paying lip service to the concept, and it needs ongoing support from the very top of the organization.

The coaching role

There is always a danger that newly acquired information is forgotten before it can be put to use. Once a learner has attended a training event, her newly absorbed skills, knowledge, behaviours and attitudes need to be reinforced. In some way what has been learned must be rapidly refreshed back in the workplace. This reinforcement of a person's learning is one of the prime roles of the coach. The diagram below shows the simple relationship linking training and coaching.

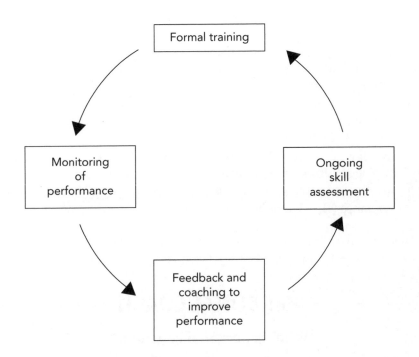

Coupled with this is the coach's role in monitoring everyday performance of his team members and in identifying opportunities for their development. Generally, the responsibility for coaching a team of people is regarded as that of the team's line manager, and coaching has become recognized as one of the essential leadership activities.

The new interest in coaching is also shown by the rapid growth in the number of organizations offering coaching services to the business community.

The essence of coaching is the development of skills, knowledge and appropriate attitudes and behaviours through one-to-one focus on the person or the team being coached.

The performance coaching role

A trainer may be required to take on a coaching role in one of a number of circumstances:

❑ Line managers are not fully trained in coaching skills and seek your assistance in the coaching of their team.

❑ Line managers have insufficient time to devote to coaching of their teams, particularly when their teams are very large or when their teams are geographically widespread.

❑ One person, perhaps in a senior role, needs to develop a particular set of skills, knowledge or behaviours but does not want to attend formal training courses.

❑ A small number of key individuals need to develop a new set of skills, knowledge or behaviours and there are no appropriate training courses available.

❑ To follow up a particular training event with individuals who feel they need additional assistance.

❑ To support e-learning initiatives should individuals require particular assistance (see Chapter 6).

This role will give the trainer/coach every opportunity of working with a wide range of people, of increasing her skills and enlarging her network.

PERSONAL COACH

What is personal coaching?

Personal coaching could be described as enabling, ie supporting, another individual to achieve that individual's personal goals. Within this context it uses a skill set that is similar to that of mentoring or counselling. To coach someone successfully it is likely that you will draw on the following: questioning, listening, observing and giving feedback; and will work within a coaching model of support and challenge. Although this mode of coaching is often used by senior executives the approach is relevant to anyone.

The difference between personal coaching and coaching can be elucidated by considering the concept of a personal sports trainer. The coaching offered very much focuses on the needs of the individual; it is driven by the individual and often looks holistically at the individual's needs as opposed to being purely work-related. You may also hear the term 'performance coach', but, while you may be helping someone improve their performance, personal coaching may not always be targeted at improving performance in a working environment. It may also be about encouraging a learner to be more reflective and to focus on behaviours rather than competency development.

Often a plan is worked out between the coach and the participant, which sets personal goals and targets and enables the participant to prepare for and take control of challenging situations. It is often very proactive, and the relationship is built up over a period of time, which enables the coach to develop a support and challenge approach.

Role of the personal coach

Being a personal coach is like accompanying someone on a journey; from this perspective it could be more accurate to describe the role as that of personal guide. As in any journey it is important to prepare, to have an overall sense of direction and then to build in special stepping stones. In acting as a guide there is the need to recognize that at certain times the individual will want 'guidance' and at other times will be ready to enjoy a process of self-discovery. As coaches we have a responsibility to get close to our learners and to help them to know themselves.

By understanding how people learn and building that knowledge in the people we coach, we are actively demonstrating the saying, 'Give a man a rod and teach him to fish.'

As a personal coach you will find yourself using a number of techniques, many of which are used in other applications, eg counselling, mentoring, facilitating or managing others. What is important is the way in which you use the right techniques for the right people, and also the way in which you build the coaching relationship, so that the individual is not aware that you are actually using techniques, and the conversation feels natural.

Right time, right place, right person

In the same way that a personal trainer would work with you to tone your body, personal coaching works with your mind and spirit. When it is done well the connectivity is seamless; your coach intuitively knows how and when to suggest meetings at times that will uplift you.

A personal coach will encourage you to step outside your day-to-day routine, help you to explore the boundaries of your learning, and support and challenge you at times of decision. The personal coach can be a sounding board, coach, mentor and friend, and can stimulate, excite and encourage you to step outside your comfort zone. Because the relationship is built on professionalism, integrity and trust, you will push yourself that little bit harder to achieve your goals. As with an athlete, you plan a training regime together and agree the times when you want to be challenged to test your resistance and personal strength of mind. Equally the personal coach will encourage you to wind down after you have put yourself through a challenging situation.

The personal coach will help you to visualize your success and to surround yourself with images and stimuli to fuel your imagination and to help you to recharge. The coach will weave in and out of your life, helping you to create a tapestry of experiences that help you to grow and develop.

The skilled partner will delight in your learning, and will help you to move forward with encouragement, giving you positive feedback. What distinguishes the experience is that it's different, it's memorable and it forms an important part of your development. Find the right time, the right place and the right person to guide your personal understanding and it will enable you to experience learning that is so profound that the memory will stay with you for ever.

The key point about personal coaching is that when it is done well it achieves the following:

❏ creates rapport
❏ set in the right environment
❏ part of an ongoing relationship
❏ focuses on the individual
❏ shares mutual respect and the opportunity to learn from each other
❏ application of higher-level skills/competencies
❏ actions agreed and followed up.

So could you be a personal coach?

Your job role may be trainer, performance coach, facilitator, developer, internal consultant or learning designer. Whatever your title, your interest will be in developing a skill set and creating an environment that is conducive to working one to one with another person.

Only the first step

Importantly this section should be read in the context of supporting personal development for coaches. A book should never be a substitute for the process of developing the skills required in becoming a coach. There are many professional qualifications available for coaches and if you are offering coaching it will be important to identify your own mentor who can help you to develop your skill set as a coach.

Also there are a number of references throughout this book to the need to refer your participants to others for additional support. There are important differences between coaching and counselling; there may be times when you recognize the need for specialist support. It is important not only that you recognize the need but that you help your participant to seek that additional help.

Client confidentiality

If you are acting as a personal coach within an organization, you need to recognize the significance of your role. Where organizations have offered counselling support it tends to be supplied by an outside agency. Personal coaches have some of the same issues:

❑ confidentiality

❑ trust

❑ relationship with line managers

❑ loyalty to the organization.

As with the role of the internal consultant, these inter-relationships need to be worked out first so that everyone is absolutely clear about the roles, responsibilities and boundaries.

Creating a climate of trust

One of the fundamentally most important parts of being a personal coach is establishing trust. Without this nothing can really start. In this context trust means confirming to the learner that everything that is said between the two of you is completely confidential. It also means creating a sense of care, empathy and total professionalism. This is the foundation of the whole relationship. It means reassuring learners that their thoughts, hopes, dreams and aspirations are safe with you. It means that through your actions and the way that you conduct the relationship they feel confident in your ability to work with them and support them. It also means that you keep your own concerns, worries and views to yourself and don't use the sessions for your own gain.

It is also important to recognize that trust once betrayed is highly unlikely ever to be regained; therefore do everything in your power to maintain it. Never *ever* repeat anything that is said to you in a coaching session to anyone else, however professional or trustworthy you believe that person to be. Once you have shared what the learner has said, you no longer have any control over how it is shared or repeated and you have broken the confidence of the learner who trusted you.

The implications of this are highlighted when you find yourself in a situation when you feel unable to offer the right support to your learner. What do you do? Importantly what you must do is gain agreement about what to do next. The options may be to encourage your learner to seek additional help or to gain agreement that on a specific issue you will seek advice from someone else on the learner's behalf. The latter can only be undertaken with the learner's express permission and with agreement on the elements of disclosure.

In many ways it is preferable to work with the learner to enable the learner to seek support; that way the learner retains ownership of the issue and also knows what information has been shared. This has particular relevance in workplace coaching where the coach may not be the line manager, but the learner may raise issues about the relationship between learner and manager. In this context it is always preferable to support the individual in working through the issue, but to encourage the learner to work with the manager to resolve the issue.

There may be occasions when you feel that your learner may need specialist help. This may be technical and skills-related, additional training, or counselling to help the learner work through a particular issue. It is very important that this is handled up front at the start of the relationship by clearly explaining your role, skills and expertise and how you would work with the learner to prepare the learner to work with others, but do not try to offer counselling within your role as a coach. The underpinning skill set may be similar, but counselling is a very specialist area, and only people properly trained and qualified in this area should offer counselling support.

Everyone is different

Everyone *is* different and gaining an understanding of the differences is essential if you are to work as a personal coach with anyone. This understanding is based on a number of key factors.

Each individual learner that you coach will be different, and you will be different to the learner. Recognizing these differences is an important part of coaching and helping others to learn. What is fascinating is recognizing how subtle these differences are. No two people will have exactly the same combination, and in this context we should never make broad assumptions about different learners.

One way that you can help an individual gain personal insight is by encouraging the individual to build self-understanding. One phrase that sums this up is 'being comfortable with yourself', which is used to describe that inner confidence that comes from knowing your strengths and areas of development. With this inner confidence also comes an ability to accept challenges and to want to explore your personal boundaries and comfort zones. Without this understanding there is a danger that the learner may not be able to respond positively to feedback from others.

Finding your own path to the future

This section focuses on you as the personal coach. Your ability to support others needs to be matched by your own ability to create your own development programme. By charting your own path to the future you create a very tangible means of empathizing with the development needs of the individuals whom you work with. Identifying personal goals and setting milestone plans for yourself will give you an intrinsic understanding of the issues and challenges faced by your people. This is not to oversimplify the process, but much of the personal coaching process is based on a commonsense approach to goal setting, and planning a route to achieve it.

How people learn

One of the most important aspects of personal coaching is recognizing the different needs of individual learners. This may also have a real impact on not only how you coach but also whom you coach. Teachers, lecturers, trainers and workplace coaches may feel they have less choice in whom they work with, and there will be those who argue that coaching is a technique that once learnt can be applied with any combination of learners.

However, if you recall the people who have really influenced your learning, it is very likely that there were very strong linkages between the way they taught you and the way that you wanted to learn. If we further develop this into the context of personal coaching, it is even more likely that an effective coaching relationship is built on something other than just the pure techniques of coaching. One of the most important places to start is to develop as full as possible an understanding of how people learn and to recognize the key influences and research in this area.

One of the most enduring models about learning is Kolb's learning cycle; he identified the key steps in how people learn (see Chapter 2, How People Learn).

If your learners enjoy the learning experience they are more likely to learn and remember. If they are *told* they need to learn something their willingness to learn will depend on the respect that they have for the person telling them and their desire to learn. If their desire to learn is driven by a personal curiosity and they learn in a way that reflects their preferred learning style it is likely that their own enthusiasm and interest will make the learning more meaningful and memorable.

Apply the following to your own learning and ask your learner also to consider the following questions:

- ❑ Have I created the right place for me to learn?
- ❑ Do I take responsibility for my learning?
- ❑ Do I use my preferred learning styles?
- ❑ Can I learn despite poor teaching? Do I seek additional coaching?

❏ Am I actively involved in the learning process?
❏ Can I learn in many different ways? Do I know what I need to memorize, what I need to understand and what I need to learn by doing?
❏ Do I seek feedback on my learning and performance?
❏ Do I learn from my mistakes?
❏ Do I regularly take a break and do something else to energize me?
❏ Do I share and celebrate my successes in learning?

Reflecting on learning

An important part of your learning is to help your learners to review the outcomes of their development activities. Encourage them to ask themselves the following after a learning event:

❏ What went well? Why?
❏ What could have gone better? Why?
❏ How could I improve next time?
❏ What have I learnt?
❏ How will I use this learning in the future?

Helping you to help others

There are so many ways in which you can develop your own skill set to enable you to help others. The very nature of personal coaching is based on the traditional ways that people have always learnt. There are the underpinning skills of effective communication, observing, questioning, listening and giving feedback, but there is also a range of other techniques and ways in which you can help individuals explore their own development.

Identifying your own style

Always recognize where your learners are starting from. You may develop a richer and deeper understanding of how people learn and their personal motivation, and may explore new philosophies and alternative ways of working. Assimilate this knowledge and use it to heighten your own understanding, but never use your learner as a guinea-pig on whom to test your half-formed theories. A little knowledge can indeed be a dangerous thing, and any reputable theory of development should have either an accreditation or a practitioner development programme.

Inviting feedback

Who gives you feedback? Do you invite it? Do you believe it? As professionals, we should be able to ask for and absorb feedback into our ongoing development. Unfortunately there are very few people who are really skilled at giving it. If you are training people to assess or coach, you will recognize the importance of doing it properly. Unfortunately it is one area that consistently causes issues in organizations, so many people give feedback that is unhelpful during appraisals or performance management sessions. With less opportunity for training, there are ever more instances of unskilled feedback.

If you do develop a clear understanding of your strengths, you are better able to help people give you feedback. By asking the right questions, you will be able to elicit information about your own performance. You will also, if you develop experience as a communicator, be able to identify other people's responses to you. There are several references to giving effective feedback in this book, but as a personal coach you really do need to consider feedback in a number of contexts:

❏ How effective am I at giving feedback? How do I know? How could I check my understanding?

❏ Do I ask for feedback? If yes, with what result? If no, what positive actions can I take to overcome this?

❏ Whom do I really trust to help me explore the areas where I feel less confident?

❏ How can I enhance my skills in giving feedback?

❏ What would I like to do differently when giving feedback?

The above questions are intended as prompts for you to consider, but as part of your personal development you may want to explore these in more depth with your own personal coach or mentor.

Selecting your own personal coach

A personal coach is more than someone you can turn to for help or advice. This person is different from your parents, partner, lover or best friend. This is someone who endures over time, will listen to your ideas, will help you talk through your deepest concerns and ultimately will allow you to make up your own mind. What personal coaches really do is provide a sounding board. You respect them for their views and they are a great source of inspiration. The nature of the relationship ought to be formalized, and there should be an agreement between you so that you are both aware of your responsibilities.

This will equally apply when you are offering personal coaching to others. They and you when acting in the role of a personal coach should adhere to a code of practice. There should be a duty of care so that, when you are being coached and when you are coaching others, everyone recognizes the full level of responsibility and acts accordingly.

Think carefully about whom you choose as a personal coach, particularly if you are offering personal coaching to others. Do not simply make an informal arrangement with a colleague because you know each other and you get on well. If you are serious about your personal growth you need to identify someone who will stretch you and help you to develop new skills. The more experienced you are, the longer it may take to find the right person. To help you in your choice you may want to consider the following checklist.

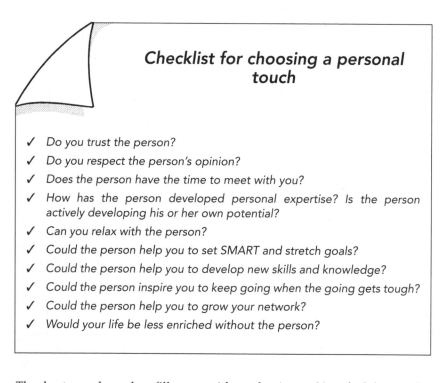

Checklist for choosing a personal touch

✓   Do you trust the person?
✓   Do you respect the person's opinion?
✓   Does the person have the time to meet with you?
✓   How has the person developed personal expertise? Is the person actively developing his or her own potential?
✓   Can you relax with the person?
✓   Could the person help you to set SMART and stretch goals?
✓   Could the person help you to develop new skills and knowledge?
✓   Could the person inspire you to keep going when the going gets tough?
✓   Could the person help you to grow your network?
✓   Would your life be less enriched without the person?

The best coaches also fill you with enthusiasm. You feel better for spending time with them or talking on the telephone to them. We often identify them over a period of time; what distinguishes them from our friends, family or colleagues is their wisdom and our respect for them. We feel comfortable with them, we accept the challenges they set us and we want them to be proud of us.

Could you be a personal coach?

As discussed earlier the role of personal coach has evolved from the principles of a variety of forms of coaching. What is really important is not attempting to work as a personal coach without developing competence. Equally important is recognizing the boundaries. In the context of personal coaching within this book it is about developing the competence to help people help themselves.

It is about skilfully using observation, questioning, listening and giving feedback to enable learners to take their own journey of discovery. The emphasis should always be on what they are going to do to take ownership of their journey, and your role will be one of personal guide, sounding board and helping them to explore options and choices.

The difference about personal coaching is that it is personal, and as such it should focus completely on the individual learner. As well as focusing on learners, you can help them to understand how they relate to others and importantly why that interconnectivity works better with some people than with others. By enabling learners to discover their uniqueness you can also help them to enjoy and reflect on the synergy of their relationships with others.

Recognizing your own boundaries

Importantly, as a personal coach you should recognize a number of boundaries. The first boundary is about encouraging learners to take responsibility for their own decisions. This rule above all others is such a fundamental point, which not only reflects your own professionalism but is critical for the individual. Although you may work very closely with individual learners you must never make their decisions for them. Another important boundary is one that is often mentioned, which is the difference between coaching and counselling. You may in your work with individuals reach a point where they are in need of counselling support. Always help them to seek this specialist help; do not attempt to offer counselling support. Even if you are a trained counsellor you need to recognize how the nature of your coaching relationship may change if you also offer counselling support to the same learner.

Setting your own development plan

One of the critical learning points for individuals is the realization that they are in fact in control of their own destiny. When you help people on their own particular journey, it is so important that they recognize and understand the process and acknowledge the insights as they occur for them. This is another important function of coaches in that they can help in raising awareness of the stages in undertaking personal discovery, not just for their learners but also for themselves.

Finally, recognize what a special role you are developing as a personal coach: the self-belief, ability to listen to others, care and compassion are not just relevant in your work. Use them to develop and share in your relationships with others: your friends, partner, parents and children.

The role of the personal coach, tools and techniques are discussed in much more detail in *Personal Coaching* by Kaye Thorne (see Appendix 3, p.237).

Using coaching skills

In each of the potential coaching situations described above the trainer/ coach follows the same guidelines:

❑ Find time and place to devote full, uninterrupted attention to the learner, the person who is being coached.

❑ Give praise whenever possible in building the relationship.

❑ Be honest.

❑ Use questioning and listening skills to help the learner identify situations where they need support and the new requirements for skills, knowledge and behaviours.

❑ Be aware of body language and any other signs which demonstrate that the learner is having difficulties with the coaching; be prepared to try a different approach.

❑ Clarify the points discussed and, when appropriate, note the agreed plans of action.

❑ Ensure that the dates and times of the next coaching sessions are agreed; coaching should be a continuous activity.

❑ Recognize when further formal training is required in addition to the coaching.

Within these guidelines trainers need to think through their own style for each coaching session. They need to think how their style will match with the learner's style. Overall, the coach should adopt a supportive, encouraging style.

Be ready to evaluate each coaching session and the overall coaching programme (see the section on the evaluation of training events, p.111).

Checklist for using coaching skills

✓ Have the coach and the learner agreed the overall goals of the coaching?
✓ Is the coach skilled in questioning, listening and feedback techniques?
✓ Are notes taken and shared?
✓ How will the effectiveness of the coaching be judged?
✓ How can the coaching style and skills be improved?
✓ Does the coach use each coaching session as a personal learning experience to review what went well, what could have been better?

Questions and answers

Q *As a trainer, can I be a successful coach? Traditionally the trainer's responsibilities have committed me to a full-time role in the training room. My impression is that coaching is concerned with continuous, ongoing evaluation, discussion and feedback. I may only infrequently meet the learner.*

A The trainer acting as a coach may not be in a perfect situation; he or she may not be as effective as a traditional full-time, line manager coach. However, particularly in the situations described above, a trainer can provide great benefit in a coaching role. The coaching will tend to be continual, ie with breaks, rather than continuous. It simply means that the trainer/coach very much needs to bring into play their questioning skills to orient each coaching opportunity. It is also especially important that notes are taken and used to record progress during and in between coaching sessions. Some organizations are moving towards more reliance on individual, desk-based, e-learning (see Chapter 10) in parallel with more conventional, workshop-based training. In these organizations a coaching role for trainers is of great importance for those learners who need assistance with newer styles of learning.

Q *In coaching a person towards improving their contribution to the business, how much does the coach really need to know about the business?*

A   Theoretically, the trainer/coach needs no direct knowledge of the topic of the coaching. The coach is armed with coaching skills built around probing questioning and active listening. With these skills they work with the learner to unravel situations and to plan progress. In reality, of course, coaches will normally have at least a general level of knowledge of the topics. This will allow the coach to focus the conversation and shorten the length of the coaching periods.

Q   *Is coaching always directed at one individual?*

A   Coaching may well be with a team. The coaching may be with a team of the trainer's own colleagues, proactively helping them to develop their skills. Additionally, the trainer should always be prepared to coach upwards within the organization. This involves the trainer in identifying with senior management situations where new training and development initiatives could be of benefit to the organization.

Q   *Will it ever be necessary for me to break the trust and openness of the one-on-one coaching environment to bring issues to the notice of senior management?*

A   There is always an overall responsibility to the organization in which the trainer works. Without naming individuals, senior management should be made aware of deep, repeated problems within the workforce that are adversely impacting on performance. The trainer/coach and the learner should both be aware of this. On the positive side, with permission the outputs from coaching sessions can be passed up the organization as good ideas for business improvement.

MENTOR

The mentoring role

A mentor is usually nominated within an organization to provide guidance and insight to others, often to younger people who are new to the organization. The mentor role tends to be far less proactive than that of the coach. A mentor usually only provides the knowledge, guidance and insight on request. Mentors are typically experienced people with a high level of knowledge of the organization and how things are done. Often they have access to the really important people within an organization. They also understand how things can go wrong and can assist their learners to cope with difficult times. A mentor may be appointed to a new starter in an organization and then stay as the learner's mentor throughout that new person's career. This will continue even when the learner moves from function to function and from line manager to line manager.

The trainer in a mentoring role

As a trainer you are ideally placed to take a role as a mentor, particularly when you have been with an organization for several years. Typically you have developed, through the training role, a wide knowledge of the organization, its aims, its ways of working and the key people. Training is often directed at new people, and the trainer develops a keen awareness of their needs and their issues. Mentors need to provide information in a digestible form or to translate input from others to reassure the new employee. They also need to be open, trustworthy, an attentive listener and a positive role model. All these are the typical ways of working of an experienced trainer.

Be ready to evaluate each mentoring session and the overall mentoring programme (see the section on the evaluation of training events, p.111).

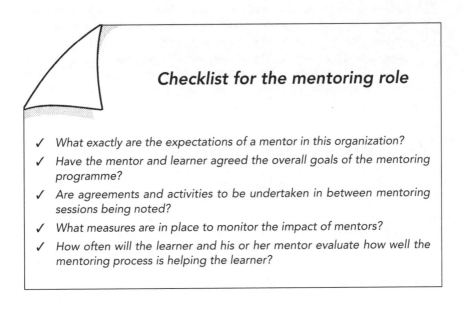

Checklist for the mentoring role

✓ What exactly are the expectations of a mentor in this organization?

✓ Have the mentor and learner agreed the overall goals of the mentoring programme?

✓ Are agreements and activities to be undertaken in between mentoring sessions being noted?

✓ What measures are in place to monitor the impact of mentors?

✓ How often will the learner and his or her mentor evaluate how well the mentoring process is helping the learner?

Questions and answers

Q   *As a trainer, what could be the problems of taking on a mentor role?*

A   As with so many things, the enemy is time, particularly if you have an intensive training commitment. The key point here is to maintain your role as the mentor. Do not be tempted to take on the role and responsibilities of the learner's manager and of other functions, such as personnel. The mentor must clearly position him or herself as that person who is available for the frank, open working sessions of mentoring and not as somebody who will willingly absorb additional responsibilities. The trainer/mentor must be absolutely sure that the guidance given to the learner is reinforcing the objectives and values of the organization.

Q   *What are the differences between coaches and mentors?*

A   There are no real boundaries between the skill sets that are applied. In most cases the roles actually *do* overlap. Coaching is basically continuous and proactive while mentoring is more 'waiting to be asked'. Again, the message for the trainer is that both these roles can bring tremendous benefit in the development of organizations and their staff. However, both roles are time-consuming and the trainer needs clear agreement as to how much time is to be devoted to these activities.

—— FACILITATOR ——

The facilitating role

Increasingly, organizations are using facilitators to run meetings and similar events. The facilitator is the controller of the process of the meeting, and ensures that all the people at the meeting keep to the agreed rules and processes. This allows the meeting delegates to concentrate on the objectives and the content of the meeting.

The trainer in a facilitating role

As a facilitator you are there to help and ease the process, using an enhanced skill set, you will work with the group through set procedures to reach a conclusion. You should have the ability to remain objective and to rise above the detail of the debate. Your goal is to enable the group to work together, respecting each other's viewpoint and participating fully.

Acting as a meeting facilitator should be a natural extension of the trainer role. An experienced trainer will normally be using facilitative skills in their work with the group. The role of a meeting facilitator is as follows:

❏ ensuring the meeting follows the agenda;
❏ ensuring the meeting uses the 'rules, processes and tools' that have been agreed for the meeting;
❏ encouraging good meeting behaviours, including full participation, no secondary meetings and the recording of commitments made by the delegates.

As well as facilitating individual meetings, you are likely to also be facilitating groups working together for long periods of time: the skill set is the same. As a facilitator you should:

❏ ask probing, open-ended questions;
❏ positively respond to each and every contribution from the group;
❏ encourage input from individuals;
❏ provide clarity in conflicting or confusing conversations amongst the group's members;
❏ draw out input from the group, redirecting comments and questions to other delegates and not interjecting your own opinions;
❏ help the group reach conclusions;
❏ be fully prepared to provide appropriate knowledge;
❏ promote and assist with decision-making;
❏ take away the outputs and return them to the group in a manageable format.

Use each facilitation session as a learning experience to improve your performance and enlarge your network. Ask for feedback from the learners, the sponsor and any co-facilitators.

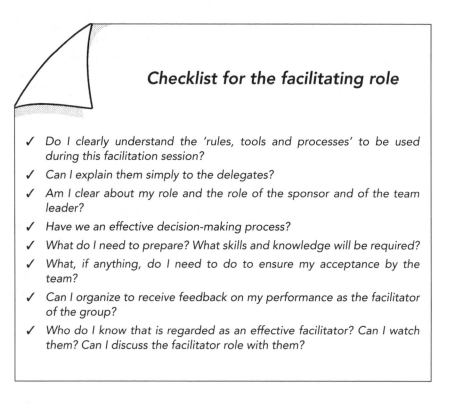

Checklist for the facilitating role

✓ Do I clearly understand the 'rules, tools and processes' to be used during this facilitation session?

✓ Can I explain them simply to the delegates?

✓ Am I clear about my role and the role of the sponsor and of the team leader?

✓ Have we an effective decision-making process?

✓ What do I need to prepare? What skills and knowledge will be required?

✓ What, if anything, do I need to do to ensure my acceptance by the team?

✓ Can I organize to receive feedback on my performance as the facilitator of the group?

✓ Who do I know that is regarded as an effective facilitator? Can I watch them? Can I discuss the facilitator role with them?

Questions and answers

Q *Should I encourage being asked to facilitate meetings when I may well have a heavy training load?*

A The more ways that you develop and use your skills, the better all-round trainer you become. The disciplines of applying facilitative skills to a meeting will undoubtedly assist you in delivering intensive training courses. The meetings you are asked to facilitate may well bring you into contact with different audiences to those from your training courses. These occasions are excellent opportunities for building your network and your knowledge of the organization.

Q *What are the major differences for me between running a training session and facilitating a meeting?*

A A lot of the things you will be doing are very similar, particularly in applying the facilitative skills discussed above. The major difference will be the way in which you control the event. In a training course, standing at the front as a trainer, you tend to be automatically the centre of attention. As the meeting facilitator you are often deliberately keeping out of the activities, but carefully helping people through the process.

 How should I prepare to be a facilitator?

A The answer to this is similar to the approach to starting out to be a trainer. That is described in detail in the next chapter. Assuming you are confident in your facilitative training skills, a good place to begin is to watch an experienced facilitator at work. Then try to share a facilitating role with an experienced person before undertaking the role alone. Facilitating a group over a number of days, or even through an intensive meeting, often requires considerable concentration that can be tiring. Prepare as you would for a training session by getting enough rest and find a way to relax afterwards (see Chapter 1, p.12).

COUNSELLOR

The counselling role

'Acting as a counsellor' has a wide range of different meanings in different organizations. In general, counselling refers to guidance given to people when their work performance is being adversely affected by circumstances that are not directly connected to the workplace. This guidance needs to be delivered by trained counsellors. These counsellors fully appreciate the experience and the skill set that are necessary to deal with such situations. In some organizations counsellors with the necessary experience and skills are provided within welfare or personnel functions. Other organizations rely entirely on external counselling services. To attempt to provide counselling when you have not received the appropriate training is potentially highly dangerous. We can listen, but should never provide advice.

The trainer in a counselling role

You will often willingly apply your trainer's skill set to coaching and mentoring. As we have discussed above, there are tremendous benefits in applying the experience and attributes of the trainer in both these roles.

You may well proactively seek opportunities to coach and mentor. Counselling situations arise for trainers in a different way. Situations where there is a need for counselling are often thrust towards you as you train. Delegates on training courses may single out the trainer when they need counselling help. Delegates can see you as a caring, listening, knowledgeable person. You may be from a different area of the organization to the delegates, or even from outside it. These facts may make you seem easier to approach than the delegate's line manager. You can easily be seen as somebody with whom to share and discuss a problem. Similarly, there is a danger with coaching/mentoring sessions. As a coach or a mentor you are seeking to develop an open, trusting environment. This will enable you to work most closely with the learner. However, this environment could also tempt the learner to seek advice that requires counselling.

Whenever a counselling situation occurs, whether during a training course or during a coaching/mentoring session, the trainer needs to reflect the best practice. A trainer may listen but should never offer advice beyond directing the learner to his own line manager or towards the organization's personnel and welfare services. The trainer may well find this difficult to balance with the aim of building an environment of trust in the training course or the coaching/mentoring session. However, you must be very careful not to step across the divide into counselling unless you are trained to do so.

Checklist for the counselling role

✓ *How is counselling handled within this organization? What exactly should I do if a counselling situation arises?*

✓ *Can I talk to more experienced trainers about the ways they handle counselling situations?*

Questions and answers

Q *What should I do as a trainer if there are a number of learners who seem to be asking for counselling?*

A Be sensitive. Identify how the organization has planned to handle counselling situations. If the trainer detects real hurdles to prevent an organization attaining its business goals, his responsibility is to bring the issues to the attention of senior management, but without betraying individual confidences.

Q *As a trainer, how easy would it be to become a counsellor?*

A If your training style is appropriate, facilitative and consultative, you have a head start. There are a number of organizations that provide programmes to develop counselling skills and certification. The certification process can take several years, particularly if your study is part time. Be absolutely sure that you are committed to this direction in your career. In addition to the skill set, it takes special behaviours and attitudes to be a counsellor. Thoroughly research your personal commitment to becoming a counsellor and the possible routes.

CONSULTANT

The business consultant and the training consultant

Often references are made to the involvement of 'consultants' in a particular business situation. When the business programme involves elements of learning, there is the possibility of confusion between the terms 'business consultant' and 'training consultant'. In our definition a business consultant is working on the overall business strategies, vision, values, objectives and business programmes of an organization. When the project involves translating business needs into training and development initiatives the work is done by a training consultant. In reality the tasks may overlap. The roles may be completed by a single person or by a single team. This section of our book primarily concerns itself with the activities of the training consultant.

Consultative training and development initiatives

The traditional approach

The typical role of T&D functions has been to respond in a reactive manner to the training and development needs of other functions throughout the organization. The relatively simple processes that have been commonly used follow this pattern:

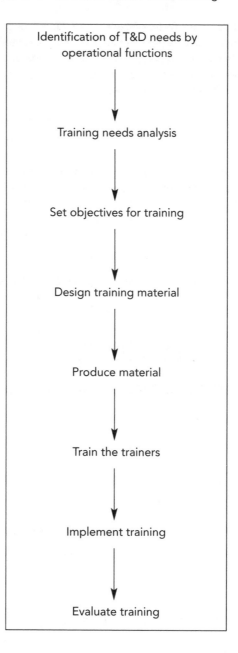

Here there are clear boundaries between roles and responsibilities. The trainer has set processes to follow and owns each stage except the first. The trainer will complete each stage and check their work with the sponsoring function before moving on to the next stage.

Moving to a more consultative approach

As the rate of business change has increased in pace, these traditional processes have often proved to be too slow and ponderous. Management has demanded large and rapid changes in the skills, the behaviours and the knowledge of the workforce. Trainers have not been able to respond quickly enough with the established processes. A different approach and a new training role are therefore evolving. This new approach, a more consultative one, is far more business-oriented and more continuous. It is demanding a wide range of advanced skills and knowledge from the training and development community. The new processes follow the following figure.

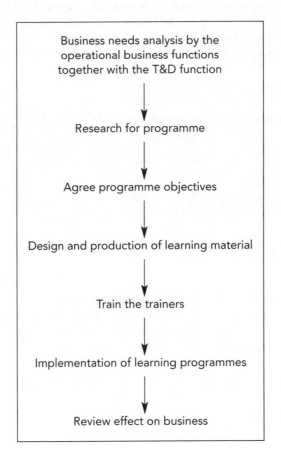

When this approach is fully implemented it is actually continuous rather than a set of discrete activities. There is an overlap of the key stages as the trainers work with business managers to ensure that the learning solutions meet the needs of the business. Its success relies on the close relationships between trainers and senior business management, and demands a very proactive role for the trainer. Here there is a definite focus on the needs of the business and the needs of the learner rather than on the training and development processes. At the same time there is an understanding between the trainer and his internal client in sharing the business risks and developing appropriate contingencies. In this context the trainer could be considered as being more of a business partner.

The trainer in a consulting role

To work in this consultative style the trainer needs to understand the business relationships and the business processes within the organization. There will also be the need to undertake an enhanced range of activities. The objectives of the consultative relationship built between, on one hand, trainers and T&D function, and, on the other hand, the remainder of the organization are broadly:

❑ quicker response to training and development needs;
❑ highly flexible, tailored solutions to T&D needs;
❑ a high concern for evaluation and speed of response to required changes in T&D programmes;
❑ proving mechanisms that allow the T&D function to proactively sell its capabilities to the organization.

In addition, the move to a consultative role will provide a stimulating, career broadening role for trainers.

Marketing the training and development function
This will involve changing the relationship between the function and the remainder of the organization. The new style will be proactive, seeking to promote internally the offer of the T&D function. Management throughout the organization is made aware of the abilities, capabilities and achievements of the function. Trainers will make themselves available to present to other functions, and to work within those functions to initiate training and development programmes (see Chapter 10, p.196, for details of marketing initiatives).

Developing a training and development strategy
This is the strategy to which the function will be working over a number of years. It is agreed with the most senior management of the

organization and widely communicated internally. It generally will include:

❑ a mission/vision statement for the function;
❑ a statement as to how the T&D strategy will be integrated with the overall business strategies of the organization;
❑ the values to which the function will work;
❑ a statement of targets and objectives;
❑ an outline of the plans to reach the targets and objectives, including the methods of T&D that will be used;
❑ an outline resource and costing plan;
❑ critical success factors for performance and evaluation methods.

This T&D strategy is totally integrated with the overall strategy of the organization and will therefore involve trainers working with very senior management. The whole document should be written in a few pages to allow it to be easily understood throughout the organization. The strategy should be reviewed with senior management at least once annually. The overall strategy should not change greatly unless there are fundamental changes in the organization. Implementation plans will normally be set for a year.

In reality, having a training and development strategy is not a particular statement of being a consultative T&D function. Published consultative strategies are certainly no guarantee of how the function will, in fact, operate! However, the manner in which a strategy is compiled and implemented within the organization, and having the skill and knowledge to write such a strategy, is a true test of a consultative trainer.

Benchmarking the T&D function

A function that is working in this new, proactive manner will be almost certainly embracing the concept of benchmarking itself against sources of acknowledged excellence. These sources will include other internal functions that are praised for excellence, particularly in client service. Benchmarking will also be done, wherever possible, with other organizations' T&D functions. Benchmarking as part of the way in which trainers and T&D functions can evaluate themselves is discussed in the section on establishing appropriate standards, p.115.

Managing meetings

The training consultant will need to develop expertise in managing meetings, particularly where there is a lot of information to discuss and where there are many different opinions. There are a number of simple rules to follow that will maximize the chances of reaching a successful conclusion:

❑ Ensure the meeting is appropriate, particularly if you are seeking agreement. Are the correct people available and have they the information to make a decision? Can decisions be made without gathering all the people involved?

❑ Keep the number of participants to a minimum. When relevant or appropriate communicate decisions after the meeting to other interested parties.

❑ Prepare extensively for the meeting, particularly if you intend to chair it. Have your thoughts in order to bring each point to a conclusion.

❑ Do not let your views limit discussion in the meeting, but have your conclusions available when they are needed.

❑ Plan the agenda to support the objectives of the meeting.

❑ Notify participants in plenty of time, ensure they see the agenda and material to be read well before the meeting.

❑ Publish clear minutes and action items.

❑ Be prepared to follow up the action item list with vigour!

Risk management

There is a significant responsibility for the trainer/consultant to minimize risk as a consultative project grows. This is particularly true when there is involvement with senior people with whom high expectations have been built. The typical risks that the trainer should be seeking to identify include:

❑ lack of involvement in the training and development by sponsor management

❑ conflicting operational programmes in other functions

❑ lack of resources

❑ lack of skills in the training team

❑ lack of commitment to critical evaluation

❑ lack of commitment to follow up by line management after training events.

It is not sufficient, however, for the trainer to identify risk. The consultative trainer will be seeking to provide recommendations for solutions to any problems, and, having gained agreement from management, to manage the implementation of the solutions.

Other skills and knowledge

In the preceding sections we have discussed five of the critical new skill areas for the trainer who is moving into a consultative role. Additionally, the trainer will be looking to sharpen the traditional skills of probing questions and active listening. To these need to be added the consultative skills of influencing, negotiating and coaching. There are also regular trainer skills that may need to be upgraded in the new role, particularly as the trainer works with more senior people. These include report writing, facilitating, brainstorming and presenting.

These new, consultative activities will necessitate the trainer building a higher level of general business skills. These need to be applied in developing a closer understanding of the business of the organization for which they work. Another development area for trainers is management of change, which we examine in more detail in the section on p.151.

Checklist for the training consultant

✓ Have you effective T&D strategies, working objectives and implementation plans?

✓ Is the approach to implementing training and development solutions sufficiently consultative? What are the major areas that could be improved?

✓ Has the T&D function been sufficiently proactive in advertising its capabilities and its successes?

✓ Is there a contact plan for regular access to the senior managers of the organization?

✓ Have exact measures to monitor the impact of moving to a more consultative approach been set up?

✓ Are you proactively looking outwards from your organization, finding out about training excellence in other similar organizations?

✓ Are there examples within your own organization of consultancy processes and skills?

✓ Do you have a personal development plan to develop both consultative training skills and a wide range of business skills and knowledge?

Questions and answers

Q *Are there any disadvantages for me as a trainer in promoting the adoption of a consultative approach to training and development?*

A Some trainers have found the change initially quite challenging. They are moving away from the controlled environment of traditional training responsibilities and from the safe haven of the training room. It can prove to be quite daunting to judge one's performance against many more criteria than the familiar 'happiness sheet' and totals of 'training days'. Although challenging, acting as an internal consultant presents trainers with a potentially new and interesting role within the organization. The trainers with whom we have worked in this way have all, given time to adjust and to learn new skills, had significant enjoyment from their new roles, including a real sense of contribution to their organization.

Q *How should the T&D function start the journey to being more consultative?*

A Actually making the decision to be more consultative is the first step. The decision tends to involve much consultation within the function and with senior management. This reflects the fact that the journey to becoming a consultative group will involve time, expense and, perhaps, additional external assistance. Traditionally, the journey has started by individual trainers starting to work in different ways. These small initiatives have been pulled together by T&D management into a development plan that has been agreed with senior management.

Q *How long will the journey take?*

A As with all journeys of business change, the answer is very difficult to quantify. You are thinking in terms of three to five years, though significant changes can be made in the short term by adopting the new approach to implementing systems and by significantly investing in changing the skills and knowledge of trainers.

——— CHANGE AGENT ———

In the introduction we talked about the changing role of T&D and with that change come changes to the role of the trainer. Training professionals today not only have to be skilled in T&D, but they also have to be business and customer focused.

They need to understand and be instrumental in the development of the organization's vision, values and practices. To achieve this often requires a new skill set, and it has also given rise to almost a new language re-engineering, transformation, downsizing, rightsizing, much of which is based on change.

Rosabeth Moss Kanter, in *The Change Masters* (1983), introduced organizations to the potential of change. This book is recognized as one of the key early sources of reference for the management of change process (see Appendix 3, p.237). Since that time many organizations faced with increased competition and stretched resources have de-layered, streamlined and transformed to become leaner, more fleet of foot, with a new customer-focused philosophy. This diagram shows an example of a change process.

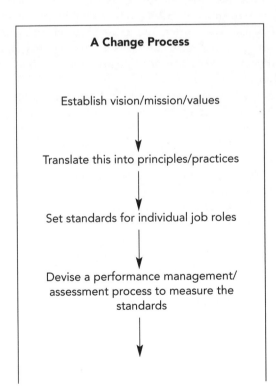

A Change Process

Establish vision/mission/values

↓

Translate this into principles/practices

↓

Set standards for individual job roles

↓

Devise a performance management/
assessment process to measure the
standards

↓

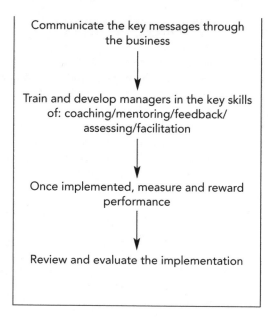

Employees in these new organizations are expected to have a more flexible approach to working, be willing to take responsibility; to understand how to work smarter not harder, and to develop self-motivated teams.

For the average employee, supervisor, or line manager this may present a challenge, particularly if there are no role models at the top of the organization.

Handling change is not easy. People feel uncomfortable when shifted from the status quo, negativity grows very easily and there is often tremendous resistance which manifests itself in statements such as 'We've always done it this way,' or, 'I don't know why we have to change, it won't work.'

Taking risks, looking at the organization from a different perspective can be exciting, but people will need extra support to help them fulfil their potential. This is why the concept of a 'change agent' has emerged; these people once identified work within organizations, fostering a positive approach to the business, working with, rather than against management. They are a force that can be mobilized, rather like a hundred candles that, once lit, will illuminate a business with a new energy.

Companies often use external consultants to provide the initial strategic support, but there are excellent opportunities for trainers and internal consultants to be involved by creating programmes designed to help managers and supervisors coach, mentor, facilitate and assess. They can also help in the internal communication process. Importantly, change by its very nature is a constantly evolving process and trainers need to keep up to date. Daily, case-studies are provided in the business pages of our national newspapers. Change is everywhere, and by adopting a positive approach you can be involved in exciting development work.

As part of this development work you may become involved in groups working on BPR.

Business Process Re-engineering (BPR)

The need for BPR has largely arisen because of the need for organizations to be flexible, streamlined, innovative, customer-focused and profitable. This requirement has also been driven by increased competition and the need to do things differently. Most large organizations are not fleet of foot; their sheer scale, size and internal bureaucratic barriers mean that they are too slow to respond to the needs of their customers and the demands of the marketplace and consequently a decision is taken to re-engineer.

What is BPR?

Re-engineering is defined in Hammer and Champy's *Re-engineering the Corporation* (see Appendix 3, p.237) thus:

> Re-engineering is the fundamental rethinking and radical redesign of business processes to achieve dramatic improvements in critical, contemporary measures of performance, such as cost, quality, service and speed. (Hammer and Champy, 1993, p.32)

A more simple definition is also given as:

> starting over, going back to the beginning and inventing a better way of doing work. (ibid., p.31).

Re-engineering is often undertaken by external consultancies, and there are two reasons for this:

1. Organizations at the most senior level believe that they need external support either because of a lack of internal expertise, or they believe that external consultants can be more objective.
2. External consultancies are more likely to have undertaken the exercise elsewhere and therefore can benchmark best practice.

Although the process may be driven by an external resource, the internal team have an important role to perform, because re-engineering focuses on processes, and so input from everyone within the organization is important. Employees are encouraged to review their working practices and to identify more effective ways of working.

Re-engineering needs to be planned and carefully implemented. Experience has shown that BPR is often only part of what is required for business success (Hammer, *Beyond Engineering*, 1996, see Appendix 3, p.237). Organizations sometimes have not realized how far-reaching the process is, or how long it takes to undertake. As a trainer you can help the organization view change positively by sharing good practice, using your network to benchmark and rising to the challenge of your new role as it develops, even if ultimately the level of change is such that your role actually disappears! (See Chapters 9 and 10 for ways in which you can continue your personal development as a trainer within a changing organization.)

ASSESSOR

Training programmes, coaching and mentoring are used to develop the skills, knowledge, attitudes and behaviours of the people within an organization. Within the organization managers and trainers need to be able to assess people's progress against agreed objectives. Assessment is about the use of:

❑ judgement of performance

❑ giving and receiving of feedback

❑ providing meaningful assessment reports.

And, if the assessment is to be of use, these steps are followed by a plan for an individual's development and ongoing assessment.

Generally, assessment of individuals and teams is undertaken by line managers and by supervisors. Assessment of performance and behaviours is at the heart of performance management, coaching and the development of people. In some organizations there is a formal requirement to assess when National Vocational Qualifications (NVQs), Scottish Vocational Qualifications (SVQs) or other qualifications are being undertaken. In the case of NVQs/SVQs there are particular assessment criteria, and assessors have to be trained and assessed themselves before they are able to assess others. This assessment is about judging evidence of specific achievements or requirements. Evidence should be gathered in a variety of ways that encourages people to demonstrate their competence. It is based on performance, knowledge, observations and responses to questions. The assessment should be based on naturally occurring events and with support from realistic simulations as appropriate.

In assessment for NVQs/SVQs there is an additional requirement to reflect national standards that need to be applied consistently. To support this process training courses and specific awards have been developed for assessors.

Assessment guidelines

Setting the standards

Assessment is only meaningful against a set of criteria for performance. This is true whether the source of the standards employed is a job specification, NVQ standards or other measures. Both the assessor and the learner have clearly to understand the standards and how those standards can be translated into the everyday workplace.

Monitoring performance

A major responsibility for a line manger or a supervisor is to observe how people are performing against the agreed standards. In the traditional workplace, the office or the factory, this is relatively straightforward. Where managers and staff do not work in the same area, the monitoring of performance is less simple. There are a number of things a manager can do to gain information about a team member's progress against the agreed standards:

❑ Visit the team member's workplace and watch them in action, particularly in intensive situations, such as when the team member is working with a client.

❑ Arrange team training sessions and watch the team members practise their skills.

❑ Listen to feedback, both formal and informal, from other managers, colleagues and clients.

❑ Ensure that there are good monitoring systems in place and that the team members are using them in the correct manner.

❑ Review portfolios of evidence and test understanding through questioning.

Giving and receiving feedback

Giving feedback is at the heart of successful coaching and therefore is very similar to the skills outlined in the section on the trainer as coach, p.121. In summary:

❑ Find the correct time and place.

❑ Start positively to build a relationship.

❑ Use questions and active listening skills.

❑ Provide real evidence when appropriate.

❑ Have the learner suggest the way forward.

❑ Gain the learner's agreement, summarize the way forward and end positively.

Taking feedback on your performance against the established standards is a vital stage in your plan for improvement. You should actively seek feedback from your managers, your peers, your team members and those you train and develop.

Writing assessment reports

Informal assessment is often given verbally during a training event. Sometimes delegates ask for personal feedback that you may send after the course by means of a simple letter. Formal assessment, however, quite often will involve the assessor in compiling a written report. These may be to a standard format, with the assessor completing ready prepared boxes on a form. If there is no form, the completed report should include details of:

❑ the standards being employed

❑ timescales

❑ the purpose of the assessment session

❑ evidence of performance

❑ an agreed action plan

❑ details of future assessment plans.

The assessor and the learner will both sign and date any formal reports. They should then be sent to the sponsor of the assessment procedures.

The trainer in an assessor role

Assessment should be a natural process for a skilled trainer. The skills involved at the heart of assessment are those of observation and the provision of feedback. These are very much the facilitative skills of the good trainer. What can cause problems for the trainer/assessor is a lack of planning and preparation. It is not at all unusual to be asked for feedback quite some time after a training event has been completed, and this can be difficult if records have not been maintained. There are a number of rules that the trainer should keep in mind to ensure the information is at hand to provide the results of assessment:

❑ Establish in the planning phase of any training event the details of any assessment that will be required and share this with the delegates.

❑ Assume that you may be asked for feedback during or after any event, whatever the original plans!

❑ Make short, discreet notes on delegates as you conduct the training event. This involves, unless you have the most efficient of memories, making notes at breaks and summarizing briefly at the end of each day. This approach becomes ever more vital the longer the mentoring or coaching continues, or the more delegates there are on a training course. Keep these notes confidential and follow the key points about feedback.

Formal feedback

When a T&D event is to include formal assessment of learners by a trainer, guidelines need to be established in the planning phase of the event:

❑ What aspects of the learner's performance and behaviours are to be assessed?

❑ What format will be used for the feedback, to whom will it be provided?

❑ What involvement will the learner have in the feedback?

❑ When will the learner be briefed that feedback will be provided by the trainer?

❑ Will this briefing come before the event from the line manager, or will the trainer be introducing the topic of assessment at the start of the event?

❑ Will the trainer share the feedback with the learner before the feedback is sent to a manager?

❑ What is in place to ensure that the assessment feedback provided by the trainer is to be properly used by a line manager? Are the line managers trained to use feedback and to manage performance and development?

The trainer as official assessor

As an assessor for an NVQ or SVQ you will be given very clear guidelines on the assessment criteria. There is also a support structure to ensure assessment is carried out effectively. This includes an internal and an external verifier appointed by the relevant awarding body.

Informal feedback

An individual learner may ask for informal feedback on his or her performance at almost any time. This is true on courses or in coaching/ mentoring sessions. The assessment may be provided in the form of a private conversation. It may require the trainer writing a short letter.

In the case of the conversation the trainer will rely heavily on the notes he has made and on the use of the correct feedback techniques. Use the questioning approach to have an open conversation with the learner. It is important to support any feedback with solid evidence of aspects of the learner's performance during the event. This will encourage the learner's ownership of what happened and of what improvements are possible.

When a letter is necessary to provide the personal feedback to a learner, it really is important to be as positive as possible without distorting the truth. You do not know where and in what circumstances your letter will be read. Try and use the sort of phrases that includes 'You might consider thinking about...'

Questions and answers

Q On a training course with a lot of delegates, is it possible to provide assessment on individuals?

A There is a limit for all of us! As a general rule, on training events of only one or two days' length and with more than six delegates, real, useful assessment becomes very difficult. On residential events a trainer will have more opportunities to get to know the delegates. When the events include a lot of discussion or a high content of individual presentation, the trainer will have increased opportunities to observe the work of particular delegates.

Q What is the impact on a training event of the learners knowing that the trainer will be providing formal feedback to their managers?

A This situation needs sensitivity and experience from the trainer. If not handled properly it can lead to a difficult, false atmosphere. The best way of handling the situation is to discuss it fully very early in the event. Explain why the assessment is being undertaken and how it will be done. Even better than this is if the situation has been covered before you meet the learners, and this includes an opportunity for self-assessment. This may be done by line managers or perhaps by the human resources function. To encourage this to happen, make sure that all the details of the assessment are fully covered in the pre-course information.

— AUTHOR —

Why be an author?

Many people at some time have an ambition to become an author. Seeing your words in print for the first time is a very positive and exciting experience. However, behind the euphoria of achieving a personal ambition is the need for a totally professional and dedicated approach. There need to be clear objectives and sound plans. As with every other developmental opportunity, it needs to be approached in a realistic manner. Part of the realism concerns your talent. The most charismatic trainer may not be the most creative writer. There are some common elements in both, but they require different skill sets.

The publication of books and articles is one very obvious way to have your name acknowledged in the training arena. The need for views and information about training and learning topics never ceases. There is a continuing flow of new people with responsibilities for training. They are searching for sources of information on developing the necessary skills, knowledge and behaviours for their new role. Additionally, there are many established trainers who are looking to understand how they can improve their skills and extend their career opportunities.

What will I write?

Having thought through the possibilities and the pitfalls, the next step is to decide the specific format for your first output. Is it to be a research paper, an article, a book or something else?

There are many books on the key topics of training and learning. However, there are certainly identifiable gaps in the market that could provide an outlet for your writing.

Writing for magazines and similar publications normally begins with making direct contact with their editors/publishers and offering a particular piece of work you have prepared. Once an appropriate article with a readable style is published, the publishers may well come back for further material. This is particularly true if your work has generated interest from the readers. Magazines normally have a schedule of topics that are to be covered in the following editions. You should start by offering to submit an article that fits in with one of the topics.

Getting into print

How to start

Whatever you set out to write and publish, you will invariably find that you will come up against time constraints. Initially you may be over-ambitious and try to address too many topics or issues. This will ensure that you will be struggling to complete the work in the allotted time! It really is vital that you approach the task with a real project management attitude, having clear objectives and timescales.

As you plan, begin with some very basic questions. The answers will give you the format for the project plan:

❑ What could I write about? What would I like to write about?
❑ Just how many words could I write on this topic?
❑ If there are gaps in my knowledge, should I consider writing with somebody else?
❑ Is it an article, a book, or an article that could grow into a book?
❑ Why do I want to do this? What am I seeking to achieve?
❑ Will I be able to write in a way that others will want to read?

Thinking through the possibilities

Having thought through the real objectives of your work, the next steps are to make sure that it is going to be worthwhile. There are a few initial steps that must be undertaken and a few vital questions to answer in investigation of the viability of your work:

❑ Research the marketplace. Is there a space for your work? Has it all been done before?
❑ Is there anything new and special about your approach to the target area?
❑ How specialist is the work? Is there an audience? Are there any specific journals and specific book publishers that would be interested?
❑ Visit libraries, specialist bookshops, university and business schools to research your topic.
❑ Network with others. Identify potential interested parties and share some of the content to establish their level of interest.
❑ Identify possible case-study material, all publishers whether of magazines or books are particularly interested in case-study material of individuals, or organizations. Always gain permission from the participants first before approaching the publisher.
❑ Approximately how large will the finished manuscript be? What format would be best for what you are trying to do?
❑ Consider online publishing.

Setting up the rules

❏ Decide which publishers and/or magazines would be suitable for your material. Consult the *Writers' and Artists' Yearbook* for details of publishers of books and magazines (see Appendix 2, p.234). Think through the magazines that you have read and investigate their criteria for the submission of manuscripts. Publishers and magazine editors are very experienced in working with potential authors and will be encouraging and helpful if your approach seems creative and well thought through.

❏ Approach your chosen publisher. They will normally expect to see an outline synopsis, a list of contents and sample contents. It will help your cause if you have researched the marketplace for your offer and can provide information as to why it should be published. If all is well you will need to agree the contractual terms under which you will work. Make sure that you clearly understand the timescales and exactly what is expected of you. It is difficult to be creative to order! Remember to leave yourself enough time to ensure you meet deadlines.

❏ If you are producing a piece of research, or a more academic paper, there are journals that would be potentially interested in the contents.

❏ Decide a pattern of working. Decide how you will research, when you will write, type and how the work will be checked. Agree these with your publisher in order that you can both keep abreast of progress and overcome any issues quickly. You will be working to an agreed time whether you are producing a book, a journal article or a research project paper.

❏ Constantly check your developing script against your objectives, your development plan and against the rules that you established.

❏ If your manuscript is going to take some time to be finished, be prepared to watch the marketplace in case a very similar book appears in the meanwhile.

Checklist for getting into print

✓ Do I know why I want to write? Have I set myself goals?
✓ Do I have something new and innovative to write about?
✓ Do I have specialist knowledge to share with others?

✓ *Can I write in a way that will interest others?*
✓ *Can I work to deadlines? Do I have the commitment to carry it through to the end?*
✓ *Can I write by myself or should I collaborate with others?*

Questions and answers

Q *Are there really gaps for new books and magazine articles about training?*

A It sometimes seems that there are already too many books and too many monthly and weekly articles. We are so busy training that we often just do not have time to read what is already available. However, the training world is a very dynamic one. We are under growing pressure to develop learners in new, innovative ways. Our experience of working as trainers in newly changed organizations is growing. We are beginning to understand how a trainer can best contribute in 'flat management' organizations. We are gaining experience in how we can take a major lead in organizational change initiatives. In addition, there are an increasing number of people who need to understand the basic elements of training. This is as a result of the growing trend for training to be delivered 'in the workplace' by line managers. There is the need to report and comment on all these things. All these trends and all these new sets of experience are offering opportunities for authoring by trainers.

Q *How can I choose a topic for my first piece of work?*

A You will obviously write best about a topic in which you are involved, but for publication it needs to be something that others will also find interesting. You will be aware from the latest publications what are the current topics. In addition there are some topics that have become standard areas of interest for the training community. These include evaluation, linking T&D to business improvement, and the development of the skills and knowledge of trainers and developers. Magazines will quite often be interested in your latest programmes if you are able to show at least the start of some business improvement in your organization that is linked to the T&D initiative. You may also become inspired about a particular topic or specialist area and find that the article almost writes itself once you start to record your thoughts. For further information see Chapter 5, Sources of Inspiration.

——— DISTANCE LEARNING DESIGNER ———

Distance learning is becoming an increasingly important way of developing new skills. More and more qualifications are being offered using this form of learning. When a trainer develops distance learning material she needs to be very conscious of the learning styles of the potential learners. As people learn in different ways, the trainer has to reflect this in the material. There is normally no direct contact with the learner, and therefore the material needs to be as interactive as possible. Pace, language and level are equally important. Common failures in distance learning materials are the author appearing to be condescending and not providing meaningful activities. In addition, many organizations are now using Internet and Intranet solutions. Therefore, before investing in any form of distance learning, carefully research the marketplace. Most countries now have regular e-learning conferences and exhibitions where you can identify supplies and their products and services (see Chapter 6, p.78, for more information).

The research process

The overall design process follows the majority of the rules for the general design of training material (see Chapter 3, p.29). The following notes discuss the particularly important items that need consideration. Careful planning and preparation are vital.

❑ Identify the needs of the learners. The material is almost certainly aimed at a number of people and therefore this research should focus across a wide sector of potential learners.

❑ Be clear about the aims, objectives and overall outcomes. What should the learner be able to do as the result of working with the courseware? Remember there is no direct delegate feedback to the trainer. The material really does have to be 'right first time'.

❑ Consider the best form of presentation for the designated audience. The majority of distance learning material has been produced in written format. There has often, when costs allow, been video-based and audio-based support material. Today more organizations are taking advantage of advanced technology. There may be a need to build your material in a multimedia format or for use in company Intranets. These options may present access issues that must be resolved before starting to prepare the material. The final format will have an impact on the style in which it is produced. It may also involve you networking with new groups of people who have skills in the development of multimedia solutions.

❑ Put yourself into the shoes of the learner. Ensure that the material will have impact and appeal for the learner. It needs to be saying, 'Pick me up and use me.'

❑ Carefully negotiate the budget, especially if you are to use outside producers and resources not directly under your control. You may need to review again the media you will use. Weigh up the costs of alternative formats with the potential impact and usefulness for the learner.

❑ Sample the learners. What is their experience of using distance learning? Have they found it useful, or difficult to use? What caused them difficulties and what was done to overcome them? What would they like to see done differently?

❑ Research the marketplace. There are many sources of excellent distance learning material. What are the style and approach of other packages? Are they easy to use, and is the content useful and interesting? While you are examining these packages, you can also take the opportunity to find out if your initiative is already covered. There may be, amongst the available material, something that already meets your requirements. This is particularly true in core development areas.

❑ Identify what support will be available to the learner. If the material is to be used in-house, are the coaches and mentors capable of providing reinforcement? Can it be arranged for the learners to meet in support groups? Will their line managers be briefed about the skills the learners are developing?

❑ What other training exists for these learners? Will the different learning initiatives support each other?

Distance learning design

You will have now undertaken enough research to be comfortable that your product is meeting a real need, and that there is not already an existing product.

You will have also decided which medium is most appropriate to meet the needs of the learners. Whichever medium is chosen, the design principles are the same:

❑ Focus on the learner, remember the different learning styles.

❑ Imagine you are having a conversation with the learner. Avoid talking down to them, use a language that is easy to understand and is non-discriminatory.

❑ Structure the content, using headings such as:

> contents
> introduction/background
> how to use this product
> aims/objectives
> modules 1, 2, 3...
> exercises/activities
> supporting handouts
> further reading
> glossary of terms
> action plans.

❑ Consider the use of colour illustrations. Remember the cost implications, but, equally, consider that too much pure text can hinder the learning.

❑ Explore the use of logos and different sizes of font to guide the learner through the content.

❑ Where multimedia or e-learning is being used, consider the linkages between the different aspects of the package. If different people are working on the different aspects, consider the retention of the 'house style' across the whole work. (See Chapter 6, p.78 for specific details about online learning.)

❑ Structure the content. There needs to be a mixture of input of information, opportunities to practise, then reinforcement of the learning through action points and checklists.

❑ Pilot the content. Remember to use a range of learners with different learning styles to test the style, approach and content.

❑ Develop guidance for mentors and/or the line managers who may be supporting the programme. This material should contain the following:

> list of contents
> background/introduction
> helping people to learn; the roles of the mentor and the line manager
> aims and objectives
> guidance on supporting learners through modules of the learning material; discussion points, answers to set questions, assessment guidelines
> solutions to activities and exercises
> supporting handouts
> guidance on handouts
> sources of further reading
> glossary of terms
> action plans.

The section on assessment will be of particular importance if the package is supporting the acquiring of a qualification. Here you may need to give specific guidance to the assessor on the gathering of evidence, or the assessment against competence.

❑ Plan the production dates for the various stages:

> first draft
> pilot
> amendments
> second draft
> review final content
> print/produce
> launch
> briefing for mentors/line managers.

❑ Set up a process for ongoing evaluation and review of the effectiveness of the material.

❑ Actively promote the availability of the package.

————— CONFERENCE ORGANIZER —————

There are real differences between running a training event and running a conference. A conference will normally be an event with numbers in excess of 20 delegates. In the largest organizations the numbers may run into the hundreds. These large events require the application of exceptional organizational skills together with the highest levels of support. Planning in advance and a true project management approach are vital to success. The following sections discuss the key points to remember as you work to implement a successful conference (see also Chapter 4, p.44).

Early preparation

❑ Identify the overall aim/objectives; be prepared to reconfirm aims/objectives as the plan unfolds.

❑ Identify the target audience; if you intend to use a mailing firm, ensure that they are reputable and experienced in your field, and that their mailing lists are current.

❑ Identify speakers well in advance.

❑ Agree a date with the sponsor, identify a venue and book it well in advance; keep careful note of the terms and conditions of the contract with the venue should it become necessary to change the details of the event, or even cancel it.

❑ Take care that your date does not clash with other events that could reduce the size of your audience. If your intended audience is international, be prepared to check national holidays across the relevant countries.

❑ Check if there is another event with which your conference has a synergy. You may be able to attract members of your targeted audience to stay on after another event.

❑ Design the marketing material, checking with the speakers that your descriptions of their expertise and experience and of their intended speeches are accurate.

❑ Plan the marketing using a variety of methods all aimed at putting the information about your conference in front of those likely to want to attend.

❑ Begin to think of contingency planning. Be prepared without becoming over worried! Keep a wary eye on some of the things that could cause you problems, particularly sudden illness of speakers, problems with the venue, train strikes and so on.

Closer to the event

❑ Mail the information about the conference to your target audience, allowing a minimum of six weeks and ideally three months before the event. There is a delicate balance between sending out information with sufficient notice and sending it out so early it fails to register as important with the potential audience.

❑ Consider other forms of publicity, including advertisement entries in training and trade magazines, flyers in magazines and e-mail. In general, print runs of material should be organized two months before they are required to ensure that time is allowed for all the processes of preparation. Check the appropriate copy dates.

❑ Consider the publication of an article in a magazine that links to and advertises the topics of the conference.

❑ Be wary of your marketing spend, costs can easily become excessive in this area.

❑ Work closely with the venue. Identify who are the people at the venue who can help you to plan and who will be there on the important day. Find out details, including how messages to speakers and delegates are handled. Discuss with the venue management their experience, anything that could go amiss, and their contingency approaches.

❑ Continually, as the arrangements gather pace and the event gets nearer, put yourself in the place of the audience, asking yourself questions like the following:

Why should I attend?
What will this conference do for me?
How will the content help the organization of which I am part?
Is it good value for money?
Is the administration efficient? Will it be easy for me to attend?

❑ Develop a tracking system for the delegates and use their responses to form the basis of your registration process.

❑ If these basic points have all been taken care of, the first registration should be with you within one month of the first announcement of the event. Be aware of the receipt of bookings in order that you can quickly react to numbers and the quality and level of those registering. Be ready to check the following:

Has there been a problem with the mailing?
Did we target (enough of) the correct people?
Is the content relevant?
Is there a clash with another event?
Be ready to use the telephone to sample some of your targeted audience and find out if there is a problem.

❑ At a set point in time you may have to decide to cancel. Consider the speakers and their willingness to talk to a smaller audience or to be able to rearrange their diaries. The planning should always include an assessment of the cost and the implications on having to cancel. If a cancellation is necessary, make absolutely sure it is handled in the most professional way possible.

❑ Work with your speakers, ensuring your expectations of their talks do coincide with theirs. Thoroughly brief them on your expectations of the venue and of any delegate response. Are they to be accommodated overnight? Who will meet them and join them for dinner? Do you want them to attend the whole of the conference? Will there be a question panel at the end of the day you wish them to attend?

❑ All these things are vital if you are using external speakers whom you may be paying. These points are equally important when you ask senior people from within your own organization to speak.

The days before the event

❑ Make all the final checks of the most important aspects, particularly:
the venue, including catering and similar arrangements,
speakers
equipment
any press or magazines that you have invited to attend.

Hopefully, everything will be going to plan, but your well-established contingency plans may just come into their own!

❑ Do all you can to be relaxed. On the day you will probably be under considerable pressure. The better you prepare yourself the more able you will be to handle difficult situations.

On the day

Everything should go well if everything has been well planned. You will need and deserve a little luck for everything to be perfect! Spend your day with the speakers and any key delegates. Leave the arrangements to the venue management – they should be able to make things happen correctly.

After the event

Continue to do everything in the professional way in which you planned and implemented the conference:

❑ Thank the speakers, the venue and any members of the press.
❑ Follow up on any actions and plans that had been discussed.
❑ Analyse all the things you planned and everything that happened. What could be done better next time?

For further information see Thorne (1998) *Training Places: Choosing and using venues for training* (see Appendix 3, p.237).

Training as a Career

HOW DO YOU TRAIN TO BE A TRAINER?

Setting up the plan for success

Learning how to be a trainer need not be an overwhelming challenge if it is approached in a logical manner. The basic steps to be followed are:

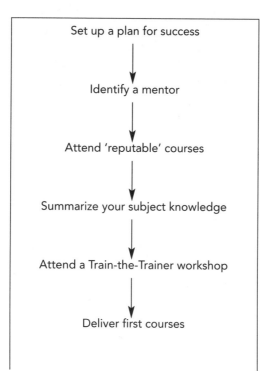

Set up a plan for success

↓

Identify a mentor

↓

Attend 'reputable' courses

↓

Summarize your subject knowledge

↓

Attend a Train-the-Trainer workshop

↓

Deliver first courses

As with any project designed for success, set yourself goals and a realistic timetable.

Initial thoughts

Think carefully through what you are trying to achieve and identify the critical aspects of both short and longer-term success. Develop your plan with these things in mind. Critically analyse your current skill set and review your relevant experience, then begin to consider the additional skills and knowledge that you will need to develop.

A good place to start is the analysis of training courses that you have attended, have enjoyed and from which you feel you gained significant benefit:

❑ How did the trainers work with the delegates?
❑ What was the style of the trainers?
❑ How did the delegates demonstrate the ways in which they were responding to the trainer, and how they were learning?

Match yourself against the best aspects of these courses and begin to think of areas in which you will need to develop yourself. The topics of detailed analysis of personal skills and of personal improvement plans are fully discussed later in this chapter. Analyse your own learning style (see Chapter 2, p.21) and decide how you might best set about developing your skills and knowledge.

Find yourself a mentor

There are many experienced trainers with whom to talk. There are many people who have already gone through the process of becoming a trainer. These established people are now involved in everyday training and in further improving their skills and knowledge. It will speed your progress to becoming a first-rate trainer if you identify such a person and gain their agreement to become your mentor. There may be experienced people in your own organization who will agree to assist you. Think through any benefits to your chosen mentor of giving you some of their time. This will help you to sell the idea of mentoring to them. People in the training community will generally be only too ready to help, they naturally like to be involved in the development of others. Mentoring is described in the section on the trainer as mentor, p.136.

Working with your mentor

Share and confirm your plan for success with your mentor. The mentor's role should be agreed as sharing experience, providing career guidance and giving feedback on your training performance. Agree with your mentor a number of specific actions that confirm your development timetable, including:

❑ regularly reviewing your plan for success;

❑ identifying courses and conferences that you will attend;

❑ agreeing materials that will be studied;

❑ agreeing dates on which you will meet with your mentor;

❑ agreeing dates when your mentor will attend parts of your early training deliveries;

❑ agreeing how your mentor will provide ongoing feedback to you on your performance and your development.

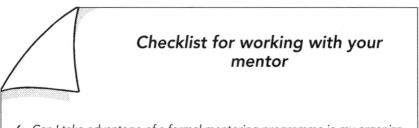

Checklist for working with your mentor

✓ Can I take advantage of a formal mentoring programme in my organiza-tion?

✓ What are the benefits to my mentor of helping me?

✓ How can I sell our business relationship to him?

✓ Is my plan for success ready for discussion with my mentor?

✓ Have I developed a regular meeting plan with my mentor?

✓ How shall I record my progress and my questions for the next meeting with the mentor?

Questions and answers

Q *Does the mentor have to be from a T&D function?*

A This is an obvious source, but certainly not the only one. You may well have access to a person who has completed a spell in a T&D function, and is now building further experience in another role. She may have a wider view of T&D's role than somebody from within the function.

Q *If there is no internal T&D function, and no obvious internal mentor, what can I do?*

A You may be able to use your personal network to identify someone. If the budget allows, it should be possible to use an experienced training consultant. Ask around to find the names of suitable trainers who could help.

Q *How much time will I be requesting from the mentor?*

A It is difficult to give a firm answer to this. Having a well-constructed plan will make the first contact with the mentor more profitable, and should reduce the overall amount of time you need from them. You are looking for somebody who will take the responsibilities as seriously as yourself, and if you find somebody, time should not be an issue.

Attend 'reputable' courses

You can learn much about training by attending a series of 'reputable' courses. You should aim for as wide a selection of courses as time and budget will allow. Your selection should include courses that are tutored by acknowledged high quality trainers and/or courses that are renowned for providing significant business benefit. Observe the successful training methods, the behaviour of the trainer and their interaction with the delegates. Talk to the delegates about their commitment to use their new skills after the course. Attend these courses as a delegate, not as an observer. This will allow you really to understand the impact of the trainer on the delegates.

Choosing the course

The difficult questions for the new trainer are how to identify these high quality courses and trainers, and how to plan to take away the best ideas. Once more the answer to at least the first question may be within your personal network. Talk to your contacts about courses they have enjoyed and found useful. Remember that the exercise is about identifying courses that are excellent examples of training and not so much about the subject of the particular course. However, do attend courses that you will understand and that will give you some overall benefit within a suitable subject area!

Using the course

Before attending the course(s), write yourself a personal list of all the things that you need to observe (see Chapter 7, p.98). Appendix 1, p.224 will provide a starting point for your personal list. During the course take opportunities to talk to the trainer and to the other delegates. Ask for their assessment of the course. Once the course is over use your personal checklist to analyse the course. Think through the following questions:

❑ What have I learned?

❑ What were the really impactful parts of the course? Why?

❑ How did the delegates react?

❑ What might have been improved?

❑ What did the trainer think about the course? Was she satisfied?

Analyse a number of courses in this way. You will have learned much about successful training and about the areas for your personal improvement. Be conscious of not simply copying the role model of the successful trainer; their techniques may not be as successful for you. Watch and understand their success and translate those things into your own strengths.

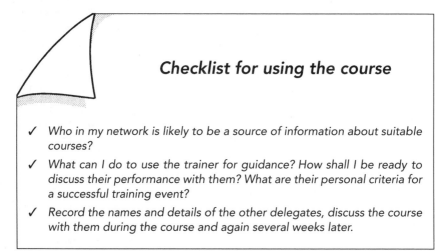

Checklist for using the course

✓ *Who in my network is likely to be a source of information about suitable courses?*

✓ *What can I do to use the trainer for guidance? How shall I be ready to discuss their performance with them? What are their personal criteria for a successful training event?*

✓ *Record the names and details of the other delegates, discuss the course with them during the course and again several weeks later.*

Summarize your subject knowledge

Choosing the correct material to include in your courses

The 'reputable' courses you have attended should have demonstrated that the trainer was using only a portion of their total subject knowledge. During the course they were almost certainly dipping further into other areas of knowledge to handle specific questions. People talk of an 'iceberg' effect, with 10 per cent of the total trainer knowledge of a subject being used in the actual delivery of a training programme. You too will certainly know a vast amount about the topics about which you will be training. But what will be the key messages of your courses and how will they be best delivered? Attendance at a Train-the-Trainer (TTT) workshop will assist with structuring your training courses and individual course modules. You will gain much more from the workshop if you have done some pre-work, preparing your subject into key training topics.

The delegate's viewpoint

As part of your preparation put yourself in the shoes of a delegate who will attend one of your future courses:

- ❑ How will they use what they will learn from you?
- ❑ What will be different for them after your courses?
- ❑ What theories and what practical knowledge will they need to learn from you?
- ❑ How will they best learn these items?
- ❑ How will the delegates return to the workplace and take advantage of what they have learned?
- ❑ Do you have a wide enough range of material to stimulate different delegates?
- ❑ Will you be able to appeal to all learning styles?

Begin to identify your important subject areas under suitable groupings. Three major messages in each training module is normally considered appropriate. Consider the training and learning techniques that will best communicate the key points of each module.

Attend a TTT workshop

There are a host of agencies providing public workshops to help the novice trainer understand and practise the essentials of the trainer's role. The largest organizations may well provide internal workshops for

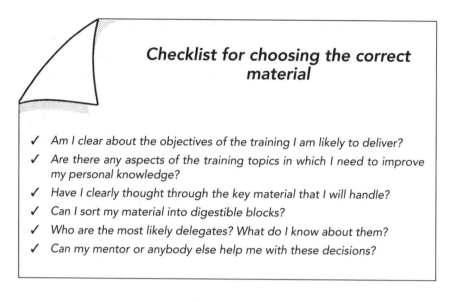

Checklist for choosing the correct material

✓ Am I clear about the objectives of the training I am likely to deliver?

✓ Are there any aspects of the training topics in which I need to improve my personal knowledge?

✓ Have I clearly thought through the key material that I will handle?

✓ Can I sort my material into digestible blocks?

✓ Who are the most likely delegates? What do I know about them?

✓ Can my mentor or anybody else help me with these decisions?

newly appointed trainers. Remember that the majority of TTT workshops will be generic in nature. Their objectives will be to prepare people as trainers rather than trainers in a particular topic area. This underlines the importance of your personal preparation for these workshops, and this was discussed in the previous section of this chapter. You must be ready to absorb the generic messages of the workshop and to translate them in preparation for your own role as a trainer.

Choosing a TTT workshop

❑ Choose a well-known training organization if you are having to use an external workshop. Some workshops offer a post-workshop service with a form of mentoring that a delegate can use to discuss particular issues and problems.

❑ Ensure that there is a good proportion of practical sessions using video recording techniques.

❑ Look for a session during the workshop that discusses, perhaps with an external speaker, some recent trends and issues in the training world.

❑ Ensure the workshop deals with training support materials such as overhead projectors, 35 mm slides, personal computers and attached presentation projectors.

❑ Think about the trainers if you are able to find details. What is their background? Have they had real experience in working with high quality training courses?

Attending the workshop

Be prepared to participate actively in the workshop; remember it is carefully designed to help you train. Be ready to use the trainer of the workshop as a guide and a coach. Talk through, during the formal learning sessions of the workshop, and also privately afterwards, the real challenges you see in your new role. Gain the trainer's insight into your plan for success. Take advantage of having other delegates on the course who, like yourself, are preparing to be trainers. Talk to them about their experiences and their own plans in preparing to be trainers.

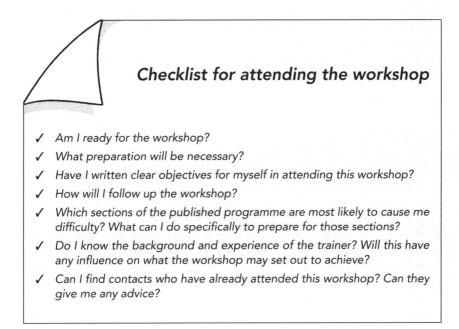

Checklist for attending the workshop

✓ Am I ready for the workshop?

✓ What preparation will be necessary?

✓ Have I written clear objectives for myself in attending this workshop?

✓ How will I follow up the workshop?

✓ Which sections of the published programme are most likely to cause me difficulty? What can I do specifically to prepare for those sections?

✓ Do I know the background and experience of the trainer? Will this have any influence on what the workshop may set out to achieve?

✓ Can I find contacts who have already attended this workshop? Can they give me any advice?

Delivering your first courses

Preparation is the key!

After all your preparation, the day will dawn when you are to deliver a course. If all the advice in this chapter has been taken and applied, there is every hope you will be feeling happy to accept the challenge! In general, there are some straightforward rules that will help you to make a success of this first challenge as a trainer. First and foremost is the option that you are able to co-train your first course(s) with an experienced trainer. Each time you co-train you take more and more responsibility for the course until you are confident with all the modules. Unfortunately, the luxury of a co-trainer is not always possible and for some first-time trainers it is a matter of taking the plunge alone. The following points will help:

❑ Develop your own checklist of preparation; this will list all the logistics and everything else that needs to be done before the course.

❑ Modify this checklist after the first course; aim to have a current precourse checklist that you will always use (see Appendix 1, p.224).

❑ Design and keep to SMART objectives for the course and for each module.

❑ Have aims and objectives that are relatively simple to achieve; this should minimize any risks and allow you to prepare for any likely problems.

❑ Have a well thought-through agenda for each module of the course, keeping to the rule of three strong learning points.

❑ Ensure that the content will not put delegates into situations that they will find trivial or embarrassing.

❑ Do not try too many different techniques of training; limit yourself to about three during this first course.

❑ Plan for a high spot in each module, with the really high-energy topics after each day's lunch and at the end of the whole programme.

Use all of these hints and read Chapters 3 and 4. With a total command of the learning topics involved in the course you will now be comfortable to deliver the course or your sections of it. You will be confident to handle debate and conflict, and you will be looking forward to a course that benefits the delegates and the organization. This first success will be highly motivational as you look forward to more challenges in the training room!

Feedback on your performance

If possible, have your mentor sit in on the first and other early courses that you deliver. With your mentor and any co-trainers critically analyse your overall performance. Consider the impact for the organization and for the delegates. Take all their feedback together with the feedback from the delegates. This will be formal, through the 'happiness sheets', and informal, from conversations during the course. Analyse all this input and plan the improvements for the next time.

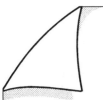

Checklist for delivering your first course

✓ Have I thoroughly checked the logistics of the course? Is there any doubt that the delegates will arrive at the correct place having undertaken the correct preparation?

✓ Have I considered the likely learning styles of the delegates and the impact of this on my delivery?

✓ What are the three major learning points for the delegates in each module of the course?

✓ Have I checked against my personal pre-course preparation list?

✓ What steps will I take to ensure that I can learn from this first course?

✓ What will I be asking my co-trainer, my mentor, my manager to do to support me through this event?

Gaining experience

Developing training experience

The hurdle of the first courses is fully out of the way. Now it is time to plan how you will further develop all the skills, knowledge and behaviours of which you have become aware. Take all the opportunities that have been discussed in this chapter to build your own experience with the help of mentors and other trainers. Without doubt, the best way to gain more experience is to deliver a range of training courses. Each time you conduct a training session, include one new technique, improve your background knowledge and continue to be self-critical. Encourage experienced trainers to watch you and give feedback. Ask the delegates to complete the end of course 'happiness sheets' with thought and accuracy. Impress on the delegates your determination to learn and improve, and the true value to you of their feedback.

Allocating training and non-training time

Trainers should be wary of the classical activity trap in which they are repeatedly delivering a small number of courses that have been well supported. Be aware of the impact of personal boredom on your performance. Almost without you noticing, you can experience ever-decreasing success in your courses. You must establish within the T&D function a reasonable spread of duties. You and all your colleagues should be ensuring that this particular activity trap does not occur. The effects are deeply demotivating.

A typical trainer's workload might be distributed in this manner:

❑ 45 per cent of time in direct delegate contact, delivering courses, mentoring and coaching.

❑ 25 per cent of time researching and developing material.

❑ 28 per cent of time developing personal effectiveness through attending courses and conferences, researching new training and learning techniques, widening skills by working in other functions, etc.

❑ 2 per cent of time in really creative pursuits, thinking outside the daily operational box, developing new approaches to the work of the organization.

These are obviously not set in concrete. They merely illustrate how a trainer can establish time away from the classroom. Many different things could impact on the figures. For example, these percentages make no allowance for administration or for marketing the T&D function. In some organizations these and other tasks are the responsibility of the trainer. Another impact on this sample diary will be the seasonal nature of training in the majority of organizations. It is not unusual for little delivery to be done around the end of the organization's financial year or at peak holiday times. At these times the percentages will be vastly different from the 'average.' For the trainer these 'quiet' periods are the times to explore the opportunities of the future and the times to build new expertise.

Gaining experience and personal development

Incorporate your plan to gain overall training experience into your personal development plan. This plan will also include a skill development programme (see later sections of this chapter). Always have an eye on your overall goals and your future career plans. As you develop your experience consider the following:

❑ Attendance at a range of courses given by other trainers. Analyse their training techniques but do not fall into the temptation of copying other trainers' best techniques. Think through techniques and sections of the course that had impact and consider the best way that you could use them.

- ☐ Take every opportunity to develop your own general business knowledge.
- ☐ Develop your own operational business information about the organization for which you work.
- ☐ Maintain the usage of your personal checklist for evaluating courses.
- ☐ Read extensively the many books and journals on T&D topics. Take care not to be carried away by the vast range of new training techniques and gimmicks. Always focus on the potential impact and the result should you use the new ideas with your typical delegates.
- ☐ Attend training conferences and meetings; debate training topics with a wide range of people.
- ☐ Attend TTT workshops specifically aimed at experienced trainers.
- ☐ Investigate the possibilities of a secondment to another function within your organization; this will allow you to gain a new insight into the organization and its business.
- ☐ If your organization is very large and has other T&D functions, investigate the possibilities of a transfer or an exchange with a member of the other function.
- ☐ In an international organization, check the possibilities of a short-term overseas appointment in a T&D function.

Checklist for training to be a trainer

- ✓ Am I regularly checking my plan for success?
- ✓ Am I keeping to the basic principles of successful training?
- ✓ Am I regularly debating my progress with my mentor?
- ✓ What else am I doing critically to analyse my progress?
- ✓ What new techniques will I be implementing during my next course, in the next month, in the next year?
- ✓ Am I organizing my diary with a view to my attendance at courses and conferences that will be useful in extending my experience?
- ✓ What steps am I taking to ensure that I find out about those courses and conferences?
- ✓ Am I networking throughout my organization and other useful areas?
- ✓ Am I networking in training organizations?

✓ *Am I engineering opportunities to co-train with experienced trainers?*

✓ *Can I organize any opportunities of work shadowing that would help me build my general experience?*

✓ *Are my courses 'special' and 'memorable'? Are there things I could do, skills I could develop, that will really help me to inspire the delegates?*

✓ *What are the possibilities of a useful secondment in the organization?*

✓ *Am I ready to provide mentoring and coaching for new trainers?*

CAREER PROGRESSION

New sources of trainers

Many of the trainers in today's commercial and public sector organizations moved into their training careers through one of three routes:

1. Human resource professionals who choose training and development as a specialism.
2. Trainers and lecturers transferring from academic organizations and bringing with them training skills.
3. Internal line managers and subject experts who acquire training skills to allow them to pass on their expertise and experience to others. These include experts in operational topics, such as marketing and sales, computing, health and safety, as well as personnel topics, such as competency, recruiting and management development.

Typically, whatever their original backgrounds, trainers stay within the T&D function for many years. Some remain there throughout their careers. They have increased their training skills and their knowledge of training and business. Quite often, their aspiration for development has been directed towards management of the training function. This section will explore how this picture of the typical trainer and their career development is significantly changing. Trainers now have many more opportunities to use their skills and knowledge in careers away from T&D. The nature of training careers is also being significantly impacted by a new, large group of people who are entering the pool of trainers. Line managers and external training consultants are delivering training in parallel with the traditional trainers. The career options for these people are adding variety to the whole subject of training as a career.

Thinking it through

Training is a demanding occupation. When you are delivering courses the days are full and there tends to be little, if any, time to devote to thoughts beyond the training room. You need to allocate time to develop your immediate skills and, more important, to plan your career. For the successful trainer, as we will explore in the following pages, there are many fulfilling and fascinating directions in which a career can develop. Find time to take stock and to consider all the possible opportunities in detail. Always be ready to capitalize when career development opportunities become available. These opportunities will undoubtedly be presented to the successful trainer.

Career progression inside the organization

Training will allow you to make many interesting and useful contacts across the organization. The more consultative your approach to training tasks (see the section on the trainer as consultant, p.143) the wider and higher in the organization will be your experience. You should be able to develop a real insight as to how other functions operate, how they are managed and the level of staff motivation. Working closely with one of the functions will allow you to judge its true impact on the prosperity of the organization. These privileged insights can assist you in a most proactive approach to planning for your career. The broad areas of career development for the trainer within an organization are:

❑ Grow to be a more senior trainer through extending your training role with higher impact training programmes.

❑ Grow in importance to the organization's staff through taking on duties including mentoring and coaching.

❑ Become a senior member of the training function by taking on more consultative projects associated with more significant operational business programmes.

❑ Become a member of the training management team.

❑ Move out of the training function to an associated one. Typically this would be the personnel function, communications, or a broader human resources role.

❑ Move to a function where your business expertise and your facilitative, consultative skills will be of use; this could be a customer service function or even sales and marketing.

❑ Be seconded to other parts of the organization where you will develop business skills and knowledge.

The possibilities outside the organization

Training as a career

The next chapter of this book examines how you can change your career by becoming a self-employed trainer, and how your business might develop.

There are other ways to develop your career when you leave the training function of one organization. You could join a training company. There is also the path into another organization's T&D function, hopefully in a different role or at a higher level. In the UK these positions are advertised in the training press. These publications include many pages of training related jobs (see Appendix 2, p.234). Senior positions in training are also carried in the broadsheet newspapers. The pages of your market sector publications often include both training positions and other opportunities for which the successful trainer could apply.

Other possibilities

In reality there are other challenging career paths. A trainer's skills and knowledge, especially one who has developed consultative business skills, are highly transferable. Many roles are open to the trainer in other types of organization including:

- ❏ becoming a business consultant
- ❏ becoming a 'head hunter' seeking specialist trainers and training consultants
- ❏ training to be a salesman or marketeer
- ❏ entering the world of publications or e-learning.

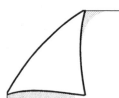

Checklist for career progression

✓ *Have I regularly discussed my career progression with my mentor and/or my management?*

✓ *Do I clearly understand the development possibilities in my own organization?*

✓ *Have I maintained my personal development in line with my potential career possibilities?*

✓ *What events should I attend? What publications should I read to keep up to date my knowledge of my own and possible new fields?*

✓ Have I placed myself on the mailing lists to find out about these opportunities?

✓ Am I maintaining a network of internal and external contacts that could
be useful if I do decide to change my career?

✓ Is there anybody I should monitor as a potential role model for my career
development?

✓ Am I building a personal portfolio of my experience and my successes?

✓ Can I organize a period of work shadowing managers within my current
organization to be able to understand their roles and responsibilities?

PERSONAL DEVELOPMENT

Your personal development plan should reflect those activities you will
need to undertake to meet your personal objectives. Such a plan may be
provided by your current organization, or you may have to design your
own. These personal objectives, both short and long term, will include
work- and career-focused items together with more individual, personal
items. The plan is focused on improving your performance in your
current position and preparing you for your future goals.

Sources of information

There are many sources of advice available to you as you go about planning your personal development and your career. It is never too early to
start. You should be seeking the advice of your managers, coaches and
mentor. Also consider people you know who seem to have planned their
way into a successful career. Use them as role models and seek their
thoughts about personal and career development. Another view of the
opportunities available to trainers can be gained by reading the appropriate pages in the training magazines (see Appendix 2, p.234). These
magazines regularly include articles about personal development and
career progression. These articles are specifically aimed at training
professionals and include interviews with training personnel who have
managed themselves through successful careers.

Formal development

Academic routes
One of the ways in which a trainer can develop skills and career
opportunities is through formal courses aimed at qualifications. These

possible qualifications include PhD, MBA and MSc at any one of a host of universities and business schools. You have to decide in what sphere of excellence you should undertake these qualifications. There are possibilities of gaining these qualifications specifically in T&D. However, you may decide to use this as an opportunity to extend your more general knowledge. You may well choose to embark on a more general business course, perhaps leading to an MBA. This is a massive career step, particularly if all or part of the funding is from your own pocket. Careful analysis of all the possibilities is necessary. Take advantage of every source of information. Discuss the possibilities with mentors, coaches, managers, human resource personnel, and with anybody in your network who has previously made the same decisions. The publications aimed at trainers and the broadsheet newspapers contain details of some of the courses. Each university, college and business school will have a registrar who will have all the information about that institute's courses. Carefully choose the best course of action with respect to your lifetime goals.

Is it an appropriate route?

The majority of people undertake these high-level qualifications through part-time courses, normally involving regular evening classes and the occasional summer school. There is an enormous commitment of time involved. The decision as to which programme to follow should therefore not be taken lightly. A personal checklist to examine the possible situations is well worthwhile:

❑   Why do I want to do this?
❑   What qualifications do I seek to have? Why are they the most appropriate qualifications for me?
❑   Where and from whom can I get assistance to find out all the possible information?
❑   Do I know anybody who has made this decision? What information can they give me? What decision criteria did they use? Are they content with the decision they made?
❑   Can I receive any financial assistance for the fees? Will my current organization help me? If so, on what terms of contract?
❑   What level of commitment of time will I have to make? How many years should I be planning to devote?
❑   What skills and knowledge will I need to start the programme? How much time will I have to spend just to be ready to start the programme?

Other possibilities

A trainer may choose to achieve qualifications closer to the world of everyday training by working towards professional or vocational qualifications. These are particularly designed to help you gather evidence of your competence in the workplace. The advantage of this type of continuous professional development is that you can often gather very valid evidence through normal activities as a trainer. As we have mentioned elsewhere, it is a very good discipline to maintain a personal development plan, because this can help you to focus your gathering of evidence and to identify training needs. You will often find there are local centres that offer this qualification together with assessor and monitoring support. As a T&D function you may wish to apply to be an accreditation centre able to offer these qualifications in-house, particularly if your line managers are adopting training responsibilities. One such qualification is based on a series of awards designed to support you in your role as a trainer. They are based on national standards set by the awarding body. More details on professional qualification bodies are available in Appendix 2.

Checklist for personal development

✓ *What are my lifetime goals?*

✓ *Is my personal development plan supporting my lifetime goals?*

✓ *Who are the useful role models for my career?*

✓ *What advice can I find in addition to that from my manager and my mentor?*

✓ *Is it worth attending a seminar on career planning? What books are available?*

✓ *Is there career and personal development advice available within my current organization?*

✓ *What journals should I be reading to gain a wide view of my potential development?*

DEVELOPING NEW SKILLS

Your personal development plan should include an overview of those skills, knowledge and behaviours you need to improve and/or modify.

When this is extended into a detailed skill development plan, it will include answers to questions such as the following:

❏ What are the likely sources of the new skills, knowledge and styles?

❏ To what levels do I need to develop these attributes?

❏ What measures can I use to test progress?

❏ What timescales can I place on my development?

❏ What help can I expect from the organization, my manager or my mentor?

❏ What other resources or sources of funding should I consider?

❏ What contingencies are there if a particular course of action becomes too difficult?

❏ What are the key milestones in the plan, and what do I need to do to ensure these milestones are attained?

Skills analysis

A personal Training Needs Analysis

Many trainers are involved in conducting Training Needs Analysis (TNA) for the organization for which they work (see Chapters 2 and 3, p.21 and p.29). It should not be difficult for trainers to apply many of the rules of the TNA process to their own skills analysis!

Understanding the current situation

The first stage for an individual trainer is to examine critically their current set of skills, knowledge and behaviours. They may be assisted in this by the results of performance reviews, psychometric tests and feedback they have received on projects both inside and outside their workplace. You will also find useful information from the personal analysis we discussed in Chapter 1. Collect all of the available information together. An interesting approach to analysing all the information described is as follows:

❏ On a large sheet of paper or a flipchart select a number of headings such as 'sales', 'business', 'personal relationships'.

❏ Now start to use the phrase 'I can' and keep writing all the things you can do under each of your chosen headings.

❏ Do not forget to include transferable technical skills under the appropriate headings. You may have developed your project management skills to a high level. You may have become an expert in computing.

This can be quite a lengthy process. However, it will probably convince you that your current skill set is much broader than you might have initially thought. Discuss your conclusions with your mentor, your manager and your life partner. Check that they all agree with your conclusions about your skill set, your depth of knowledge and your general patterns of behaviour.

The target skill set

The next major stage of the analysis process is to collect together information on the target skills, knowledge and behaviours that you will need to develop in pursuit of your chosen goals. These targets will be established through reference to your goals and objectives. There will be a mass of information, particularly if your goals are not completely defined. To analyse all this information you might consider this approach:

❑ Write three column headings: 'required skills, 'required knowledge' and 'appropriate behaviours'.

❑ Within the columns list the information you have under groupings, such as 'company needs', 'personal needs', 'input from coaches and mentors' and 'life partner view'.

Another approach, in conjunction with 'I can' as described above, is to undertake an 'I need' review under your chosen headings and use this to identify new areas of skill development.

Bridging the gaps

You are now ready to make plans to fill the gaps between attributes you have and those you need. Carefully list:

❑ those skills that need to be developed
❑ a priority order
❑ the likely ways to improve each attribute
❑ a realistic timescale for each part of the plan
❑ measures that will allow you to test your progress.

Discuss the plan with your manager, coach and mentor. If the whole exercise has been done thoroughly there will be extensive plans to implement. The plan will extend over several years. It is most important to conduct reviews regularly. These reviews should include both progress against the plan and also reconfirmation of company and personal objectives. In this way you can reassure yourself that the plan is aimed in the correct direction.

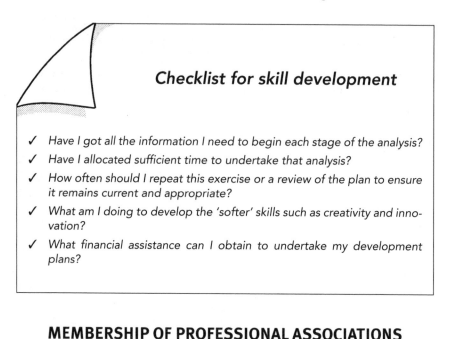

Checklist for skill development

✓   *Have I got all the information I need to begin each stage of the analysis?*

✓   *Have I allocated sufficient time to undertake that analysis?*

✓   *How often should I repeat this exercise or a review of the plan to ensure it remains current and appropriate?*

✓   *What am I doing to develop the 'softer' skills such as creativity and innovation?*

✓   *What financial assistance can I obtain to undertake my development plans?*

MEMBERSHIP OF PROFESSIONAL ASSOCIATIONS

Sources of vital information

We have mentioned several times in this chapter the need to have information about news and current trends in your own chosen 'industry' of training. Through their publications, local meetings and conferences the trade and professional associations are the chief source of this information. Trainers are recommended to join an association, such as the CIPD (Chartered Institute of Personnel Development) in the UK, whose Web site is given in Appendix 2, p.234. Most of the important market sectors also have professional associations and these are well worth joining for their supplies of information.

Other useful services

Joining such professional associations can provide you with more than a supply of news and views about developments in the marketplace. The majority have a range of events which you will have the opportunity of attending and contributing to. This is an excellent way of building your personal network. These organizations, including the CIPD, are often the leaders in setting standards for trainers that are accepted across many organizations. Membership is offered at a number of levels and there are ways of being assessed or taking further qualifications to move to a higher level.

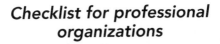

Checklist for professional organizations

✓ Do I know the professional organizations in my market sector? Who can I ask about the organization and its value?

✓ What could I contribute? Can I present at a local meeting? Are there articles I could submit to their journals?

✓ What professional or vocational qualifications do they offer? Are those qualifications appropriate for me now or for my longer-term plan?

MANAGING YOUR SUCCESS

We have discussed the possibilities of developing your skills, broadening your position within your own organization and becoming known in your professional associations. As part of your development plan you should be thinking about marketing your success. This is particularly true as you implement your strategy to progress your career. You are developing a personal brand, and in common with all brands it should be marketed.

Internal activities

You are now involved in self-marketing! Internally you should let your manager and the personnel function understand what you have achieved. You will also have the opportunity of talking to management in functions across the organization. Ensure that they are also aware of those of your skills and knowledge that could be of use to them. Publish successful projects in your organization's internal newsletter. These actions will, at the very least, build the influence of the T&D function throughout the organization. They may result in new personal opportunities.

Be proactive. Use your newly developed skills to plan and promote business initiatives to your T&D management. Ask them if they want you to promote such ideas into the organization.

External activities

Spread your influence externally by offering to become involved in initiatives in your professional associations, the local chamber of commerce, local colleges, even with local charitable voluntary organizations. Offer to write papers, to speak at conferences and to do any other things that could promote your name and your abilities.

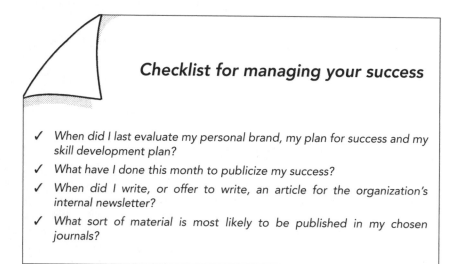

Checklist for managing your success

✓ When did I last evaluate my personal brand, my plan for success and my skill development plan?

✓ What have I done this month to publicize my success?

✓ When did I write, or offer to write, an article for the organization's internal newsletter?

✓ What sort of material is most likely to be published in my chosen journals?

NEURO LINGUISTIC PROGRAMMING AND OTHER DEVELOPMENTS IN TRAINING

As a responsible trainer you will regard it as important to keep up to date with recent developments in training, We have already discussed how to encourage networking (pp.73–75 and do so again on pp.220–221). It is one of the most useful ways to find information about what is happening and about recent trends and issues in T&D. However, networking is not the only source of such information. Most of us are bombarded with information about courses, events, books, videos, training games and other publications. Each and every item is suggested to us by the promoter as being highly relevant. You will need to become an expert in identifying what is important and useful to you rather than just being interesting.

With a personal development plan you will already have identified the broad areas of development that are important to you. Having done this you will be able to apply a filter to the information. You will be able to ask yourself if this is important, relevant and helpful to your development. If you actively network, other people will also alert you to those relevant, important events you should investigate. Equally, subscription to one or two relevant training journals will ensure that you are regularly alerted to the latest developments.

Keeping up to date really does require focus, with all this information so readily available. It is possible to spend a lot of time and money unwisely. One key test is, will this concept, initiative, process, trend, stand the test of time? Training can be a little like the fashion business in that initiatives have a habit of coming in and out of fashion. One technique that has stood the test of time is Neuro Linguistic Programming (NLP).

Neuro Linguistic Programming

NLP has gained respect within many organizations in the areas of personal development and communication.

NLP practitioners describe it as an art and a science of personal excellence. It is based on a set of models, skills and techniques for thinking and acting effectively.

It was started in the 1970s by John Grinder and Richard Bandler. From their initial work NLP developed in two complementary directions: first, as a process to discover patterns of excellence in any field; second, as the effective way of thinking and communicating used by outstanding people.

What does NLP mean?

The 'neuro' part of NLP refers to the neurological process of seeing, hearing, feeling, tasting and smelling, ie our senses. The 'linguistic' part refers to the importance of language in both our thought processes and our communication, for example:

❑ *Visual:* You think in pictures, you represent ideas, memory and imagination as mental images.
❑ *Auditory:* You think in sounds. These sounds could be voices or noises of common everyday sounds.
❑ *Feelings:* You represent sounds as feelings that might be internal emotion, or the thought of physical touch. Taste and smell are often included in this category.

'Programming' refers to the way we can programme our own thoughts and behaviour, in much the same way a computer is programmed to do specific things.

NLP is a practical technique concerned with outcomes and has developed the concept of modelling excellent performance.

There is not the space within this book to explore the full potential of NLP. There are now a range of books available on the subject, including one that is widely recognized by practitioners as a key source of reference: Joseph O'Connor and John Seymour *Introducing NLP: Neuro linguistic programming* (see Appendix 3, p.237).There are also courses that will introduce you to NLP in more detail, and can lead to your achievement of practitioner, or master practitioner in NLP.

NLP, as well as building your own skill set, also has many applications within organizations, for example in customer service and helping people communicate more effectively.

Before embarking on any process of self-development in new areas of training, you should ask yourself the following questions:

- ❑ How will this help in my personal development?
- ❑ Is it relevant to us as an organization?
- ❑ Can I justify spending money on it either to myself or to my organization?
- ❑ Will it enhance our offer, help my organization or me to generate more revenue?
- ❑ Does it have credibility?
- ❑ Have other people heard of it? Use your network to investigate.
- ❑ Are there reputable providers?
- ❑ Is it likely still to be relevant in three years' time?

Not all information about trends involves training; we gather much through reading and sharing information through our network, and as we discussed in the section on using resources on p.75, it is important to have reliable sources of data gathering that respond promptly to requests and have up-to-date and relevant information.

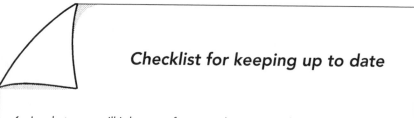

Checklist for keeping up to date

- ✓ In what ways will it be easy for me to keep up to date?
- ✓ Will my network regularly supply me with details of new and useful material?

✓ *What information services are available in my organization or in my professional association?*

✓ *Why do I want to attend/subscribe to this event/publication?*

✓ *What new information will it give me that I cannot get elsewhere?*

✓ *When was the last time this source gave me something of real use?*

✓ *How quickly could I access data on a new European training initiative?*

✓ *Who can I contact who has the latest information on UK government training programmes?*

✓ *Where can I find out about external training courses in my chosen development areas?*

✓ *How much do I use the Internet for accessing relevant information?*

If you cannot respond positively to most of these questions, then serious thought should be given as to the usefulness of your current sources of updates and new information. We have tried to help you in this process by suggesting some sources of information in Appendix 2, p.234, but training is such an evolving area that you constantly need to be updating your sources of reference.

A NOTE OF CAUTION

A trainer must have the key skills of recognizing important information, absorbing it and translating the key components into their own work. However, a little knowledge can be dangerous. Make sure you really do understand the concept or approach, and do not be tempted to simply dip in by attending one conference or by reading one or two articles. If you are going to work with people as an expert in your field, make sure that your claim to expertise is valid. There is a real responsibility for trainers to work with people in a positive and caring manner. This development of other people has to be achieved professionally, and you should never train in areas that are beyond your levels of true expertise.

Training as a Business

THE FIRST STEPS

Running a training business has a lot in common with being a retailer. Anybody can open a shop, but how long will it trade? Will it be capable of building client loyalty? Will it be possible to run it at a worthwhile profit? At some stage in your career as a trainer you may well decide that you want to manage your own training business. Such a venture can be worthwhile, rewarding and fun. However, as with all of life's major decisions, deciding to start a training company should not be undertaken without careful thought and planning. In common with any potentially self-employed person you need to assess carefully every aspect of running a business. Importantly, you need to assess whether you want to run a business, or just want to operate as a sole trader. By identifying which route you wish to pursue, it will help you in the subsequent decisions you make about developing your brand and your potential offering to clients. There is a host of specialist help available from people, including your bank manager, accountants who specialize in small business start-up and Business Link. Try to build as wide an understanding as you can of running your own business, and talk to people in your own network who have already had the experience.

Why are you doing this?

You are taking a massive step. You should be carefully identifying in these early stages the reasons why you want to run your own business. Many people contemplate the idea of being a self-employed trainer and many are successful – usually because they have clear objectives and because they are able to make things happen. Unfortunately, others fail. You must establish the goals, both short and long term, to give substance to your ideas. The real accent here is on 'you'. What is it, in the face of the competition, in the prevailing marketplace, with your skill set, that *you want to do?* Your business plans should coincide with your personal long-term goals, and they should provide you with work in an area that interests you. Without these guidelines, the task of establishing your company and your offer may become overwhelming! On a more positive note, this really is a time when you can evaluate what you want to do and what those short- and long-term personal goals should be. If this is your first experience of self-employment, you are about to enter an exciting and challenging period. Warn your partner and your family it is all-encompassing and totally time-absorbing!

Is there a mentor?

In the previous chapter we discussed the importance of a mentor as you develop your career within an organization. In that organization it is likely that there are established processes, rules and guidelines within which you will have worked with your mentor. The value of a mentor to a newly forming independent business is possibly even greater than in an organization. For the smaller business, those processes, rules and guidelines are less obvious, and the guidance of a mentor is really valuable. If your training business is going to be as a sole trader, initially your life will probably be a lonely one, especially in the first few months as you search for the elusive initial contracts. A mentor, with whom you can handle the loneliness, and with whom you can critically discuss plans and progress, can be the difference between success and failure.

To find the appropriate mentor may prove to be more difficult than in an organization. Ask a member of your own family with suitable experience, or a friend who has already developed a small business. These people may be very willing to help but have only an outline understanding of the skills of mentoring, so agree exactly what the mentor will do. Build a list of the topics you will discuss each time you meet. Give the mentor as much detail of your business ideas as possible and time to consider the ideas so they can be ready to provide accurate, honest, critical feedback to your strategies and your plans. Most people who have a business background will have experience of training and should be able to help you work through your ideas.

CREATING A BRAND

One of the most exciting parts of starting your own business is the creation of the brand. Your brand will consist of your:

vision/mission
values
style and approach
service/product offer
measures of success.

If you have not previously been involved in a brand creation exercise, this may appear a challenging list. The task is large, but without it a start-up business will have a fragile foundation and a high likelihood of failure. The brand will be the real strength of your developing business. It will allow you to be most comfortable in presenting your offer to potential clients. In addition, it will be invaluable if you need to build a presentation to somebody who will be a source of funds.

Where to start?

The brand should reflect your total belief in your offer and, as such, should come 'from the heart'. When you write the details and when you explain your business to others it must sound genuine; you should be proud of your business.

Begin the branding exercise by examining other examples. Research statements of mission, vision and values from large, medium and small organizations. Check to see how training companies express their brand. Begin to jot down initial thoughts and ideas. Words that work for you will start to form and you will be able to write a first draft. Take a few days to work on this, refining the phrases and individual words. Does it sound appropriate for the training company you had initially considered?

Once you have a draft with which you are reasonably comfortable, become really pragmatic. Apply a critical approach to it. Can it be measured? Is it realistic? Can you believe in it? Can you explain it to others and have them understand it and believe in it? Once the description of the brand passes those critical examinations share it with your mentor, with colleagues and with friends. However hard you have worked on it, listen with an open mind. If there is feedback indicating change, be prepared to return 'to the drawing board'. Spending time at this stage can make the remainder of the development much more straightforward.

Choosing a name and a logo

This can present the greatest challenge of all. Many self-employed trainers simply choose to use their own name and add the words

'Associates' or 'Training.' Unless you are a limited company or a public limited company you cannot use Ltd or plc within your business name. Should you wish to be more creative and reflect your brand in the title of your new company, there is work to be done. Company names are registered through Companies House. Searches are available from company formation agents; for a nominal fee they will search to find if your chosen name is already in use. Companies are highly protective of their name and their logo. Logos and trademarks can be protected by patent; if you wish to search this area a patent agent will undertake the work for a small fee. If your accountant handles start-up businesses, he or she will certainly know the name of a reputable company formation agent. You may also wish to involve a design company in designing the logo. This can be costly, particularly as we would strongly advise that you choose an experienced designer.

After the design work, when you are comfortable with the logo and the name, discuss their impact with your mentor, friends and colleagues. What may appear really creative and different to you may be just too complex to others! A lack of time devoted to these early stages could prove costly at a later stage when you begin to produce brochures and stationery.

IDENTIFYING YOUR OFFER

The overall offer consists of many parts, some tangible and others intangible. It includes you, your service/product(s), your marketing material, as well as your reputation as somebody who provides quality training. This is an important part of your brand. It will involve you in a good deal of research about markets, the competition and yourself. This is time-consuming, but, in the same way as when researching a name and a logo, can potentially save you from critical mistakes.

Initial research

Marketplace evaluation

It is unwise to progress further without a period of basic research. Just what is being offered in the marketplace and how will it influence what you are thinking of doing? Are you building a training offer into an already saturated marketplace? There are already in existence many specialist offers in a seemingly endless list of areas, including assessment centres, training design, change management, outward bound management development and training consultancy. Other offers concentrate on particular markets, such as retail, health care or financial services. You need to be clear where you are placed against this competition and that you appear to offer something new and interesting. The research will be a major help in formalizing your offer. In addition, you will have learned a lot about the marketing that is being done by other training companies.

There is another potential benefit from this marketplace research. The evaluation of your possible competition may have identified other organizations that actually appear to match your own. You may wish to investigate the possibilities of working in association with them or even in a business partnership. This needs to be considered carefully and there will have to be a clear understanding of the respective roles. Both sides should be sure that the benefits outweigh the potential hurdles and business conflicts. Should you decide to pursue such a relationship, you may well have the first test of your marketing and sales skills. This will involve selling to an existing training company the features of your offer and its advantages to the partnership.

Personal skills and knowledge evaluation

You will by now have at least an outline of your offer to the marketplace. Now spend time looking at how well your current skills and knowledge can support that offer. What can you do now, what will you find difficult and what will you need to learn? You can gain tremendous insight by starting with an 'I can' and 'I need' analysis (see the section on developing new skills, p.187). Undertaking these analyses in detail and with a lot of personal honesty should give you real insight into the starting point of your venture. Talk through your views with your mentor and start to implement your skill development programme. You should plan not to over commit in the early stages of the training business. Remember, people will be paying for your service. They will not expect to pay while you are completing your own learning.

Your personal brand

Earlier we identified the importance of the performance (p.15). Your personal brand within your training business is just as important. If you are operating as a sole trader, you are the brand, and it is you the clients will measure. When you are developing your offer and writing your marketing material, you will constantly need to assess what you are offering. Can you actually deliver what you have promised? Are you reflecting your carefully thought-out brand? In a highly competitive marketplace with many organizations appearing to offer the same service or product *you* have to be the difference. You are the brand that builds the 'chemistry' with the clients to make you successful, winning business against competition. Elements of the personal brand and how you should portray yourself to clients is discussed in Chapter 1, p.12. You are building in the mind of the client a picture of yourself as somebody who is genuinely interested in them and who really wants to be involved in a business partnership.

You constantly need to be appraising your image and how you are presenting yourself. Are you always appearing professional and competent? This is a time of self-evaluation that goes beyond examining your trainer skill and knowledge set. The offer you are making includes your sales calls, the branding shown by your marketing material, the way you look as you stand at the front of the training room. Working for many years as a trainer, or even as a training manager, in a large organization, may possibly take the edge off our performance. Working as a self-employed trainer means every appearance, every performance is critical. A personal audit, with the assistance of a life partner and/or your mentor, is well worthwhile. Funds are at a premium, but are some new clothes a worthwhile investment? Perhaps you really should go on that diet, join that gym! Stand in front of the mirror and ask, 'Would I be happy doing business with this person?'

Your brand needs to be reflected in literally everything you do and in every contact you have with a client. This can be difficult if your training business is to be run from your home. The telephone needs to be handled professionally. This may involve an additional line with a professional messaging service when you are not available. If a client is to call a more general number, make sure they do not become involved in a conversation with your three-year-old who believes he is talking to his grandfather!

Thinking about the future

In the early days of your training business as a self-employed sole trader life can be lonely and frustrating. We have already discussed networking (p.73) and will enlarge on the topic later in this chapter. We have also discussed preventing 'burn-out' and handling pressure (Chapter 1, p.12). Other pressures also exist. Managing your time is critical, especially as the first business arrives. Do not stop planning, evaluating and marketing. Be critical of how you are dividing your overall time. Are the competing needs of the business and the family leaving you no time for yourself? What happened to that monthly day for golf or that day at the fitness centre you promised yourself and that you know you need in helping you unwind? One of the elements you should be building into the plan is the need for a balanced lifestyle. Self-employment and building a successful business is a wonderful experience. This is particularly true if it is balanced against lifetime goals. If your business has begun with a cushion from a redundancy package, you will be able to reach a reasonable compromise situation between work and other important things. Your professionalism in handling clients and in delivering training will be bringing you a fairly constant flow of work. You will have some time for other things. Remember though to maintain the overall brand, your personal brand and to maintain all the business aspects of the small company.

Building the offer

The approach to building your training business is, in common with any start-up business, based around a familiar business building strategy:

❑ Crystallizing your brand in preparation for presentation to the market place:

> logo
> vision
> identity.

❑ Writing the details of what you will be offering to the marketplace (these should be considered through the eyes of a potential buyer):

> yourself, your style, your approach, the way you work with clients; your expertise and your experience;
> the possible supporting mechanisms, such as your network, your contacts;
> the offer itself, the specialist areas, the measures of success.

> What are the business benefits that you are providing for your clients?
> What are the likely training needs in your target markets?
> How can you express your offer as something necessary and exciting in that marketplace?

❑ Outline your potential market (further details in the section on p.204):

> market sectors: retail, financial services, etc

> types of target organization: plcs, small and medium businesses, public utilities, etc

> geography: local, regional, international.

❑ Outline a first-cut marketing plan (further details in the section on p.210):

> To whom will you market?
> How will you market?
> What methods will you use to break into the market?
> What can you allocate to marketing budgets?

❑ Plan a launch. Will it be an event or a low-key, gradual entry to the market? Can you afford something more grand?

❑ Think very carefully through your financial plan. It will often take three months to find the first real business, and it may take at least six months to receive payment. Once the business is flowing, establish an overall plan that is aimed at a regular flow of business and income.

Your training offer

With a background as a trainer it is likely that your major offer will be as a training consultant. However, as you undertake your research and seek to offer something to the market, remember your other skills. You may well have developed quite specific skills and knowledge during your previous career. These skills may enable you to build a more targeted and more exciting offer than simply as a training consultant. Your exact offer might be constructed from an integration of:

❑ your specialist knowledge in the design and implementation of training solutions from items such as computer-based training or distance learning packages;

❑ your experience of auditing training solutions;

❑ specific details of training requirements in narrowly defined market sectors;

❑ project management of very large, international training projects that may have included language translations;

❑ true experience with advanced computing techniques or perhaps training issues on the Internet;

❑ handling the human resource implications of a merger/acquisition.

These special types of experience may well allow you to build a very specific offering to potential clients. Because it is specialized it will be necessary to be very clear in your marketing. It may take time to find your first business, but it is quite likely that once you are established you will do well. You could be in that extremely powerful position of making, and therefore dominating, a market (see the section on p.207).

Pulling it all together

There are obviously a challenging number of key tasks to complete as you build your brand and your offer. We will discuss many of these tasks in more detail in the following sections. You need to work steadily through the stages of building the offer, but ensure you have enough energy remaining to take the offer to the marketplace. The overall process, beginning the plan to the winning of the first business, can occupy as short a time as a month, or as long as a year. The time depends on many things, some of which can be very difficult for the trainer to control:

❑ the size of the organizations you will need to target with your offer;

❑ the complexity of your offer;

❑ any time you need to devote to enhancing your skills and knowledge;

❑ the urgency of the business need and your abilities to establish the need with your clients;

❑ client decision-making processes;

❑ early agreement as to contractual and payment terms;

❑ the facilities for implementation.

As we have previously highlighted, the successful trainer or training business will ensure that all the stages of the business cycle are fully covered. None can be ignored. Many smaller training companies fail when they are successfully delivering because future business isn't being identified and won.

ASSESSING THE MARKETPLACE

Your brand is now established and you are certain about your offering. You may already be able to market and sell to your former organization and to the first contacts made through your network. This is a perfectly acceptable part of your overall marketing and sales plan. However, business won through these sources should really be regarded as a bonus. They are quick and easy wins that can provide practice for your training skills, welcome revenue and an introduction to the first stages of handling client relationships. However, if you want to build your business consistently, the majority of your energies will now be applied to the next stage of the overall business cycle, the detailed assessment of your potential marketplace.

What do people want?

The needs of today's businesses

The majority of new training ventures will not be offering too much that is different. You will certainly have little or no direct experience in your new business role, and little success to broadcast. To maximize the chances of success, there is a need for a clear understanding of what is happening in the chosen marketplace and what is needed in training/learning solutions. You need to be asking the following questions:

❑ What, specifically, are organizations currently looking for in training and development?
❑ Why are these important areas? What are the connections to business trends and to organizational requirements?
❑ What are the accompanying trends in staff selection and staff development within the target organizations?
❑ What solutions are being bought from training companies?
❑ What are the most popular formats of those solutions? Three-day training courses? CD-ROM? Self-paced learning books? Coaching programmes? Online learning?
❑ Why are these successful training companies (and not others) selling their products in these marketplaces?
❑ What role are the organizations' training functions taking in the purchase and implementation of training solutions? What about line management? Purchasing functions?
❑ What decision criteria are organizations using when they choose a training company and a training solution?
❑ What level of fees are clients paying for the training services they are using?
❑ What is stopping organizations from buying training solutions? Lack of funds? Lack of the appropriate solutions from training suppliers?
❑ What is the impact of e-learning?

Building the vital information

The answers to these questions are obtained from a number of sources. The closer you really are to understanding the answers and the business issues, the better able you will be to assess the needs of the marketplace. You should be building data from the following:

❑ Your personal knowledge of training from your previous experience.
❑ Extensive reading and attendance at conferences and meetings.
❑ Publications on training trends (see the section on using resources, p.75, and Appendix 2, p.234).
❑ Every possible opportunity to discuss training in the type of organization you are targeting.

❏ The results of organizing a survey of trainers in typical organizations within your target market. This will take the form of a questionnaire sent to training buyers. The questionnaire is normally preceded by a telephone call to investigate the names of the appropriate people in each target organization. Don't aim your questions at commercially sensitive areas. Be conscious of how busy people are, and do not antagonize potential buyers. However, trainers inside corporate training functions are often prepared to complete and return a survey form if it arrives on their desk. Make things as simple as possible for those who receive your survey by making the questions multiple choice whenever possible. Provide a self-addressed envelope. Do not include too many questions, and ensure they are clearly written and unambiguous.

❏ Make use of e-mail and the Internet as appropriate.

The results

If the research has gone well, you will now have a host of data that you need to collate into useful information. Collect the information under similar headings to the list of questions in the section on the needs of today's businesses, p.204. Analyse it for trends and gaps that your offer may be able to match. Most important, ask yourself what are the reasons for these trends and gaps. Find answers to any further questions that may have arisen, and generally extend your knowledge. Use the telephone or e-mail to contact people who have completed your survey and attempt to probe deeper for information. Always be aware of the pressures on people's time. Establish that they do have time to talk before you take the conversation further.

You may, through your research, find that there is lack of knowledge in the marketplace about a particular T&D topic. If this is the case, you could consider undertaking a benchmarking project in that area. This will provide you with a very strong reason to approach the training buyers that you have identified in your initial searches. It is an excellent opportunity for you to enhance your brand and reputation as a premier player in training in that business area.

Who is offering what?

As your research helps you to build a general picture of your marketplace, you will be finding out about other training suppliers. Some of these will obviously be competition to your direct services. Your calls and your reading, particularly of advertisements and catalogues, are contributing to your picture of these training suppliers. Continue to build and analyse this competitive information:

❑ What are the characteristics of the successful training companies?

❑ Are there any common areas between the successful companies?

❑ Are there training programmes that all training companies seem to be selling?

❑ What type of programmes are being bought by many organizations?

❑ What level of fees are training companies winning?

❑ How are they winning business? Are they marketing extensively? How are they marketing?

❑ Could any of these competitive companies be potential future partners?

What is special about your market positioning?

Having assessed the marketplace, it is important to establish where you and your offer will fit. Do not be discouraged by the weight of competition in the crowded marketplace. Clarity of offer and careful marketing can still win the business. Your market assessment should have helped you identify where the potential lies. Developing your unique offer will take time as you sensitize the market place. Be prepared to have to call on your personal motivation and all your optimism! There is a lot of strong competition! The world of training is occupied by many experienced trainers and training companies. This only serves to underline one of the basics of establishing your marketing and selling plans – regularly asking yourself what are the special, different things in your offering that will help you to sell. In addition, you have to assure yourself that these are things that could be made important to your potential clients. Your unique points of difference will be built into your sales campaign. Check your potential uniques with the 'so what?' test. Each time you think of a feature of your offer and think it is important, put yourself into the shoes of the potential client and ask 'so what?' Will the client think the feature is important in helping achieve business success? If yes, then the feature can be legitimately included as one of your unique selling points (USPs) when approaching that client.

Can you create a new marketplace?

You will be working very hard to search for and develop any USPs of your offer. Unfortunately you will normally be responding to an existing marketplace that was built by forces in which you had no part. The marketplace is already heavily populated by other training companies. Can you be in the position, as you develop your marketing plan, to have a really proactive approach to the market? Can you build a market, even in just one business sector? You may have identified a potential service or product you believe is unique. If that is the case, continue to refine and focus on this area. Test the service/product offer with a number of carefully selected clients to establish the viability of the offer. Have you a training/learning offer that is so unique, so full of client benefit, that you can define a new marketplace and then dominate it? Your chances of doing this will be at their highest when:

❑ your background is in a market sector where there is traditionally only a limited amount of training expertise;

❑ you have undertaken a large amount of focused research;

❑ you have expertise in unusual approaches and methods of training and development.

Checklist for assessing the marketplace

✓ As a result of what I have learned, should I go back and re-evaluate any aspects of my offer? Even my overall brand?

✓ Have I set my expectations too low? Too high?

✓ Am I planning to offer anything that is really different?

✓ Am I sure that it is not too different and difficult to market?

✓ What have I learned from other companies' offerings, successes, experiences?

✓ What, in general, will be my USPs?

✓ How shall I build my marketing and sales material around making these USPs attractive to my potential clients?

✓ Have I found a really different offering? Can I take advantage of it in the dominance of a marketplace?

SETTING A BUSINESS PLAN

Establishing a business plan needs to be undertaken against a framework of these three questions:

1. Where am I now? This is an assessment of your current position, the people, resources, assets and cash.

2. Where am I going? This is the visioning part of the process. What are your personal objectives, why do you want to run a business? To generate a high income? To act as a retirement springboard? To leave to future generations? Where do you want to be in five years' time?

3. How am I going to get there? What are the milestones?

Your research will have given you the information to set realistic business targets for future periods of time. The targets should firmly relate to your overall goals, business objectives and personal financial commitments. It is important to be realistic in these targets, but also to be optimistic. You will need an optimistic challenge to keep you focused, particularly in the opening months of your sales efforts. However, be wary of being too optimistic in your first year, when failure can be both financially damaging and extremely demotivating. Do seek help with your business planning if you have not previously undertaken such an exercise. There are many books on the subject, the banks in the UK all have helpful booklets and your accountant will undoubtedly be able to help. Remember, though, in every case you will need the basic facts and well-thought-through numbers before you can start to produce the plan.

The sales forecast plan is at the heart of your business plan. The other important parts of that business plan are:

❑ the marketing plan
❑ a financial plan including projected costs and a revenue plan
❑ risks and contingencies.

The vital questions you must answer are:

❑ What, realistically, is the amount of work you will have in each of your financial periods?
❑ How many days do you want to work each month?
❑ What fees are you expecting to charge? (Your marketplace assessment will help you with this.)
❑ What set-up costs will you incur? The purchase of capital equipment, including office equipment and a car, needs careful consideration. They are expensive to buy outright, though there are other methods of financing the purchase. Talk to your accountant.
❑ What assets do you have already? You can obtain tax relief on assets brought into the business.

❑ What other ongoing costs will need to be included? Just how much can you allow for marketing, brochures, advertising, etc?

❑ Can you provide any other services or products that can generate early revenue?

❑ Have you considered VAT registration?

As you start your sales campaign you will be controlling your business through comparing actuals with the plan. A certain amount of variation is unavoidable. However, if actuals move wildly from plan, examine your plans in detail to see where things need to be rethought. As your business builds, you will gain experience in planning your finances and you will be expecting to work within much tighter tolerances.

MARKETING

Everything is now prepared for you to take your message to the marketplace. You will have seen during your research how other training companies market their products and services. Although yours is a small training company, the marketing processes you may consider are the same as for a large organization. Take care not to plan to spend large amounts of money that will bring little return. Your intention should be to stimulate the buyers' interest, arouse their curiosity and to make it easy for them to buy.

So how does a training company, particularly one yet to establish success, market itself to its clients? Where and how should you be planning to spend the marketing budget? What will you be doing to check that the marketing plan is correct, and what will you be able to do quickly to make any necessary changes?

Your first goal should be to establish your brand as a provider of a quality service into your chosen marketplace. Your first task is to achieve this. Your choices are as follows:

❑ direct marketing;

❑ telemarketing using a specialist service;

❑ advertisements in national, regional, local trade magazines or in newspapers;

❑ hosting a seminar, conference or workshop;

❑ having a stand at an exhibition;

❑ writing or telephoning individual clients with a focused offer;

❑ using network contacts;

❑ meeting people socially through associations, clubs, etc;

❑ building a Web site.

In reality, the list is immense. As you grow your business you will develop a wide range of contacts from a wide range of sources.

Marketing material

Importantly, whichever route you choose, you will need marketing material. At the most basic level you will need printed stationery. There are now many franchised operations that provide professional printing services. They can provide cost-effective stationery for you. In addition there are many local printing companies. Always shop around and obtain estimates. Ask to see examples of work. Consider one- and two-colour options rather than full colour, and always proof-read very carefully. You can also create your own using specialist software packages.

In the early days a full brochure may not be appropriate. It can be expensive and you may not yet be totally clear about what it should contain. An A4 folder with the company logo is a good marketing vehicle. Into this you can insert details of whatever is appropriate for a particular client. Try and include details of your vision, mission and values, products and services, all of which should be reinforcing your professional image.

Marketing approaches to the clients

Direct approaches
Initially you may find that a focused and targeted mail shot to selected potential clients followed up with a telephone call to arrange a visit is the most productive route.

'Cold calling' by telephone requires particular skill, and you may find attendance at a professional training course helpful. Some small companies use direct mail or telemarketing companies to support them. This can be timesaving for you, but will be expensive if you are not able to focus them into your targeted marketplace and targeted clients.

Initial contacts made by any form of approach need to be followed up by you very quickly.

General advertising
Advertising is another option to consider, though again cost will be an important factor. In addition to buying the space in magazines there

will be the cost of the artwork. There are a number of possible types of publication from which to choose:

- ❏ Generalized human resources magazines that are read by training management. These are normally associated with one of the professional bodies (see Appendix 2, p.234).
- ❏ Magazines designed for the training community. These are circulated to training managers in a wide range of organizations.
- ❏ Local business papers designed to be read by business managers of the organizations in your geographical area.
- ❏ The magazines in your targeted market sectors.
- ❏ Local business broadsheets that are built by organizations, including the local chambers of commerce.

Talk to the publishers and to the magazines and newspapers themselves. Investigate their circulation, talk to their readers and find out if they are influenced by advertisements. Some magazines offer 'directory'-type entries that tend to be cheaper, but again you need to establish the likelihood of success versus cost.

If this approach is of interest, look at the style of the current advertisements and make sure your design is more professional and more eye-catching than the others. Recognize that a one-off advertisement will have less impact than a series, however this obviously increases the cost. Always negotiate on price for a series.

Other ideas

In addition to this traditional, paper-based advertising the small training company can advertise itself through other 'deliverables'. There are many advertising companies offering to sell you promotional materials, such as personalized pens, paperweights and paper openers. These are expensive to buy and to distribute and therefore need to be carefully selected. They are, however, talking points and can be part of satisfying the overall need to 'be different' to the competition. Think carefully about the quality of the product and how it reflects your brand.

As the business grows, you should consider extending your brand through sponsorship, promotional products, exhibitions and other types of event. Always review cost against potential business benefit and always be conscious of any possible impact on your brand. Keep the professional image uppermost and ask yourself the question, 'How will this help promote the brand?'

Your most powerful marketing tool should be yourself. You need to take any reasonable opportunity of putting yourself and your expertise in front of potential buyers. These include many of the possibilities we discussed in the previous chapter under the general heading of personal development. As a trainer you should be exploring the potential of writing articles and books, speaking at conferences and meetings and finding other ways of meeting people.

You might consider making yourself available for teaching at a local college. This might involve teaching 'day release' or 'evening school' programmes. The financial reward is restricted, and the motivation of some delegates is not always high. It is, though, another way of promoting your expertise. It is also an opportunity to practise your training skills when most of your time is spent on the telephone and away from the training room.

Launching your company

You will need to decide how your company is to be launched. Local newspapers, particularly in smaller towns, are a useful source of introduction. They will allow you to write a few column inches about your new business venture. The skill here is to build into the article something interesting and special about you or the company. If these special features can have a particular relationship to the town, the article is likely to have greater prominence. There is normally an understanding that you will also buy advertising space in the same newspaper.

Exhibitions

Another approach to the launch could be to take a supplier stand at the next business fair organized by your local business group. You may meet some potential clients, you may find that your training offer is the only one on display. You may also consider a stand at one of the regular nationally promoted T&D conferences. Examine very carefully all the associated costs, including the production of stand display boards, marketing material and the incidentals, including travelling and accommodation. Make your stand simple and attractive and be prepared to give away a lot of literature. It is often better to focus on one product or service than to confuse your visitors with too much information. Remember not to block your stand ready to pounce on potential visitors. Stand to one side or sit in a relaxed manner awaiting their questions. Encourage existing clients and friends to drop by, making the stand appear busy but never crowded. It is probably worthwhile having a one-page 'flyer' version of your marketing material for events like these. Consider sharing your stand with an organization that is not a competitor. You may also be able to negotiate a discounted rate nearer the date of the event.

Building a database of contacts

All of your marketing will be bringing you into contact with potential clients and with many other people with whom you will network. You need to build and maintain a database of these contacts. There are computer-based databases that can link directly into mailing software. In the early days of your business this may seem a luxury, and your database will consist of a well-organized paper system. The key elements to be maintained are:

❑ names;

❑ telephone/fax/e-mail numbers; Web site details;

❑ addresses;

❑ details of contacts, meetings, telephone calls, any literature sent;

❑ likely areas of interest in your products;

❑ any other interesting information, including other networked contacts, training companies they have bought from, etc;

❑ an action plan, at least a date for a next contact.

Be aware of data protection legislation.

Reviewing your marketing

Marketing, whatever methods you employ, will be time-consuming and costly. Marketing your brand and your services/products needs to be maintained even when you start to win business. You must maintain the marketing flow to keep your name in the mind of buyers. Web sites should be maintained so that they are kept up to date and details of special offers refreshed. If you are using your Web site as a marketing tool consider very carefully ways of encouraging your visitors to return. There are service providers who will monitor your site for you and provide details of the hits you have received. Equally, you must be able to decide what marketing approaches work for you. Be rigorous in examining the impact of any marketing initiatives.

WINNING THE BUSINESS

You now have contacts where you have established some elements of need for your training solutions. You are ready to prepare your sales calls and ready to win business. Experience says that these calls are the result of significant time and effort. You must not waste them! It is vital to be

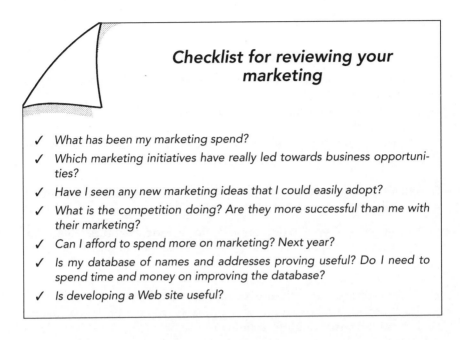

Checklist for reviewing your marketing

✓ What has been my marketing spend?

✓ Which marketing initiatives have really led towards business opportunities?

✓ Have I seen any new marketing ideas that I could easily adopt?

✓ What is the competition doing? Are they more successful than me with their marketing?

✓ Can I afford to spend more on marketing? Next year?

✓ Is my database of names and addresses proving useful? Do I need to spend time and money on improving the database?

✓ Is developing a Web site useful?

fully prepared to handle the meeting, to sell your offering against the client's needs and be sufficiently confident to ask for an order. In reality, every contact with a client is a potential selling opportunity. Be prepared to discuss their business, your business, progress with a current training initiative or anything else that reinforces your professional brand and may lead to winning business.

Preparing the call

Initially you should allocate at least three hours to prepare carefully for each call, particularly if you have little experience of making sales calls. Work with your mentor if possible, preparing your ideas and practising the likely events in the meeting.

Work through the following plan of preparation:

❑ Collect your knowledge about the market sector and the target organization. Visit their Web site, read the business press. What are the business trends and opportunities? How are you likely to be of help to this organization? In which of your training/learning solutions are they likely to have an interest?

❑ What do you know about training in this target organization? What methods of training have they used? Are they used to working with training companies similar to yours?

❑ What might stop the buyer wanting to work with you? These are the classic 'buyer objections'. Prepare to handle them in your sales call where the standard approach is to:

> ask clarifying questions to ensure that you really understand the issue;
> check that understanding with the buyer;
> answer the objection;
> discusss any significant objection the buyer has and be prepared to remind her of the many positive points in your offer.

❑ What have you available to support your case? You may have any of the following:

> Examples of your work; these could include examples from your previous experience, though you must be conscious of client confidentiality.
> Reference letters.
> Newspaper and journal extracts that will support your presentation; for trainers these will probably come from newspapers, trade journals and the training press.
> Your brochure or other marketing material.
> Take care during the meeting not to hand over material to the buyer that will encourage him to read and stop him listening to your presentation.

❑ Remember you are trying to build a relationship. If it really isn't working, be prepared to agree you are not the right trainer for the work. You can win the client's respect by not trying to be all things to all people.

Making the call

The call is obviously the key part of the sales cycle. Do not waste the call by failing to cover the following points:

❑ Complete the preparations discussed above.

❑ Telephone on the day of the call to confirm the arrangements.

❑ Dress professionally, looking your best and arriving in plenty of time.

❑ Scan the business press and the local papers on the morning of the call to be aware of any important news for the organization, its market sector and its most important competition.

❑ Write a letter of thanks after the call and confirm commitments made during the meeting (see section on 'proposals' below).

❏ Learn from the experience and ensure an even better performance in subsequent calls.

The essence of a successful visit to a client is to take the first steps towards building a positive relationship. You want to establish contact, identify their needs and reach a point where you are invited to present a proposal. This often has to be achieved within a very short time-frame:

❏ Establishing with the buyer business objectives and business needs with which you can associate your training offer. If there are no established needs, spend time helping the client explore business objectives to investigate his training needs.

❏ Establishing the success criteria for a training solution. Ask the buyer what she would like to be different as a result of this intervention.

❏ Gaining agreement from the buyer that the benefits of your solution really match his needs. This may well involve you describing your product in a way that aligns to his needs. You should use any of the supporting material that you have prepared.

❏ Politely handling any objections that the buyer has to your approach.

❏ Understanding any client timescales and budgets together with his criteria for choosing a solution and a training company. These may not always be readily forthcoming, particularly in a competitive situation.

❏ Asking for the order you are seeking. This will not be possible in every meeting. At the very least, agree further actions that will lead towards the order. If the meeting has shown that this client has no clearly established needs, you may start your consultancy by selling a short study in which you investigate and report on their potential uses of training initiatives.

The vital skills in these meetings are questioning and listening. Do not be tempted to fill the meetings with descriptions of your offer and your experience. These may be important, but only after you have established the client's needs.

Always check the time available at the start of the meeting and ensure that you use the time carefully. Take notes, but do not scribble so much that you cannot concentrate on the buyer. Use mind mapping techniques to build the picture of the needs as the conversation flows.

Writing the proposal

As soon as possible after the meeting, while the details are still fresh in your mind, write any proposal that is necessary.

Your proposals should be short and designed to have impact. They should be confirmations of commitments already made, including implementation plans and costings. They can be one or two page letters together with any supportive material that adds credibility to your proposal.

When a more detailed proposal is required the following headings are useful:

❏ Introduction and Background to the Proposal. This is the scene setting section.

❏ Our Understanding of Your Needs. This should clarify what you believe is the client's need. This emphasizes the importance of having asked the correct questions during the meeting.

❏ Our Proposed Methodology or Approach. This is your opportunity to show how you would professionally approach the particular solution. Be careful not to provide too much detail in case the client chooses another provider, but do provide enough to demonstrate your competence. This may include sample aims, objectives and outline content if it is a training programme solution.

❏ Measures of Success. Your suggestions for evaluation.

❏ Proposed Fee Structure. Your estimate of fees and expenses against the list of proposed activities. Always reference full additional costs including VAT and material production.

❏ Relevant Experience. Include career summaries of the proposal team together with summary information about other related activities that you or your associates have undertaken. Supply references as required.

Include multiple copies of proposals if this will be helpful to your client. The overall document, whatever the length, should be professional and focused on the client. The presentation does not need to be excessively expensive, but it should be neat, clear and easy to read. Bind it, or present it in a folder for increased professionalism. Also include any relevant articles that you may have written, or brochures of your company in the appendix of the proposal.

Occasionally you will be offered the opportunity of replying to a detailed tender or request for proposal (RFP). These will have been circulated to you, and probably to (many) competitors. Be very wary of completing these if the client is not prepared to grant you a meeting before the submission of the proposal. A worthwhile proposal will be difficult to complete without checking and amplifying the information.

Maintaining the clients

Clients are hard to win and they should always be respected. Your immediate goal is to honour all your commitments and deliver training solutions of the highest quality. 'Delight' the client and over-achieve with your total deliverables. Your existing clients will always be your most likely source of further orders. Try to establish an ongoing, professional relationship with your clients. Talk to them in a businesslike way, add your knowledge to their thoughts. You are seeking to be one of their preferred suppliers of training solutions. In addition you will hope that they may pass business possibilities to you through their own networks. Make them feel special, think about their needs, share information with them that is helpful and useful in their own development.

As you grow, you may start to think about hospitality events to which you invite clients and guests. These include golf days, theatre and concert trips or a meal at which you will try to get to know your clients in a more relaxed and informal manner. These are not overt selling events! All these events need to be well managed since they reflect your marketing brand. Be aware that many large organizations have strict rules about accepting hospitality from suppliers.

Checklist for marketing

✓ Is everything I am planning to do in support of the brand?

✓ Am I personally prepared?

✓ Have I identified a clear marketing offer?

✓ Have I set a marketing plan with a budget?

✓ Can I create a professional image with my business stationery?

✓ Can I develop supporting material to illustrate my offer?

✓ Will there be people who will be able to act as referees for my competence?

✓ Have I carefully researched my chosen marketplace and identified potential clients?

✓ Can I prepare a set of questions that will help me identify with a client's potential training needs?

✓ What am I going to do to plan speculative approaches to the target clients?

✓ *Am I prepared to make client visits to identify their needs?*

✓ *Am I prepared to follow up all leads and to act promptly on any business opportunity?*

✓ *Have I access to any successsful proposals against which to benchmark my own?*

✓ *With whom have I discussed my proposals? My mentor? Could I discuss a proposal with a client from whom I have won business? Where I have not succeeded?*

✓ *Can I construct a 'loss report' to analyse when I fail? See Appendix 1, p.224.*

✓ *What am I doing at each stage of the marketing and selling cycle to learn and to improve?*

NETWORKING

As we discussed in Chapter 5, p.67, the key to success for many trainers is their network of people. These networks can be the source of much, if not all, of their leads to business opportunities. It has often been stated that without access to such a network it is extremely difficult to grow a new training company. The major sources of these networks are as follows:

❑ Former business colleagues.

❑ Social contacts who themselves are involved in business ventures.

❑ Satisfied clients who tell colleagues in their organizations and people in their own networks about you.

❑ Local business groups and trade associations.

❑ Groups of people with whom you have shared attendance on training events. If you have recently left a large organization you may well have attended workshops designed to help cope with your new life. Keep in touch with your fellow delegates. As they grow their businesses they could be looking to share a contract with your sort of company.

Trainers building their own businesses must take time to establish and to grow their own network. Everybody in the network should believe that there will be potential benefits for themselves. This can be encouraged by regular contact and by the passing on of business information and interesting social news. Try to give more than you request, be known as somebody who will give well-thought-through advice. Be prepared to be a good listener. You will occasionally receive calls from other entrepreneurs who are less successful than you. Help people talk through their bad times and reinforce their motivation. One day it could be your turn!

Keep the network fluid. Look to increase the network from those people that you meet and with whom you can establish mutual business benefits. Occasionally review your network and check those people with whom you have not had regular and useful contact. Try not to lose contact completely. If people were once of value in your network they could be of value in the future.

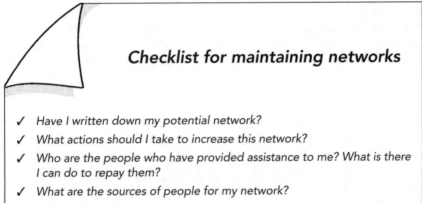

Checklist for maintaining networks

✓   Have I written down my potential network?

✓   What actions should I take to increase this network?

✓   Who are the people who have provided assistance to me? What is there I can do to repay them?

✓   What are the sources of people for my network?

✓   How do I feel about turning social contacts into business contacts?

✓   Could I go and sell training solutions to a friend? Am I sufficiently convinced of the value of my solutions I could sell to that friend?

MANAGING OTHERS

Bringing new people into your company

As your business grows, you may well consider bringing other people into your company. There may currently be a large amount of available work and you may wish to stop working quite so hard! This is a very exciting time, as you see evidence of the success of your venture. However, be totally convinced that adding staff is the correct course of action. Talk it through carefully with as many people as possible. It is a massive step for a small business. It will involve a new business approach, the dedication of time to managing others and a new cost structure. There are legal and taxation considerations to be taken into account. You will need specialist advice, so talk to your accountant. It may prove easier to establish a partnership or even sub-contract.

Once the overall decision has been made, you will need to decide how new staff will be used. Will you split the work between existing clients and new accounts? Or would it be simpler to split by market sector or by geography? Will you continue to market and sell with the new staff only delivering? Or should you encourage them to sell on a commission basis?

These are significant decisions, and your criteria for making the decisions need to be focused on ensuring the continued quality of your training delivery to your clients. Be aware of the brand you have carefully created. Your clients may be less prepared to accept your offer if it will be provided by another trainer. Spend time checking the synergy between you and people who may potentially join you. Discuss their aspirations and really check their competence. Work together initially in a safe environment. Jointly prepare proposals and attend sales calls together.

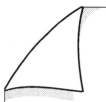

Checklist for bringing in new people

✓ Am I giving myself time in my busy schedule of selling and delivering training solutions to analyse my company?

✓ With whom can I discuss the possibilities?

✓ What similar organizations to my own can I benchmark against?

✓ Should I consider a loose partnership with one or a number of local trainers?

✓ Is there any point in building a network of trainers who are offering similar training solutions to mine? What would I offer to such a network? What would they bring to me?

✓ Do I understand enough about being an employer?

✓ If I attract associates what will be the contract between us? What happens if I am unable to find them work?

Building the team in other ways

Several training companies are currently taking a different approach to growing their number of available trainers. These companies have built their own small groups of 'associate' trainers who themselves are independent. This approach obviously provides a very flexible size of training group. It should mean that any client's training request can be answered quickly. This approach is simple, but the arrangements have to be carefully managed. There has to be a really workable agreement between the training company and their associates. The integrity of the brand and your company's relationship with your clients must be maintained. As with your own staff, the contractual arrangements need to be carefully considered. Will you encourage the associates to sell? How will you reward sales? Again, check contractual arrangements with your accountant.

Appendix 1:
Forms and Models

Time	Topic	Subject/resources	Comments/skills
10.30	Coffee		
10.45	Session 2: role-play	OHP 4: 'Using role-plays', Delegates Guide, p7 Introduce delegates to use of role-plays: supervisor/coach team member observer Delegates to use pp 3–6 of exercise pack	Practical session to reinforce learning points of session 1, 'Introduction to coaching' Stress opportunity for delegate who role-plays coach to really try skills
11.20		Debrief role-play learning If necessary briefly refresh communication skills	Check use of questioning/listening/feedback skills
11.40	The supervisor in a coaching role	Use flipchart to lead discussion on opportunities and perceived barriers to coaching Park on flipchart any issues for further discussion OHP5: Coaching summary (1), Delegate Guide, p8 Add to issues flip if necessary	Pull out all perceived issues Discuss delegates' roles in working with managers in proactively 'making it happen' Check acceptance of coaching responsibilities
12.00	Second role-play	Teams are same, different roles. Use OHP 4: 'Use of role plays' to remind delegates of roles	

SURVEYING THE T&D FUNCTION

This survey is about your personal perception of the T&D function. Your views will be added to those of other people within the organization, and the overall result will be a major input to the continuous review of our activities. Please give your rating of the T&D function against each statement. A score of 0 is lowest and indicates absolute disagreement, 5 is highest. If you feel unable to score any point, please score the # sign. Wherever you wish, please provide any comments and examples that amplify your scoring.

Name .... Function ....

STATEMENT	SCORE	COMMENTS

In my opinion, the T&D function:

1. Consistently *provides* training and development appropriate to support the organization's goals   # 0 1 2 3 4 5

2. Clearly *broadcasts* its own strategy and plans within the organization   # 0 1 2 3 4 5

3. Regularly *updates* the organization about the status of training and development activities   # 0 1 2 3 4 5

4. Regularly *discusses* with other functions the success of the T&D programmes in assisting those functions to reach their goals   # 0 1 2 3 4 5

5. Is prepared to work *away from the training room* to provide facilitation of meetings, on the job training, direct coaching or mentoring   # 0 1 2 3 4 5

6. Proactively *sells* its services within the organization   # 0 1 2 3 4 5

7. Is *staffed* by professional people who understand the organization, and who consistently deliver high-quality T&D   # 0 1 2 3 4 5

8. Is consistently *measuring* its own activities with a view to improvement   # 0 1 2 3 4 5

9. *Talks knowledgeably* about new T&D initiatives and how these could help the organization   # 0 1 2 3 4 5

10. Is *recognized as a source of change* initiatives across the organization   # 0 1 2 3 4 5

Please circle your answers to these questions:

How many times have you attended a course in the last 12 months?   *0–1, 2–4, 5+*

If you *lead* a team, on average how many days of training has a member of the team received in the last 12 months?   *0–1, 2–4, 5–8, 9+*

Note to trainers: This form should be modified to capture the information in which you are most interested. Use language that will be familiar to people within your own organization, eg you may wish to substitute 'learning' for 'T&D'.

SAMPLE COURSE EVALUATION FORM

Please devote a few minutes to completing this form. Your input will receive serious consideration as we seek to improve our overall performance and our contribution to business success. Thank you.

Your name: .... Job title: ....

Training course title: .... Start date: ....

Please circle the numbers to mark questions 1–10

1. The course met the stated objectives	slightly	1 2 3 4 5	completely
2. The length of the course was too short	too short	1 2 3 4 5	too long
3. Your skill development during the course met your expectations	hardly	1 2 3 4 5	completely
4. The trainer's knowledge appeared to be	poor	1 2 3 4 5	excellent
5. The trainer's teaching methods were	poor	1 2 3 4 5	excellent
6. The amount of practical/practice sessions was	too low	1 2 3 4 5	too high
7. Your level of confidence in using your new skills is	low	1 2 3 4 5	high
8. Your level of confidence to improve your contribution to the business is	low	1 2 3 4 5	high
9. You would recommend this course to others	not at all	1 2 3 4 5	definitely
10. The facilities were	poor	1 2 3 4 5	excellent

Were you prepared for the course? Did you have a briefing with your manager? What else would have been useful to know before you attended this course?

Please describe your feelings about the course. Which parts were handled well, which could be improved (in this case, what improvements)? Would you change the amount of time devoted to any part of the course? Would you increase or decrease practical/practice sessions?

Is anything missing from the course?

How will attending this course help you in your everyday role? Will it help you significantly improve your contribution to the business?

Do you expect to have a debrief with your manager after the course to discuss your reactions to the course? How will you plan to reinforce what you have learned? What steps will you take to use the new skills?

Note to trainers: This is only one example of the many types of course evaluation form. The actual form is 2 pages in length, encouraging the written answers. We have found this form has been readily accepted by delegates and useful to us in evaluating our progress with a training course.

SAMPLE COURSE EVALUATION FORM

Please devote a few minutes to completing this form. Your input will receive serious consideration as we seek to improve our overall performance and our contribution to business success. Thank you.

1. What were your expectations before the course? Did you agree these expectations with your line manager?

2. How well did the programme match up to:

    the published objectives?
    your personal objectives and expectations?

3. What are your views on the course content? Were things covered in sufficient depth?

4. What could have been amplified? What occupied too much time?

5. Were practicals, videos and other materials used correctly?

6. Did you feel personally involved? Did you feel you contributed to the course?

7. Were there sufficient skill practising sessions? Were they of sufficient depth?

8. Are you able to apply the course to your role? How will you use the course information?

9. Are you ready to discuss your personal activity plans with your manager?

10. What else do you need, training, coaching etc to implement your knowledge? Are there any other follow-up actions required?

Please make any general comments about the logistics and facilities provided.

Note to trainers: This is only one example of the many types of course evaluation form. The actual form is two pages in length, encouraging the written answers. We have found this form has been readily accepted by delegates and useful to us in evaluating our progress with a training course.

PERSONAL DEVELOPMENT CHECKLIST
Skills development

In the training room
Motivating, energizing
Facilitating, communicating, influencing
Patience, adaptability
Monitoring, evaluating, improving
Giving and receiving feedback

Client service
Proactive relationship building
Understanding key client requirements
Reflecting requirements in training initiatives
Evaluating, improving, reporting
Assessment, monitoring, evaluation

Management and leadership
Coaching, mentoring
Motivating my team, my peers, the T&D function

Organization
Developing, implementing, using appropriate systems
Developing, implementing training strategies and plans
Developing a brand for the function
Advertising capabilities and the successes of the function
Evaluation, standards

Knowledge development

Training developments
    Training and development trends
    Change processes and training
    Developing a learning organization
Training mechanisms, systems
    E-learning and computer-based training systems
    Distance learning and books
Business skills
Organizational direction, strategies and plans

Personal development

Building a network, externally and with business unit managers
Understanding availability of conferences, seminars
Reading list; books, journals, magazines
Authoring plans
Investigating work shadowing, secondment, transfer
Personal development plan
Co-training, mentoring, coaching

Note to trainers: A trainer in an organization's T&D function should modify this form for their personal use in conjunction with the personal development processes of the organization.

ASPECTS OF TRAINING FOR EVALUATION AND BENCHMARKING

This is a list of areas that could be considered for evaluation by the T&D function and by individual trainers. The topics included are 'how' rather than 'what' and therefore should be capable of being included in an external benchmark. They are not, generally, commercially sensitive.

1. The T&D function's ability to build and implement a strategy and an implementation plan that are integrated with the organization's business strategies and plans, and are integrated with HR processes including assessment and career development.

2. Working with senior and line managers to understand the organization's needs from T&D programmes.

3. The ability and willingness to use benchmarking of internal and external sources of excellence in improvement of the T&D function.

4. Agreeing priorities for current and future training needs with the organization.

5. Promoting the implementation of a learning environment and the personal ownership for development throughout the organization.

6. Monitoring and evaluating all aspects of training with a view to continuous improvement.

7. Providing high-quality T&D services integrated with the organization's business needs.

8. Initiating appropriate training needs analyses across the organization, integrated with a competence framework.

9. Publishing clear documentation about all aspects of training programmes.

10. Working proactively with line management to encourage all aspects of learning, including course attendance.

11. Proactively offering mentoring and coaching to the organization.

12. Building a high-quality T&D function with skilled, knowledgeable staff within budget.

13. Proactively seeking feedback on individual trainer's performance from delegates and all other possible sources.

14. Seeking to make appropriate changes in the methods of operation of trainers, towards 'change agents' and 'training consultants'.

15. Adoption of a blended learning approach.

Note to trainers: This is obviously not an exhaustive list. Use this list as a starting point to consider the areas that would be of most interest and benefit to you.

EVALUATING THE 'REPUTABLE' COURSE: YOUR PERSONAL CHECKLIST

Before the course

What was done to ensure my correct attendance and pre-course preparation?
What was done to let me know about what was to happen both in terms of the course objectives and content and about the surrounding logistics?
What would I do differently?

As the course starts

What did the trainer do to ensure the delegates were comfortable?
How did the trainer introduce the course?
What commitments to use the new skills and knowledge were made by the delegates (a) during the course and (b) after the course?
Did the delegates get involved early in the course?
What did the trainer do to encourage the delegates to take ownership of their learning?
What would I do differently?

As the course develops

What were the strongest features of the trainer's approach?
What were the weaker features of the trainer's work?
What could have been improved?
How did the trainer continually demonstrate interest and expertise in the topics?
To what extent were delegates involved? How did they show learning?
Was there an overall pattern to the course?
Which parts of the course really worked?
What could the trainer have done to improve the weaker parts?
How were the slower learners encouraged?
How were conflicts resolved?
What would I do differently?

At the end of the course

How did the course finish? On a high note?
Did the delegates (re)commit to using the new skills and knowledge?
Did the trainer appear to have learned from the programme?
What did the trainer think about the course? What did she think went well? How did the trainer think things could have been improved?
What would I do differently?

Three weeks after the course

What do I remember about the course? About the trainer?
What do other delegates remember?

Note to trainers: This is designed to allow a trainer to build her own checklist when attending another trainer's course. It is only a framework and the trainer should add any questions that are particularly personally useful in her own skill development. Use your form in conjunction with the sections in Chapter 7 on evaluating trainers and courses.

TRAINER PRE-COURSE PREPARATION CHECKLIST

Pre-course documentation

Invitation letters to delegates, line managers, guest speakers
Co-trainers identified
Training materials prepared: trainer notes, delegate materials, exercises/practicals

Location details

Room booking: training room and breakout rooms
Comfort: temperature, air conditioning, light, acoustics
Food, refreshments organized
Equipment:
    Seating arrangements
    Training equipment
        Video, screen and films
        Flipchart and pens
        Overhead projector
        Computer equipment
Delegate materials organized:
    Training materials: exercise/practical materials
    Paper, pens, name cards
    Course evaluation forms
    Any corporate materials for use during course (eg annual reports, brochures, product details)

Preparing

Examine training material: parts you need to read in more detail
Timetable: any parts that will be rushed and how to overcome
Delegates: are they confirming attendance and are there any issues
Guest speakers briefing
Line manager briefing, discussion
Meet and plan with any co-trainers
Reconfirm guest speakers, location, facilities

On the day

Trainer guide available. Acetates
Room prepared to plan
Comfort: temperature, air conditioning, light, acoustics
Materials delivered
Equipment checked and working
Food, refreshments available
Availability of breakout rooms
Details of the logistics of venue and event available:
   fire drill, locations of food, refreshments, toilets

Ready to start

First acetates ready
Opening remarks prepared
Ready to discuss course aim and objectives, rationale with organization's business directions
Ready to introduce clearly self and any co-trainers
Ready to discuss briefly logistics of venue and event
Ready to build delegate involvement and ownership of learning

LOST BUSINESS ANALYSIS

OPPORTUNITY: French & Willers. South Poges. Furniture restorers. Two-day
                  time management training course for sales force
CLIENT: Ian Smith-Fellows. Sales Director
CONTACT SOURCE: Personal network; George – one of his customers
OUR BID: Two days delivery, one day preparation all at standard price

Client commentary

NUMBER BIDDING ORGANIZATIONS: 5
WERE WE THE SECOND CHOICE?: Y
WINNING BID IN COMPARISON TO OURS:

Bid price:	Higher	Lower	Similar
Organization:	Larger	Smaller	Similar
Previously known to client?	y		
Previous supplier?	y		
First contact with client:			
Client's personal network	y		
Supplier advertising	y		
Supplier approach	n		
Supplier listing	n		

CLIENT OPINION OF WINNING BID IN COMPARISON TO OURS:

More specifically tailored to client needs	n
Showed more understanding of client	y
Demonstrated greater experience	y
Contained more details of solution	y
Showed greater determination to win	?
Showed greater flexibility in approach	y
Showed more flexibility in price	n
Included more supporting material of interest to solution	y

PLEASE NOTE ANYTHING ELSE THAT MAY HELP WITH OUR BUSINESS DEVELOP-
MENT, ESPECIALLY IF WE WORK WITH THIS CLIENT AGAIN:

Client said the decision was very close. Winning competition knew their client and his organization from previous work and therefore had put in a bid with lots of reference to the way
the organization worked.

Most of the competition had very glossy brochures describing themselves and their products.

Good chance to win future business with this client.

Appendix 2:
Useful Contact Names
and Web Site Addresses

This section is designed as a first step to help trainers build their own resource bank of useful information, it is not a detailed directory. We would instead refer readers to *The Skills and Training Handbook* (2000), published by Kogan Page in association with The Institute of Management, which is a comprehensive listing of providers and other organizations classified by training category, specialism, industry sector and geographical location.

In addition we list some relevant Web sites.

ASSOCIATIONS/PROFESSIONAL BODIES

American Society for Training and Development (ASTD):
  www.astd.org
Australian Institute of Training and Development (AITD):
  www.aitd.com.au
Australian Institute of Management (AIM):
  www.aim.com.au
American Management Association International (AMA):
  www.amanet.org
Chartered Institute of Marketing:
  www.cim.co.uk
Chartered Institute of Personnel & Development (CIPD):
  www.cipd.co.uk
Commission for Racial Equality (CRE):
  www.cre.gov.uk
Department of Trade and Industry:
  www.dti.gov.uk

Department for Education and Skills (DfES):
  www.dfes.gov.uk
Equal Opportunities Commission (EOC):
  www.eoc.org.uk
Institute of Management:
  www.inst-mgt.org.uk
Institute of Directors:
  www.iod.co.uk

We have also made specific reference to the following:

Basic Skills Agency:
  www.basic-skills.co.uk
Tony Buzan Mind Map® method, contact:
  Buzan@mind-map.com
Honey and Mumford Learning Styles Questionnaire, contact Peter Honey:
  www.peterhoney.com
John Seymour (NLP), contact:
  www.johnseymour-nlp.co.uk
The Masie Center, contact:
  www.masie.com
Brook Manville, contact:
  brook_manville@mckinsey.com
Nathaniel Foote, contact:
  nathaniel_foote@mckinsey.com
Fast Company, contact:
  www.fastcompany.com
Transitions:
  www.tdatransitions.co.uk
@Brint.com:
  www.brint.com
Campaign for Learning:
  www.campaign-for-learning.org.uk
Learning and Skills Development Agency:
  www.LSDA.org.uk

Special Note: New Web sites are becoming available all the time, in your own region use a search engine to identify the ones that are most relevant for you.

PUBLICATIONS AND JOURNALS

People Management:
  www.peoplemanagement.co.uk
Personnel Today:
  www.personneltoday.com
Tmag:
  www.tmag.co.uk

Other useful sources of information are the *Times Educational Supplement* and the *Higher Educational Supplement*. *Fortune Magazine* and *Forbes* are a useful source on US business. Trade magazines such as *Marketing*, *Retail Week*, *Campaign*, *The Grocer*, *Caterer and Hotel Keeper* supply information from the various sectors. The *Writers' and Artists' Yearbook*, published annually by A. C. Black gives further information on publishers and other relevant publications.

Appendix 3: Recommended Reading List

Belasco, James A. (1990) *Teaching the Elephant to Dance: Empowering change in your organisation*, Hutchinson Business, London

Belbin, Meredith B. (1981) *Management Teams*, Heinemann, London

Black, Jack (1994) *Mindstore*, Thorsons, London.

Bohm, David and Nicol Lee (1996) *On Dialogue*, Routledge, London

Brown, Mark (1993) *The Dinosaur Strain*, Innovation Centre Europe Ltd, Polegate, East Sussex

Buzan, Tony (1995) *Use Your Head*, 4th edn, BBC, London

Buzan, Tony and Buzan, Barry (1993) *The Mind Map Book*, BBC, London

Csikzentmihalyi, Mihalyi (1990) *Flow*, Harper & Row

Goleman, Daniel (1999) *Working with Emotional Intelligence*, Bloomsbury, London

Grigg, Joanna (1997) *Portfolio Working: A practical guide to thriving in a changing workplace*, Kogan Page, London

Hammer, Michael and Champy, James (1993) *Re-engineering the Corporation*, HarperCollins, USA, and (1993) Nicholas Brealey, London

Handy, Charles (1994) *The Empty Raincoat*, Hutchinson, London

Handy, Charles (1995) *Beyond Certainty*, Hutchinson, London

Heller, Robert (1998) *In Search of European Excellence*, HarperCollins, London

Helmstetter, Shad (1998) *What to Say When You Talk to Yourself*, Cynus

Jaworski, Joe and Senge, Peter (1998) *Synchronicity*, Berrett-Koeler

Kanter, Rosabeth M (1983) *The Change Masters*, Allen Unwin, London

Kanter, Rosabeth M (1989) *When Giants Learn to Dance*, Simon Schuster, London

Kolb, David A. (1984) *Experiential Learning: Experience as the source of learning and development*, Prentice-Hall, London

Kolb, David A., Rubin, I. M. and McIntyre, J. M. (1994) *Organisational Psychology: An experiential approach to organisational behaviour*, 4th edn, Prentice-Hall, London

McNally, David (1993) *Even Eagles Need a Push*, Thorsons, London

Malone, Samuel A. (1997) *How to set up and Manage a Corporate Learning Centre*, Gower, Aldershot

O'Connor, Joseph and Seymour, John (1990) *Introducing NLP: Neuro linguistic programming*, Mandala, London

O'Connor, Joseph and Seymour, John (1994) *Training with NLP: Skills for managers, trainers and communicators*, Thorsons, London

Peters, Tom (1992) *Liberation Management*, Knopf, USA; Macmillan, London

Peters, Tom, (1997) *The Circle of Innovation*, Hodder & Stoughton, London

Peters, Tom and Austin, Nancy (1985) *A Passion for Excellence*, Collins, London

Redfield, James (1998) *The Celestine Vision*, Bantam Books, London

Scott, Amanda (1997) *Learning Centres: A step-by-step guide to planning, managing and evaluating an organizational resource centre*, Kogan Page, London

Semler, Ricardo (1993) *Maverick*, Arrow, London

Senge, Peter M. (1990) *The Fifth Discipline*, Doubleday, New York

Slater, Robert (1998) *Jack Welch & the GE Way: Management insights & leadership secrets of the legendary CEO*, McGraw Hill

Thorne, Kaye (1998) *Training Places: Choosing and using venues for training*, Kogan Page, London

Thorne, Kaye (2001) *Personal Coaching*, Kogan Page, London

Thorne, Kaye (2003) *Blended Learning: How to integrate online and traditional learning*, Kogan Page, London

Thorne, Kaye (2003) *Managing the Mavericks*, Spiro Press, London

Thorne, Kaye and Machray, Alex (1998) *Training on a Shoestring*, Kogan Page, London

Thorne, Kaye and Machray, Alex (2000) *World Class Training: Providing training excellence*, Kogan Page, London

Index

styles 21–24, 34, 129–30
see also online learning
Learning Management System (LMS)
80, 84
learning organization   4–5, 27–28
Learning Styles Questionnaire   21–22,
27
left brain/right brain   26–27
line manager, as trainer/coach
10–11

Machray, A   115
management development
programmes   19
Manville, B   6–7
market positioning   207
marketing   210–15, 219–20
marketplace
assessing   204–08
creating   207–08
research   199–200
see also needs identification
MASIE Center   96
materials
costings   42–43
design   41
marketing   211
non-arrival of   64
production of   39–43
scheduling   41–42
see also marketing material
Mayer, J   7
media   92–93
meetings, managing   147–48
mentor   74, 136–38, 171–73, 197, 215
mentoring   136–38
evaluation   114
mind mapping   27, 33, 71–72, 94
Mumford, A   21, 86
music, use of   19

needs identification
blended learning   85
businesses   204–05
client   30–31
individual   25–26
nerves, coping with   62–63
networking   73–74, 192, 220–21
Neuro Linguistic Programming
192–95
NVQs   154, 157

objectives
business 30–31
SMART   24, 34, 35, 113, 178
O'Connor, J   194
online learning   88–95
Ornstein, R   26–27

PDA (Personal Digital Assistant)   81,
97
performance guidelines   15–16
personal coaching   124–36
personal development   12, 114–15,
133–34, 171, 180–81, 185–87, 192,
229
pragmatists   22, 23
presentations   39, 40
pressure, handling   17–18, 201
priority planning   18
problem solving, creative   72–73
product champion   70, 83
professional associations   190–91,
234–35
proposals   217–18
psychometric tests   13, 14
publications   236
pull/push theory   7

qualifications for trainers
academic 185–86
vocational   187

reflectors   22
refreshments   47, 51, 59
research   33, 63, 163–64
residential events   53
resources for training   75–77, 92–93
see also materials
risk management   148
role-play   36
room arrangements   58–59

Salovey, P   7
security   65
self-employment   196–223
Seymour, J   194
skills   187–90
analysis   188–90
checklist   190
development plan   115, 180, 229
SMART objectives   24, 34, 35, 113, 178
speakers, external   57